"The Best School"

"The Best School"

★

West Point, 1833–1866

★

James L. Morrison, Jr.

The Kent State University Press

KENT, OHIO, & LONDON

© 1986, 1998 by The Kent State University Press, Kent, Ohio 44242

All rights reserved

Library of Congress Catalog Card Number 98-13132

ISBN 0-87338-321-4 (cloth)

ISBN 0-87338-612-4 (pbk.)

Manufactured in the United States of America

05 04 03 02 01 00 99 98   5 4 3 2

All photographs courtesy of the U.S. Military Academy Archives and Special Collections.

Library of Congress Cataloging-in-Publication Data

Morrison, James L., 1923–

"The best school" : West Point, 1833–1866 / James L. Morrison, Jr.

p.   cm.

Originally published: "The best school in the world." 1986.

Includes bibliographical references and index.

ISBN 0-87338-612-4 (pbk. : alk. paper) ∞

1. United States Military Academy—History—19th century.

I. Morrison, James L., 1923–   "The best school in the world."

II. Title

U410.L1M67   1998

355'.0071'173—dc21   98-13132

British Library Cataloging-in-Publication data are available.

To my comrades of the regular army,

my colleagues at York College of Pennsylvania,

and my students.

I believe [the U.S. Military Academy is]

the best school in the world.

—Andrew Jackson

Contents

CONTENTS

Preface

The military academy at West Point represents the oldest continuing experiment in federally sponsored higher education in the United States. Although founded during the administration of President Thomas Jefferson, the academic scope of the institution never broadened sufficiently to fit the great Virginian's concept of a national university, but in its accessibility to boys of all classes and its dedication to measuring human merit with mathematical precision the academy did in a peculiar and limited way promote the aristocracy of talent so cherished by Jefferson. Yet West Point is something more than a quaint relic of the American Enlightenment and therefore deserves study for reasons quite apart from antiquarianism. Through its graduates who played major roles in some of the most crucial events in the history of the United States, the institution has left its mark on the American experience. The reverse also applies; the flow of American history has molded West Point. Throughout its existence the corps of cadets has mirrored with fair accuracy the socioeconomic composition, the tensions, and the prejudices of the American middle class. Because of this it is no exaggeration to say that an understanding of the military academy is essential to a full appreciation of the history of the United States.

For the student of institutions the academy holds a special appeal. In some respects a typical creature of the government, West Point makes a convenient vehicle for analyzing the evolution of a bureaucracy in action. Close examination of the military academy reveals the degree to which a formally designated control structure conforms to the actual distribution of power, a feature of the academy and other bureaucratic organizations frequently overlooked by casual observers. Likewise, a study of West Point brings to light clashes between men with opposing ideas and the importance of those clashes in stimulating or inhibiting institutional growth. In addition careful examination discloses how the antipodal pulls of political expedience and academic excellence have affected the evolution of the military academy. The history of West Point is in part, then, a case study of institutional development in a politically charged atmosphere.

Despite its historical significance the academy has seldom undergone serious examination. There is an overabundance of devotional and anecdotal literature which may amuse the general reader and inspire the undiscriminating alumnus but provides little guidance for the thoughtful student. Nowhere is the dearth of accurate information and dispassionate analysis more acute than in the period between the relief of Sylvanus Thayer, the ostensible "Father of the Military Academy," from the superintendency in 1833 and the removal of the institution from the jurisdiction of the corps of engineers in 1866. This era is particularly significant. The graduates who went forth in those years explored, surveyed and pacified the West, built railroads, dams and canals, served as junior officers in the Mexican War, and held high commands on both sides in the Civil War. Their panegyrists and their bitterest critics all agreed that the academy had uniquely influenced the ways these men thought and acted. The precise extent to which this was true must remain an open question, but even so, an accurate comprehension of the forces at work on their minds and personalities in the years they were passing from adolescence to manhood should contribute much to an understanding of the graduates themselves.

Antebellum West Point merits study on still other grounds. Boys from all walks of life mingled on intimate terms at the academy. It was also there, as in no other institution in the United States, that the opposing forces of sectionalism and nationalism coexisted in uneasy equilibrium—but equilibrium, nonetheless—until the coming of the war destroyed the delicate balance. At the military academy in the antebellum era the polished aristocrat—a Du Pont, a McClellan, a Maury, or a Lee—dwelled side by side with the rough-hewn commoner—a Jackson, a Grant, a Sheridan, or a Bragg. There Henry Heth, Virginia bluebood, and Ambrose Burnside, Indiana tailor's apprentice, lived together in boisterous camaraderie for four years, and Oliver O. Howard, the Maine abolitionist, made friends with a hot-blooded young Virginian called "Beauty" Stuart. And it was at West Point that the sectional drama played itself out with heartwrenching poignance until, finally, classmate drew the sword against classmate.

The span between 1833 and 1866 is important for yet other reasons. The earlier date signified the end of Thayer's tenure at the academy, but not his influence. How was that influence preserved after his departure, and what was its effect on the academy in the years that followed? These questions are particularly significant because of the sentimental reverence accorded Thayer; they can only be answered by surveying the period following his relief. The other terminal date, denoting the end of the hegemony of the corps of engineers, raises pertinent questions too. What had been the impact of the engineers on the academy during the years of their administration? Why was a change in the arrangement thought necessary, and why did it come about in 1866? More importantly, what did the change produce?

This study is an institutional history of the military academy in the years between 1833 and 1866. It examines the people and forces which induced or retarded change and their effect on the evolution of West Point. The work also evaluates the academy as an antebellum institution of higher learning and assesses the influence of West Point on its student body, the corps of cadets. The book is not simply a history of the curriculum and administration of a school, although the narrative includes these aspects, but an examination of the academy as an educational, social, military, and bureaucratic institution.

The volume is divided into three parts chronologically. The first section deals with the period between 1833 and 1854, during which the academic program of the preceding era continued in full force; the second investigates the years between 1854 and 1861, the term of the five-year course, one of the most radical departures from tradition in the history of the military academy. The final section explores the Civil War and the immediate postwar period when the command structure underwent drastic modification.

The goal is a more detailed and less distorted view of a crucial period in the history of the military academy than has been available heretofore. In keeping with that aim every effort has been made to analyze objectively but in a manner which does not reduce the institution or the men associated with it to lifeless laboratory specimens. All of this has been done in the hope that the reader will find the chronicle of antebellum West Point, stripped of gilt and tinsel, as interesting as—and far more realistic than—the musings of the academy's apologists and enemies.

Among the many people deserving my special gratitude for contributing to this work are: Professor Eric L. McKitrick of Columbia University who patiently shepherded it through the dissertation stage; Dr. John T. Hubbell,

Director of the Kent State University Press and Editor of *Civil War History,* whose guidance proved invaluable in bringing the project to fruition; Brig. Gen. George A. Lincoln, deceased, former head of the Department of Social Sciences, U.S. Military Academy, and Brig. Gen. Thomas E. Griess, former head of the Department of History, U.S. Military Academy, both of whom provided time, advice, and resources; Robert E. Schnare, former Chief, Special Collections Division, U.S. Military Academy Library, together with archivists Kenneth W. Rapp and Marie Capps, all of whom went beyond the dictates of duty to assist me; Joseph O'Donnell, deceased, formerly of the same office, whose cheerful willingness to lend a hand eased the burden in many ways; Col. Edgar Denton III, retired, and Col. Walter S. Dillard, retired, now an Episcopal priest, former colleagues and constant friends, whose scholarly studies provided valuable insights; Dr. Richard J. Sommers, U.S. Army Military History Institute, who generously gave his time to help me exploit sources I would not have found otherwise; Dr. Robert V. Iosue, Dr. William A. DeMeester, deceased, Professor Chin Ha Suk of York College of Pennsylvania together with William H. Ashbaugh, formerly of the same institution, now retired, whose unflagging support, guidance, and friendship were vital to the accomplishment of the task; and my parents, James L. and Brander Wyatt Morrison, both deceased, whose considerable material assistance was overshadowed by their gift of the inspiration to carry on in the face of seemingly insurmountable obstacles. Above all others stands my wife, Carol Brown Morrison; to enumerate her contributions or describe what her inspiration has meant would be impossible. Simply stated, without her there would have been no book; indeed, there would have been no reason to write one.

Some of the material in chapters four, five, and nine of this book was used earlier in articles for *Civil War History,* and *Military Affairs,* and for portions of *The Memoirs of Henry Heth.* I wish to express my thanks to the editors of those journals and of Greenwood Press for their permission to use the same material in the present work. I am also grateful to the archivists and librarians of several institutions for permission to use material from their collections in this book. These institutions include the William H. Perkins Library, Duke University, the Ohio Historical Society, the Rutherford B. Hayes Presidential Center, the Historical Society of Pennsylvania, the Virginia Historical Society, and the Hagley Museum and Library.

The Old
Army,
1833–1860

★

In his comments on a plan to reorganize the United States Military Academy in 1844 Richard Delafield, then superintendent at West Point, took occasion to delineate the mission of the institution. As Delafield saw it, the academy existed

> To provide capable and well instructed officers for the several arms composing our army, in sufficient numbers for a peace establishment based upon the principle of skeleton regiments and corps, susceptible of sudden enlargement through the influence of well educated officers . . .
>
> To introduce into the country military science and tactics and to diffuse them throughout the militia . . . the army serving as skeleton garrisons in the fortifications and along our inland frontier to economize the valuable time of the militia . . .
>
> To obtain, and have some means of preserving and diffusing the improvements in the science and art of war . . . and to afford officers of all arms of service an opportunity of gaining from such a nursery of their profession everything new in the lines of their respective arms.[1]

This statement of purpose suggests several factors which are requisite to a full and accurate comprehension of the military academy as it evolved in the years between 1833 and 1866. To begin with, Delafield's assertion affirmed that West Point was no longer the mere technical school for artillerists and engineers its founders had envisioned[2] but had become an institution devoted to educating and training officers for all arms, the cavalry and infantry as well as the more specialized technical branches, the artillery, ordnance and engineers. The broadened scope, in turn, points to another important feature, the distinctiveness of American military education in the years before the Civil War. In Great Britain and France, the foremost military powers of the time, cadets aspiring to commissions in the infantry and cavalry attended different schools and pursued different studies from those wanting to be officers in the artillery and engineers; most of the other European states also provided specialized branch training for officer candidates. The United States, however, could not afford the luxury of specialization; consequently, West Point had to prepare cadets for service in all the arms and at the same time give them a scientific education.

The evolution of the military academy into an institution capable of performing the missions enumerated by Delafield came about as much by chance as design. Beginning in the Revolution and continuing throughout the Federalist era, experienced soldiers such as George Washington, Friedrich von Steuben, Henry Knox, and Alexander Hamilton advocated national military schools to train a professional officer corps, but invariably Congress rejected or ignored these proposals. Ironically, the United States Military Academy came into being during the administration of Thomas Jefferson, a staunch opponent of standing armies who as a member of Washington's cabinet had once voted against the establishment of a national military school.

Scholars have usually explained away Jefferson's apparent inconsistency by arguing that his primary aim was to found a school of science and engineering. In a thoughtful article Theodore Crackel has challenged that interpretation. Crackel maintains that Jefferson thoroughly understood the implications of his act. He had come to realize the necessity for a professional army but wanted to break the Federalist hold on the officer corps. Obviously, a military academy which would train and educate the deserving sons of the masses at public expense in exchange for a term of service in the regular army would be an ideal means of obtaining his goal. Certainly Crackel's argument squares with the facts. By the time Jefferson left office in 1808 more infantry and artillery officers than engineers had graduated from West Point, and this would hold true for the future as well; furthermore, it was not until 1812 that a professorship of engineering was established and not until 1817 that a true engineering curriculum was imposed.[3]

The law of March 1802 which created the academy specified that the corps of engineers would operate it. Accordingly, the president selected Maj. Jonathan Williams, a grandnephew of Benjamin Franklin, to head the school. Although superintendent of the military academy, Williams also had to serve as chief of engineers, but despite these conflicting demands on his time, he managed to establish the infant West Point on a sound basis. The first class consisted of eleven students; some were cadets detached from their parent regiments or corps; others were already commissioned officers. They studied mathematics, fortification, and surveying at first; however, French and drawing were soon added to the curriculum. Until 1816 when a four-year program was instituted, students remained at the academy for varying lengths of time. Whenever a suitable vacancy occurred, the secretary of war would order a cadet to rejoin his corps or regiment as a commissioned officer.

This haphazard procedure was modified in 1812; thereafter, cadets received appointments in the general service of the United States rather than to specific corps or regiments. Other significant changes took place the same year. Professorships of engineering and natural philosophy were established. Also, Joseph Swift, the first graduate of West Point, replaced Williams.

Colonel Swift, like his predecessor, had to serve as chief of engineers and superintendent of the military academy simultaneously. Finding it necessary to devote most of his time to supervising the construction of harbor fortifications in New York City, he left the day-to-day operation of West Point to Capt. Alden Partridge, an engineer officer who had remained on duty at the academy ever since his graduation in 1806. Unwilling to delegate authority, Partridge attempted to do everything himself from teaching engineering sections to drilling squads of cadets. He also had a knack for antagonizing practically everyone who met him: the faculty, the secretary of war, the president, and finally even Swift. In 1817 following conviction by a court-martial for disobedience, Partridge resigned from the army and devoted the rest of his life to vilifying the military academy.

Swift resigned in 1818. Although his administration had been plagued by the troubles with Partridge, it was also marked by solid achievements. Swift had instituted the board of visitors, a group of distinguished citizens who inspected the academy annually; he also began the practice of holding examinations twice a year. In addition, Swift encouraged instructors to teach by the question and answer method rather than lecture. Finally, it was during his term that the four-year program went into effect. All of these reforms became permanent elements of the West Point educational system.

Sylvanus Thayer, the third superintendent, had graduated from the military academy in 1808 after only one year as a cadet. Before returning to West Point in 1817 Thayer had spent two years in France studying the military educational system of that nation. L'École Polytechnique, the engineering school in Paris, had particularly impressed him, and he used it as a model for shaping the academy during his extended tenure as superintendent. Unlike Williams and Swift, Thayer did not hold office as chief of engineers; therefore, he could devote all of his attention to West Point. Also, during the early years of his administration he enjoyed the full support of Secretary of War John C. Calhoun. These advantages permitted

3

Thayer to add substantive reforms to those which had been made by Williams and Swift. An able administrator and disciplinarian, he restored the sense of order which Partridge had almost destroyed. Thayer also introduced other beneficial changes. One of these was the establishment of the academic board, a collegiate body consisting of the superintendent, the heads of the academic departments, and the commandant of cadets. The board decided on curricular matters, conducted the semiannual examinations, and ranked the cadets in each class according to their performance in every subject. The academic board also recommended each graduating student for a particular branch of the service based on his overall class standing for the four years. In addition, Thayer imposed a precise system for grading cadets' daily recitations in the classroom, requiring each instructor to submit a weekly compilation of these marks to the superintendent. This not only kept Thayer abreast of the progress of every cadet, it also enabled him to implement another reform: assigning students to sections according to demonstrated competence. The brightest cadets in a given subject were grouped together in one section; the next best group into another, and so on. Composing sections in this manner allowed each instructor to teach at a pace commensurate with the abilities of his students.

Thayer also established the rule that any cadet who received more than two hundred demerits a year was deficient in conduct and liable for discharge; previously, there had been no specified limit. Another modification of older, more informal procedures took place during Thayer's administration, but in this instance the impetus came from Washington, not West Point. In the 1820s, the secretary of war began allocating one cadet appointment to each congressional district, two to every state "at large," and a dozen or so to the president for disposal as he saw fit. It was not until 1843, however, that this practice became law.

When Calhoun left the war department in 1825, Thayer lost a valuable ally. A few years later the superintendent's insistence on enforcing the conduct regulations without regard to partisan politics brought him into conflict with the Jackson administration. After losing a protracted dispute with the president over the dismissal of a cadet who had powerful political connections, Thayer resigned the superintendency in the summer of 1833.

Thayer's influence lingered at the military academy long after his departure. The men whom he had appointed to the key professorships retained their positions until the early 1870s, and throughout their long tenure worked to ensure that the academy continued to operate in accordance with the principles laid down by Sylvanus Thayer. An appreciation of the strength of this Thayer mystique is essential to understanding why West Point followed the path it did in the years between 1833 and 1866.

The regular army for which Thayer's disciples prepared cadets numbered

4

a little more than six thousand in the early 1830s.[4] Small though it was, this force undertook a variety of tasks. The regulars' routine duties included manning the coastal defenses, exploring, mapping, and policing the West, and building bridges, railroads, and canals. In addition, the regular army, along with the militia and volunteers, participated in several major combat operations during the antebellum period.

The coastal defense mission, shared by the engineers and heavy artillery, embraced the construction, maintenance, and garrisoning of a string of fortifications stretching initially from Maine to Florida and along the Great Lakes; following the Mexican War this perimeter was extended to include the Gulf and Pacific coasts.[5] The infantry, dragoons, light artillery, and later, cavalry guarded the inland wilderness and the major wagon routes.

In addition to, and sometimes in conjunction with, its protective mission the army sponsored exploring expeditions in the West during the antebellum era. Most of the soldier-explorers set out with the primary aim of finding railroad routes or lines of communication to support military operations, but in carrying out those duties they also collected scientific data about the region. Civilian scholars made extensive use of this information in their own work. For example, Henry R. Schoolcraft, a pioneer American ethnologist, drew heavily on material contained in official reports of army explorations in writing his monumental study of the American Indian. The tie with science was not coincidental. Representatives of the Smithsonian Institution, the American Philosophical Society, the Philadelphia Academy of Natural Sciences, and similar groups occasionally participated in planning the scientific aspects of the expeditions; furthermore, civilian scholars and artists frequently accompanied the military explorers. But even when civilians did not take part, the expeditions still yielded valuable and accurate scientific data. Their West Point education had equipped army officers to serve as competent observers and artists in their own right.

Among the West Pointers who added to the store of geographical knowledge about the antebellum West were George G. Meade who helped survey the Sabine River Boundary of the Republic of Texas; Capt. Randolph Marcy who began his brilliant career as an explorer by making a trek from Fort Smith, Arkansas to Santa Fe, New Mexico; and Lieutenants William Henry C. Whiting and William F. Smith who jointly explored western Texas. Also, there were Maj. Isaac I. Stevens and Capt. George B. McClellan who led an elaborate expedition to the Pacific Northwest. During this journey McClellan gave an early display of the excessive caution which was to mar his performance in the Civil War. While searching for possible railroad passes through the Cascade range, the future commander of the Army of the Potomac failed to examine what may have been the

5

most suitable one in the mistaken belief that the snow cover was much deeper than it actually was.

Politics was a major determinant in selecting railroad routes, but safety and construction costs also influenced decisions. For instance, when Paiute Indians massacred Capt. John W. Gunnison's party near Manti, Utah, in 1853, enthusiasm for a rail line along the thirty-eighth parallel route which Gunnison had been exploring quickly diminished. The next spring, however, Lt. Edward G. Beckwith completed Gunnison's mission, carrying the survey into the Sacramento Valley of California; the first transcontinental railroad eventually followed the route Beckwith had laid out.

On an eight-month journey from Fort Smith, Arkansas, through New Mexico and Arizona to San Diego, California, Lt. Amiel W. Whipple discovered one of the best routes for a transcontinental railroad, but because he had grossly overestimated the cost of construction Whipple's route was not given due consideration. Even so, the expedition proved worthwhile from a scientific standpoint. W. W. Turner, a civilian linguist who had been a member of the party, compiled vocabularies of the Indian tribes along the way and then classified the tribes according to linguistic groups. Turner also found that the Apaches of the Southwest were linked linguistically to a Canadian tribe, thus strengthening the Bering Sea land bridge theory of migration.

The need to establish convenient supply routes to support troops engaged in operations also led to important scientific discoveries. It was while engaged in such a task that Lt. Joseph C. Ives became the first white man to explore the floor of the Grand Canyon. In addition, Ives and his party found a tribe of primitive Indians who had never seen whites before. On a similar mission in 1859 Capt. John C. Macomb discovered the relics of an ancient Indian civilization in what is now Mesa Verde National Park.

Further north Lt. Gouverneur K. Warren and Ferdinand V. Hayden, one of the first paleontologists to investigate the West, explored the Yellowstone Valley, the Powder River country, portions of Nebraska, and the Black Hills of South Dakota in connection with operations against the Sioux. Hayden found numerous fossils which he sent back to the Philadelphia Academy of Natural Sciences. Warren went on to become a leading American mapmaker. Secretary of War Jefferson Davis appointed him to draw the summary map which accompanied the official report of the transcontinental railroad surveys. To do this the young lieutenant had to extract, reconcile, and then incorporate data from all the individual reports. In accomplishing this formidable undertaking Warren created, in William H. Goetzmann's words, "one of the climactic maps in the history of American cartography."[6]

In contrast Lt. John Pope made a negative contribution to knowledge about the West. Between 1855 and 1858 Pope conducted a series of unsuccessful experiments digging artesian wells in Texas. His failure to find water lent further strength to the "Great American Desert" image which did so much to delay opening the West to farming.

West Pointers also shed new light on the origins of the American Indian. Not long after the Mexican War Lt. William H. Emory, one of the foremost antebellum explorers and an expert on the Pima and Maricopa tribes, found among ruins in Arizona evidence which flatly contradicted Alexander von Humboldt's thesis that the Aztecs had migrated to Mexico from ancestral homes in the American Southwest. At about the same time Lt. James H. Simpson made similar finds in Chaco Canyon and Canyon de Chelly, New Mexico. These discoveries laid the foundations for the study of southwestern archaeology.[7]

Yet important though they were, such activities as exploring and surveying the West remained secondary. Guarding the national boundaries, pacifying Indians, and defeating foreign enemies were the main ways the regular army earned its keep in the years before the Civil War.

The first of the large-scale conflicts, the Florida, or Second Seminole War, began with the massacre of Dade's Command on 28 December 1835. A total of 107 regular army officers and men died in this prelude to a six-year campaign of frustration. By the end of the war more than fourteen hundred soldiers, almost one-fourth of the regular army, had paid with their lives,[8] and there was no clear-cut victory to justify the cost. In marked contrast stood the Mexican War, the second major military venture of the antebellum era. This struggle, with its more conventional style of campaigning, decisive battles, and rewarding triumph restored the regulars' self-confidence and gained them a measure of popular acceptance they had not enjoyed before.

When military crises arose, such as the Florida and Mexican Wars, Congress granted temporary increases in troop strength, but at the cessation of hostilities withdrew these augmentations, leaving fiscal penuriousness and public indifference, rather than strategic necessity, to dictate the size of the army. Moreover, the strengths authorized by Congress seldom corresponded to the number of men actually in uniform. Military service was unpopular among Jacksonian Americans, and recruiters rarely met their quotas; also, desertion was common. Thus, regular army units habitually operated at less than their authorized strengths.[9]

Gradually the army increased in size during the antebellum period. There were 6,102 officers and men on the rolls in 1833; by 1841, as a result of the Second Seminole War, the total had jumped to 11,169, but by 1845 had declined to 8,349. Then, under the impetus of the Mexican War, the figure shot up to 21,686. Thereafter, the strength hovered between nine and eleven thousand until augmentations in 1855 and 1858 boosted it to about eighteen thousand. The authorized strength remained at that level through December 1860; however, the number of military personnel actually on duty at that date was only 16,367, a figure soon to be drastically reduced by the resignations of Southern officers and the surrender of the Department of Texas to the Confederacy.[10]

To meet the requirements imposed by its variegated tasks the regular army was divided into a scientific corps, a general staff, and the line. The first-named group consisted of the engineers, topographical engineers, and ordnance. The general staff included the offices of the adjutant general, inspector general, and judge-advocate general, and the subsistence, quartermaster, medical, and pay departments, while the line comprised the regiments of artillery, infantry, dragoons, cavalry, and mounted rifles. A commanding general and several brigadier generals presided over the organization.[11]

The corps of engineers enjoyed the envy of the rest of the army. Except for occasional exploring and surveying expeditions in the West and projects related to railroad, canal, and road construction, the officers of this branch could count on spending most of their careers in or near cities where they worked on fortifications, harbor improvement, and erecting bridges and buildings. For example, Montgomery Meigs, future quartermaster general of the Union Army, passed most of his time in the vicinity of Philadelphia, Detroit, and Washington, save for a short surveying expedition with fellow engineer Robert E. Lee along the Mississippi in 1837.[12] Perhaps even more importantly, the intellectual requirements for entry into the corps of engineers exceeded those for the other branches, and this too added a touch of glamour. Until 1846 the engineers consisted solely of officers, but in May of that year Congress authorized a hundred-man company of sappers, miners, and pontooneers; this remained the only engineer troop unit until the Civil War.[13]

Closely allied in function, though less prestigious, was the second of the scientific corps, the topographical engineers. In theory the "topogs," as they were popularly known, had primary responsibility for surveying and mapping, but in fact other branches also did some of this work, and by the same token, the topographical engineers at times undertook projects that properly were the preserve of the corps of engineers. Because of this overlap in functions the topogs were absorbed by the corps of engineers in 1863.[14] Throughout its existence as an independent branch the corps of topographical engineers consisted of officers only. Organized in 1821 at a strength of ten, the corps gradually rose to a peak size of thirty-seven in 1855.

While serving as officers on duty with the army engineers and topographical engineers, graduates of the military academy built lighthouses, erected public buildings, dug canals, and removed hazards to navigation, as well as exploring, surveying, mapping and building roads and railroads. A few of the more important construction projects undertaken by antebellum West Pointers were: the Minot Ledge Lighthouse in Boston Harbor, the Spectacle Reef Lighthouse on Lake Huron, the Davis Island Dam and the Louisville Canal on the Ohio River, and the Delaware Breakwater. Graduates also designed and built several public works in the vicinity of Washington, D.C., including the Georgetown Aqueduct, the Capitol extension, the Pension Office, the State, War, and Navy building, and the Washington Monument. In New York Charles P. Stone of the class of 1845 laid the base for the Statue of Liberty.

Other graduates made important innovations in engineering technology. William S. Smith, for example, built the first all-steel bridge to span the Mississippi River and Hermann Haupt, the distinguished Civil War railroader, invented the pneumatic drill.

John Newton made what were probably the most spectacular technological innovations in his attempts to clear New York Harbor of hazards to shipping. Newton, a member of the class of 1842, had been a corps commander in the Army of the Potomac during the Civil War. Afterward he reverted to the grade of lieutenant colonel of engineers and obtained an assignment to river and harbor duty in New York. To remove Pot Rock, an obstacle in the East River, Newton invented a steam-powered scow with a well in the bottom through which a framework supporting a large number of drill bits could be lowered into the water. He also devised a way of levelling the framework so that all the bits would drill holes of equal depth in the rock. After the holes were drilled divers filled them with explosives; the charges were then set off by an electric battery. Newton's method of breaking up a three-acre reef which jutted out into Hell Gate channel was equally original. First, he sank a shaft on the shore, then tunneled from the floor of the shaft to the bottom of the reef. Next, workers drilled forty-five hundred blast holes through the roof of the tunnel into the base of the reef above; twenty-five tons of dynamite were than tamped into these holes. To achieve the desired results all the charges had to detonate at the same time. The idea of such a tremendous explosion alarmed people living nearby; however, Newton, who had carefully calculated the effects of the blast, calmed the fears of the public by stationing his wife and family on the banks opposite the reef and by having his small daughter push the button that ignited the charges.

In the West graduates of the academy played roles in developing new techniques for surveying the Sierra Nevadas, a range so rugged it was impossible to use standard systems of measurement. The solution eventually employed was to compute horizontal distances by triangulation and altitudes by barometric readings. Josiah D. Whitney, a civilian, claimed credit for this innovation, but, as William H. Goetzmann has pointed out, army explorers such as John W. Gunnison and William H. Emory had used similar techniques earlier. Still, the West Pointers could not lay claim to having invented the triangulation-barometric method either, for they had borrowed their ideas from other sources. Nevertheless, they are more entitled to recognition as pioneers in the use of the technique than Whitney.

Some West Pointers took their engineering skills to civilian life. Ever since the academy had opened in 1802 a number of graduates had left the service and pursued other careers. Although they engaged in a wide variety of civilian occupations, more of them entered engineering and its allied fields than any other. This trend continued in the classes which graduated between 1833 and 1866. Twenty-four members of that group became civil engineers; thirteen practiced some unspecified kind of engineering; seven became mining engineers; and seventeen worked for railroads either as engineers or in some position requiring a knowledge of engineering. Not all of these graduates were veterans of the corps of engineers or the topographical engineers. For example, Hermann Haupt, chief engineer of the Pennsylvania Railroad, and Henry Heth, assistant civil engineer in the district of Georgetown, South Carolina, had been infantry officers. And William T. Sherman, who directed a street railway in St. Louis for a short while, was an artilleryman. The ability of these men and others with similar backgrounds to switch to engineering after careers in other fields speaks well of the education they had received at West Point.[15]

The ordnance corps, last of the scientific branches, had begun as a separate organization, but in 1821 merged with the artillery. Kindred interests in weapons and munitions should have produced harmony among the members of the amalgamated branch; the opposite proved to be the case, however, so in 1832 the secretary of war dissolved the mésalliance, restoring the ordnance to its former autonomy. This corps did not operate as a unit, but in small detachments assigned to posts where large bodies of troops were stationed. In 1833 the ordnance corps numbered 14 officers and 104 men. Its strength doubled temporarily during the Mexican War, but in the subsequent demobilization declined to an aggregate of 302, remaining at that level until the outbreak of war in 1861.[16]

The artillery, part scientific corps and part combat arm, began to increase its capabilities for mobility and close support on the battlefield in the Jacksonian era. In 1838, under the enlightened supervision of Secretary of War Joel Poinsett, a few units were converted to light, horse-drawn batteries, the beginning of a new trend. The older fortress defense mission retained primacy for a long time to come, but the shift toward improved mobility continued. Its enhanced capabilities enabled the artillery to play decisive roles in the Mexican and Civil Wars and in some of the Indian campaigns as well.[17] The combined strength of the four regiments of artillery in 1833 was 192 officers and 1,988 men; by 1847 this number had doubled but was reduced following the Mexican War to approximately 3,000. It remained at that level until 1861.[18]

The largest branch in the years between 1833 and 1860 was the infantry. The troops of this branch, unlike those of the scientific corps, spent little time in the East; instead, they occupied the frontier posts and patrolled the wagon trails. In addition, the infantry bore the brunt of the combat burden in the Florida and Mexican Wars. In 1832 there were seven regiments, making a total strength of 3,829. By 1838 the number had almost doubled because of the Second Seminole War. Nine years later, at the end of the Mexican War, sixteen line regiments and one of *voltigeurs* (light infantry) remained on the active list. In 1848, however, half the line regiments and the *voltigeurs* were inactivated, bringing the overall strength down to 4,464. Then, in 1855 Secretary of War Jefferson Davis organized two new regiments, raising the total infantry strength to 5,580 where it remained until the beginning of the Civil War.[19]

"Walk-a-heaps," the derisive term the Plains Indians applied to foot soldiers, was indicative of the frequently demonstrated inability of infantry to cope with the style of warfare encountered in the American West. This limitation grew increasingly apparent as the army's area of protective responsibility pushed further into the domain of the horse Indian. The pressing need for a more mobile striking force finally overcame entrenched prejudice, and in 1833 a dragoon regiment was formed from a nucleus of mounted rangers which had been raised the previous year for the Black Hawk War.[20] The advent of the regiment of dragoons marked the return of cavalry to the army after an absence of twenty years. In 1836 a second dragoon regiment was added, and by 1855 the mounted force had expanded to two regiments of cavalry and one of rifles in addition to the two dragoon units. The designations "dragoons," "rifles," and "cavalry" then in vogue did not carry the same connotation in the United States as elsewhere. American horse units, regardless of regimental names and despite minor distinctions in organizational structure, uniforms, and weapons, performed all the usual cavalry missions: reconnaissance, raiding, light combat, screening, and pursuit; rather than specialize in any one of these tasks as was the practice in European armies. Another difference was that, more often than not, American horse soldiers rode to the scene of action but dismounted to fight. Saber charges at the gallop were the exception, romanticists notwithstanding.[21]

With respect to strengths, the First Dragoons had been organized in 1833 at 34 officers and 749 men. The addition of the Second Dragoons in 1836 doubled this figure. With the activation of the Mounted Rifles in 1847 the total rose to 3,007. Post-war reductions brought the number of cavalrymen down to 2,100, but with the creation of two new regiments by Secretary Davis in 1855 the total rose to 3,401; this level remained in force until the outbreak of hostilities in 1861.[22]

The infantry and cavalry, generally in company-sized units, were stationed at small, isolated posts in the frontier regions and along the major wagon trails. Once in a while large forces of mixed composition would assemble for operations such as William S. Harney's march against the Brulé Sioux in 1855, George Wright's campaign against the Yakimas in 1856, and Albert Sidney Johnston's Mormon Pacification Expedition of 1858, but otherwise the Walk-a-heaps and the horse troopers earned their pay by maintaining the tiny posts and patrolling the surrounding territory.[23]

To control and administer the widely dispersed little army more effectively, the high command had split the area of responsibility into Northern and Southern Divisions—each commanded by a major general—after the War of 1812, but in 1821 this structure was replaced by one organized along east-west lines. However, the latter arrangement also proved inadequate and was supplanted in 1842 by another which divided the country into nine geographic departments.[24] Periodically thereafter the number of departments changed, but the geographic command concept remained in effect until the Civil War. In 1860, for instance, there were seven departments: the East commanded by Bvt. Maj. Gen. John E. Wool, the West under Col. Edwin V. Sumner, Texas commanded by Bvt. Maj. Gen. David E. Twiggs, New Mexico under Col. Thomas T. Fauntleroy, Utah under Bvt. Col. Charles F. Smith, Oregon commanded by Brig. Gen. William S. Harney, and California under Bvt. Brig. Gen. Newman S. Clarke.[25] In principle the geographic command scheme was sound; it permitted the extension of national control over a vast stretch of territory while simultaneously affording local commanders freedom of action, a vital necessity in view of the lag in communications between the outposts and Washington. That the system failed to work properly at times was less due to faulty basic design than to niggardly politicians who refused to provide adequate resources and to unimaginative commanders who did not use the forces they did have to best advantage.

The secretary of war, a civilian, presided over the military establishment. Of the twelve men who held that office between 1833 and 1861 only two, Joel Poinsett and Jefferson Davis, made any consistent effort to influence military policy. The others, more interested in patronage and political advantage than national defense, readily deferred to Congress and other partisan interests in matters pertaining to the army. The ineffectiveness of these secretaries, coupled with public indifference, congressional stingi-

12

ness, and the lack of a credible enemy abroad, permitted several long-standing deficiencies to go unchecked throughout most of the antebellum era. For instance, the disasters of the War of 1812 had spurred the government to embark on a program for constructing coastal defenses, but the project was carried out in such a lackadaisical fashion that key fortresses, such as those in Charleston Harbor, were still unfinished when the Civil War broke out. Then too, politicians customarily used the argument that the militia was the main line of defense to justify keeping the regular army on a starvation budget, yet those same politicians did nothing to stop the rapid deterioration of the militia which was taking place at the time. Moreover, despite the obvious need for highly mobile forces on the western frontier, mounted troops remained in short supply simply because Congress thought them too expensive to maintain.

Poinsett and Davis, the only two exceptions, did manage to introduce several badly needed reforms. In addition to increasing the mobility of the artillery, Poinsett standardized procedures for commissioning officers directly from civilian life. He also developed a rational system for defending the frontiers; however, the proposal was never implemented, and the old practice of locating forts according to the whims of politicians and settlers without regard to military effectiveness continued in full force. Jefferson Davis added four regiments, two of which were cavalry, to the regular army. He also experimented with camel transport in the southwestern desert and dispatched a group of officers to observe the Crimean War. Aware that the advent of rifled small arms and cannon would profoundly affect warfare, Davis also took measures to revise tactical doctrine accordingly; the officers assigned to carry out the effort, however, failed to give the new technology sufficient consideration in their studies and experiments as the Civil War was soon to demonstrate.[26]

Just below the secretary of war stood the commanding general of the army, the senior professional officer in the military bureaucracy. Winfield Scott, who occupied that position from 1841 to 1861, never openly challenged the principle of civilian control, but he steadfastly refused to acknowledge the secretary of war as his superior and resisted in every possible way any usurpation, real or imagined, of his prerogatives. In keeping with this spirit of independence Scott insisted on maintaining his headquarters in New York for much of the antebellum period, making it almost impossible for him to supervise effectively the staff bureaus in Washington When Jefferson Davis, a man as determined and knowledgeable as "Old Fuss and Feathers," became secretary of war, a collision was inevitable. Soon the two became embroiled in a vicious vendetta over what should have been a relatively minor matter.[27] Although stemming in this particular instance from a clash of monumental egos, the feud was symptomatic of a larger

13

issue, the anachronistic nature of the ill-defined, multi-headed command structure. Secretary of War Lewis Cass had sensed this organizational deficiency as early as 1834, but his and subsequent attempts at reform came to grief on the shoals of political expediency and bureaucratic inertia. As a matter of fact, the ambiguous situation was not rectified until the Root reforms of 1903 which eventuated in a general staff charged with advising, planning, and coordinating under a chief answerable directly to the secretary of war.[28]

The term "general staff" had been used since the 1820s to designate the Washington-based heads of the administrative and logistical services—for example, the adjutant general and the quartermaster general—but neither these nor the chiefs of engineers, topographical engineers, and ordnance, who were also tenanted in the capital, functioned as a modern general staff. Rather, each acted as an independent departmental administrator, responsible for only one specific area of support. This had become painfully evident in the Mexican War when Scott had to make both the operational plans and the detailed estimates himself. Moreover, there was no clear-cut delineation of staff responsibility with respect to the secretary of war and the commanding general. Until 1821 the bureau chiefs had dealt directly with the secretary; after that date they became responsible to the commanding general also, but in practice continued reporting directly to the former. John B. Floyd, who headed the War Department under James Buchanan, complained of this practice and the concomitant reduction of the commanding general's authority but to no avail.[29]

These obstacles to operational efficiency were to some extent overcome by the extended tenure of the bureau chiefs; this enabled each of them from experience to work out effective techniques for conducting business. In the process, of course, the chiefs also found ways to insulate their departments from undue interference by secretaries of war, many of whom did not stay in office long enough to learn ways of handling the veteran department heads who occupied the same positions for decades. Thomas Jesup, for instance, became quartermaster general in 1818 and, except for field service in the Florida War, retained that office until his death forty-two years later. Roger Jones was adjutant general for twenty-seven years, and his successor, Samuel Cooper, had been in office nine years when he left to serve the Confederacy in the same capacity. George Bomford remained chief of ordnance for sixteen years; John J. Abert acted as chief of topographical engineers from 1834 until 1861, and Joseph G. Totten died in office after serving twenty-five years as chief of engineers.[30] Obviously, even a moderately competent man could learn to function effectively when he held the same job for so long.

The air of immutability surrounding the commanding general and the heads of the staff bureaus did not permeate the rest of the regular army in the antebellum period. Profound changes were taking place in the officer corps, with the older generations who had entered the service from civilian life or risen from the ranks before the military academy had opened gradually giving way to West Pointers. The transformation began in the lower grades and slowly worked upward; in fact, no alumnus of the academy reached the status of general in the regular army until 1860. But as early as 1833 over half the officers on the active list were graduates of the military academy, and by 1860 more than 75 percent were. The proportion of graduates as officers did not grow in a straight, linear progression, however; the percentage, even though showing a general increase for the period, varied from year to year according to circumstances. In 1837, for instance, 117 officers resigned because of dissatisfaction with conditions of service in Florida; 99 of these were West Pointers. As a result the percentage of graduates on active duty declined overnight from almost 71 percent, the proportion in 1836, to a little over 53 percent in 1837. By 1838, however, the percentage had climbed to 64 and continued to increase except for a 1 percent dip in 1855 when officers were brought in from civilian life to fill vacancies in the newly activated regiments.[31]

Graduates of the military academy were not uniformly distributed among the branches of the army; the scientific corps contained the highest proportions of West Pointers and the combat arms the lowest. The percentage of graduates in the corps of engineers was the largest of all; indeed, only one officer of that branch was not a West Pointer.[32] This distribution was not coincidental. It reflected an official War Department policy, enthusiastically supported by the authorities at West Point, of reserving the scientific corps for those graduates who had stood highest in their classes. The others, together with the occasional civilian augmentations, were relegated to the infantry and cavalry.[33] The wisdom of concentrating the available intellectual talent in branches of the army that would play minor roles in a war is questionable, but there was a shred of logic behind it. The engineers, topographical engineers, ordnance, and, to a lesser degree, the artillery required skills and knowledge that only the military academy taught, whereas the intellectual demands of the infantry and cavalry were less stringent.

The increasing percentage of West Pointers in the regular army periodically gave rise to charges of monopoly; these were hotly debated in Congress where, almost as a matter of course, florid rhetoric and sheer ignorance obscured the truth. To begin with, graduates of the academy never achieved anything approaching a monopoly, as the above figures demon-

15

strate; however, West Pointers did receive first priority in filling the existing vacancies—a policy dictated by the law requiring them to serve in the regular army after graduation. Secondly, civilians and noncommissioned officers could obtain commissions whenever there were sufficient openings. But in periods when Congress imposed stringent budgetary and personnel limitations, and these were frequent in the 1830s and 1840s, West Pointers filled all the vacancies; as a matter of fact, for much of the antebellum era, graduates of the military academy had to serve a year or more as brevet second lieutenants, awaiting openings in the commissioned ranks. Under such circumstances civilian and noncommissioned officer applicants could not be considered.[34]

There were three periods between 1833 and the Civil War when sizable numbers of non-West Pointers obtained appointments as commissioned officers. The first, 1836 to 1838, came from vacancies accrued as a result of the Florida War and the activation of a second regiment of dragoons. The second, 1846 to 1848, grew out of the Mexican War and the creation of new units, namely, the Regiment of Mounted Rifles and the Company of Sappers, Miners, and Pontoneers, together with the addition of two companies to each artillery regiment. The final period, 1855–56, resulted from the activation of two infantry and two cavalry regiments with the specific proviso that a portion of the officers for each come from sources other than West Point.[35]

Candidates who were not West Pointers had to be unmarried, between the ages of twenty and twenty-five, and physically fit. They also had to meet certain mental standards, though these were considerably lower than those demanded for graduation from the military academy, the non-West Pointers being required merely to demonstrate proficiency in arithmetic, geography, American history and government, and international law. Each September, whenever vacancies remained in the officer corps after the academy graduates had been commissioned, civilians and noncommissioned officers desiring to compete for appointments appeared before examining boards. These bodies originally convened in Washington but subsequently moved to West Point where the professors served as examiners.[36] The low level of attainment required of the aspirants drew the fire of Professor Dennis Hart Mahan, a member of the faculty. In a letter to Secretary of War Poinsett he pointed out that "As these young men are commissioned only in the Infantry and Cavalry, the requirements need not certainly be of a very high order; but there are certain attainments which every officer should possess . . . amongst these . . . are the Means of Military Reconnaissance and a knowledge of the simple elements of Field Fortification."[37]

The wisdom of Mahan's caveat went unheeded. The army continued to employ a dual standard in the selection of professional officers, a procedure which fostered divisiveness within the commissioned ranks.

The Jacksonian politicians who decried the alleged West Point monopoly and advocated opening the officer corps to more appointees from civilian life were opposed by an equally resolute group that bitterly resented the commissioning of non-West Pointers. For example, an article in the September 1839 issue of the *Army and Navy Chronicle,* an unofficial but influential professional journal, complained, "To the introduction of young men from private life there are many objections. The first and most obvious is their want of early training and discipline. . . . Then the want of harmony of views, and of the chain of early associations and common reflections, deprives them of ready sympathy and welcome; while their comparative ignorance of the profession they are entering exposes them to the pity if not the sneers of their new associates."[38]

A piece in another issue of the same journal quarreled with the practice of commissioning ex-cadets who for some reason or other had left West Point without graduating. A few of these men actually became officers before their classmates had completed the course at the military academy. The author, who styled himself "An Officer of the Western Division," asked "Can any practice be better calculated to wither the hopes and crush the ambitions of the aspiring student than to see and learn daily, that idleness and incapacity must and will insure greater and speedier rewards than talent and application?"[39]

The writer was touching on a particularly sensitive point. Regulations and War Department policy prohibited commissioning former cadets before their classes graduated, but ingenious politicians sometimes found ways to circumvent these restrictions, much to the chagrin of those who had remained at West Point for four years.[40]

Awarding commissions to enlisted men also caused problems. In fact, so strong was the bias against this that a group of noncommissioned officers complained to Congress in 1837, maintaining that West Pointers were blocking their entry into the officer corps. And the following year Secretary Poinsett felt obliged to chastise Colonel Zachary Taylor and the other officers of the First Infantry who had refused to accept former enlisted men as colleagues. In his reprimand Poinsett stated: "The department regrets to see a feeling adverse to the promotion of non-commissioned officers. . . . It is foreign to the military character and institution to exclude from advancement a gallant soldier who has earned his promotion by long service and uniform good conduct. There can be nothing degrading in associating with such a man."[41]

17

Pro- and anti-West Point biases were not the only sources of friction among officers in the pre–Civil War regular army. Branch parochialism, sectionalism, and politics also provoked dissension. In fact, the officer corps of that era could hardly have been called a tightly knit "band of brothers."[42]

American society remained largely unaware of and indifferent to the intramural squabbles and everything else pertaining to the regular army. Civilians seldom saw soldiers and when they did, tended to view them with contempt. In his memoirs Ulysses S. Grant recalled how, as a new lieutenant walking the streets of Cincinnati, a small boy had taunted him with the jibe, "Soldier! Will you work? No siree, I'll sell my shirt first!" Leonard White in *The Jacksonians* quoted an *Army and Navy Chronicle* editorial bemoaning the fact that "The military profession in this country has been so poorly encouraged that but little incentive is held out to devote exclusive attention to it. . . . The distrust of military men, so prevalent among politicians, . . . it might be supposed, would long since have yielded to the light of reason and experience."[43]

In a similar vein White maintains that "Congressional parsimony and republican mistrust kept the army and the War Department in a constant state of frustration from 1829 to 1860," a contention which Russell Weigley, Robert M. Utley, and Samuel P. Huntington sustain.[44] Further proof of American antipathy toward military service can be found in the recruiting statistics. As early as the 1840s 47 percent of the regular army enlistees were Irish and German immigrants. With the possible exception of white Southerners, few native-born Americans looked on the profession of arms with affection or interest.[45]

Ironically, the psychological and geographic isolation of the regular army gave rise to the very thing the Jacksonians claimed to fear—military professionalism. The insular environment, together with the special demands of their calling, fostered among regular officers a corporate identity which, factionalism notwithstanding, separated them from their civilian contemporaries. In a like manner, the continuing evolution of military technology and thought called for a distinctive expertise which increasingly differentiated between the full-time soldier and the amateur. The trend toward professionalization was further stimulated by the advent of publications such as the *Army and Navy Chronicle, The Military and Naval Magazine,* and *The Military Magazine,* periodicals devoted exclusively to military affairs. Hence, the years between the early thirties and the Civil War constituted a milestone in American military history, a point where the semiprofessional citizen-soldier began to give ground to the educated military practitioner. Even though still incomplete at the outbreak of war in 1861, the process had gotten well underway in the preceding decades.

West Point was crucial to the rise of military professionalism in the United States. Up until the end of the Civil War the academy was, for all intents and purposes, the army's only school of tactical training as well as an institution of higher learning. It is true that the old Hamiltonian concept—a basic military college surmounted by schools of application to prepare officers for a particular branch—still survived, but barely. For instance, schools of artillery, infantry, and cavalry operated sporadically throughout the period; also, a few officers went abroad to study in European military schools.[46] However, only a small fraction of the officer corps managed to partake of these benefits. For the majority, West Point represented the sum total of their formal education and military training.

The academy nurtured professional growth in yet another way. During the pre–Civil War era West Point served as a proving ground for new weapons, materiel, and tactical concepts. Cast-iron gun carriages, breech-loading rifles, small arms ammunition, pontoon bridging, and cavalry saddles were tried out at the military academy prior to adoption by the army; in addition, the local siege battery was employed to test the effects of heavy artillery on the construction materials used for permanent fortifications. Moreover, manuals on the rifled musket and on infantry and cavalry tactics were revised after trials involving the corps of cadets and the enlisted detachment. As a general rule, the testing officers came from the field rather than the staff and faculty of the academy. A notable exception, however, was William Hardee who, just before beginning a tour of duty as commandant, used companies of cadets to determine the feasibility of his new infantry maneuvers. Normally, cadets did not participate in the experiments either, beyond acting as guinea pigs for Hardee and, later, for Philip St. George Cooke who was revising the system of cavalry tactics. Yet in one instance the West Point authorities did provide a student with facilities for experimentation. In 1857 Cadet Edward P. Alexander, subsequently a noted Confederate artilleryman, was issued a weapon to test a musket ball he had invented. Not only Hardee, Cooke, and Alexander, but Ambrose Burnside, George B. McClellan, Silas Casey, and Henry Heth also participated in the testing program at antebellum West Point.[47] That these innovators later became generals in the Civil War was undoubtedly coincidental, but the relation of their experiments to that bloody conflict was not. A comparison of the technological developments the tests represented with the tactical revisions made in the same period starkly reveals two facts pregnant with significance for the coming bloodbath. In the first place, such an examination discloses a continuing dependence on European military developments, particularly French; the ideas of American tacticians and inventors were mainly derivative, paying scant heed to the peculiar requirements imposed by the geography of the United States. An even

19

more ominous revelation is the chasm dividing changes in military technology from the updated tactical concepts that were supposed to take those changes into account. The reasons for these oversights may remain debatable, but there can be little disagreement about who would be called on to pay for them.

The young West Pointer entering the army in the years between 1833 and 1860 probably did not concern himself very much with the contributions his alma mater was making to the growth of military professionalism. To him the pursuit of his calling meant slow promotions, frequent separations from his family, physical hardship, the drudgery of military routine, and possibly an occasional encounter with danger, all of this on a less than munificent income and no pension plan.

In the 1830s pay scales ranged from $760 annually for a second lieutenant of infantry to $2,245 for a colonel of the same branch. Mounted officers and certain others drew a little more than this because of a supplementary allowance for forage. Salaries slowly increased throughout the period until by 1860 second lieutenants received $1,242 and colonels $2,616, the pay of officers in the intermediate grades being proportioned accordingly.[48] A colonel's salary roughly equalled that of a Harvard professor, whereas a second lieutenant's approximated that of a teacher at one of the smaller colleges such as Williams, Wabash, or Emory. The chief engineer on a large construction project, on the other hand, could earn as much as $6,000 a year in the early 1830s and a superintendent of construction at the lower end of the managerial scale in civil engineering made about $2,000; after 1838, though, engineers' salaries declined to a level approaching military pay,[49] a drop that was of some consequence to the army. As the financial incentive for leaving the service to become an engineer diminished, so did the resignation rate of regular officers.

The improvement in military pay was not matched by reform of the promotion system. Advancement was based on seniority alone, and there was no provision for removing the superannuated. Thus, a young officer had to wait until his seniors died, resigned, or moved up before he could get ahead. Moreover, promotion through the grade of captain depended on vacancies within the officer's regiment; therefore, a new lieutenant assigned to a unit in which the turnover of officers was low could expect to stay on the bottom rung of the ladder for a long time. One possibility of escaping the dead hand of seniority lay in the activation of additional regiments. At such times relatively junior officers, if fortunate enough to obtain transfers to these new units, could win promotions to fill the vacancies in them. Brevets, honorary promotions for valor or meritorious service, could also be used to accelerate advancement, but only under narrowly prescribed conditions, and then only temporarily.[50]

Although he could expect neither wealth nor rapid advancement, an officer stationed in the East could at least enjoy the amenities of civilization. Life for his fellow soldier on the frontier was vastly different. There, officers could anticipate years of duty at small, one-company posts, living in sod, log, or adobe huts and devoting most of their time to the dull round of garrison duties. Even the patrols and expeditions which relieved the monotony of cantonment life provided precious little in the way of adventure, for only rarely did they culminate in actual combat. As one historian has pointed out, a frontier soldier, on the average, took part in one real Indian battle every five years. Otherwise, the sorties beyond the confines of the post consisted of long, hard marching, sometimes under extreme weather conditions, vainly searching for an enemy who could be found only when he wanted to be. The cumulative effect of such an environment was encapsulated in Richard Ewell's frequently quoted aphorism that on the frontier an officer learned all there was to know about commanding forty dragoons but forgot everything else he had ever been taught.[51]

Yet the same, intellectually enervating frontier service which drove men like Grant out of the army and turned others into drunkards, time-servers, or petty tyrants held a unique appeal for some officers. Evidently, Lieutenant William Grier of the First Dragoons was feeling that attraction when he requested a transfer from the comforts of West Point with the comment: "The first five years of my service have been spent on the Western frontier. —To that kind of duty I have become so attached that I cannot . . . consent to remain here."[52]

Kindred sentiments motivated Henry Heth to speak of the years he spent at Fort Atkinson, a small post on the Kansas prairie, as among the happiest of his life. Others too, though less rhapsodic, savored some aspects of the experience. For instance, the journal Lieutenant John W. Turner, First Artillery, kept while participating in Wright's campaign against the Upper Columbia River Indians in 1856 dutifully records the tedium, a discomfort Turner made more bearable with an occasional toddy; however, it also captures the color of Indian life and the grandeur of the Cascades. Similarly, Lieutenant John C. Tidball of the Second Artillery could only take sardonic delight in "trampdoodling through the swamps" of Florida under the critical eye of General "Davey" Twiggs, but being an artist as well as a soldier, Tidball must have relished sketching the vistas he saw while accompanying the Whipple Expedition overland from New Mexico to California. Furthermore, the journals, memoirs and biographies of still other regulars, men such as Phil Sheridan, Dabney Maury, J. E. B. Stuart, Eugene A. Carr, Zenas R. Bliss, David S. Stanley, and August V. Kautz make clear that whatever its drawbacks, army life on the frontier did appeal to those of appropriate temperament.[53]

21

One of the compensations of frontier service was the opportunity it provided for relatively junior officers to exercise independent command, far removed from the scrutiny of higher headquarters. This freedom to train and employ a unit pretty much as he saw fit must have proved rewarding to a competent, self-reliant young lieutenant. Another compensation was that even though discipline was severe, the frontier army was less inhibited by social restraints and military punctilio than was the case in the East. In addition, the antebellum West was a sportsman's paradise. Indeed, if their writings are accurate indicators, some officers seem to have spent as much time hunting, fishing, gambling, and racing horses as they did on military duties.

Such, then, was the antebellum regular army of the United States, the force which justified the existence of the military academy at West Point. Small, far-flung, isolated and ignored, that army nevertheless served the nation far better than the civilians had any right to expect.

The Military Academy: The External Hierarchy of Control, 1833–1854

★

When he left West Point in the summer of 1833 following the dispute with President Andrew Jackson,[1] Sylvanus Thayer could look back with honest pride on his fourteen-year term as superintendent. First, he had brought order out of chaos, no trifling achievement considering the muddle he had inherited from Alden Partridge. Subsequently, he had not only preserved and refined the reforms of Williams and Swift, but had made substantial contributions of his own. These achievements earned Thayer the title "Father of the Military Academy";[2] however, the term "Midwife" seems more appropriate since some of the most notable innovations associated with him, namely, annual inspections by boards of visitors, a four-year curriculum, semiannual examinations, and teaching by the question and answer method actually should be credited to Joseph Swift, Thayer's predecessor. Furthermore, the reforms Thayer himself inaugurated were borrowed from L'École Polytechnique and American colleges. Nevertheless, it is true that by 1833 the essential components of the "Thayer System" were firmly in place at the military academy. A blend of the reforms of Williams and Swift with those of Thayer,[3] the system served as a guidepost for the men who controlled West Point in the antebellum period and for a long time after that.

Perhaps the most singular characteristic of the Thayer System was the emphasis on mathematics, science, and engineering in a curriculum purportedly designed to educate officers for all branches of the army. Using L'École Polytechnique as a pattern, Thayer created what was essentially an engineering school at West Point and gathered about him a faculty dedicated to keeping it that way in the face of all opposition.[4] As early as 1819, for example, Col. John E. Wool, the inspector general of the army, had felt compelled to remind Secretary of War Calhoun that "the great victories which had called forth the admiration of every age were not achieved by 'the rule and compass' or 'the measurement of angles.' " Then in an even more pointed reference to the curriculum at the academy, Wool expressed the fear that stress on mathematics would produce graduates capable only of "thoughts like the blasts from the polar regions which at every breath freeze the imagination and lock the heart from those generous and noble qualities which are the result of inquiry and liberal investigation." Forty-two years later a congressional investigatory commission headed by Senator Jefferson Davis found similar faults, and in the interim several boards of visitors had criticized the priority accorded mathematics, science, and engineering at the military academy. But none of the protests brought change. As late as 1866 the curriculum canted as much in the direction of these subjects as it had in 1833.[5]

Other hallmarks of the Thayer System were less controversial. The practices of dividing each class of cadets into small sections for academic instruction and having instructors frequently quiz their students antedated 1817, as did semiannual examinations. Thayer refined these innovations by requiring instructors to grade the performance of each student daily and submit weekly progress reports to the superintendent. He then used this information to assign cadets to academically homogeneous sections in every subject, thus permitting each section to progress through the course at a pace appropriate to the abilities of its members. The daily grades were also used in conjunction with the scores on final examinations to compute each cadet's annual order of merit standing; the cumulative annual order of merit standings, in turn, determined the student's graduation, or general order of merit ranking. The introduction of the order of merit concept was one of Thayer's most significant reforms.

The board of visitors inspection, initiated by Swift, became another permanent feature of the Thayer System. Ostensibly, the boards were made up of disinterested experts who carefully examined every aspect of the academy and then reported their findings, together with suitable recommendations, to the secretary of war. Actually, political expedience generally dictated the selection of board members; furthermore, the boards saw only what the authorities at West Point wanted them to see; consequently, the reports were, with few exceptions, mere encomiums camouflaged to resemble objective observations. Thayer went along with this charade during his administration but refused to take it seriously. As he pointed out, the board reports "would not be worth a feather with anyone who knows how the board is composed."[6] Still, the board of visitors did provide a convenient barometer of opinion and public relations tool.

In contrast, the academic board, organized by Thayer, became a linchpin of his system. Like the body which directed L'École Polytechnique, the academic board at West Point determined curriculum content, conducted the semiannual examinations, computed order of merit standings, and recommended graduating cadets for branches of the army. The chief of engineers, the secretary of war, and, of course, the president could override the board but rarely chose to do so. And even in cases where the higher authorities did seek to impose their will, the board usually found ways to circumvent any directive which conflicted with its desires.

When Thayer established the academic board, he may not have realized that it would help perpetuate his influence at West Point for many years to come. But several factors made that almost inevitable. Four of the department heads who sat on the academic board had been cadets under Thayer's tutelage: Dennis H. Mahan, professor of civil and military engineering and the art of war for forty-one years; William H. C. Bartlett who chaired the department of natural and experimental philosophy for thirty-seven years; Albert E. Church, chairman of the department of mathematics from 1837 to 1878; and Jacob W. Bailey, professor of chemistry, mineralogy, and geology from 1838 until his death in 1857. Mahan and Bartlett had additional ties to Thayer; while superintendent he had recruited both for the faculty. Also, Claudius Berard, head of the department of French for thirty-three years, had taught at the academy throughout Thayer's administration. Then too, three of the four superintendents between 1833 and 1854 had attended West Point during the Thayer era. Being intimately familiar with what the putative Father of the Military Academy had accomplished, such men would naturally be inclined to respect and maintain the Thayer System, but the former superintendent was not content to rely on natural deference. Instead, he actively endeavored to extend his sway over the institution.

Convinced that he had created a perfect system, Thayer attempted to frustrate any subsequent modification, no matter how trivial. For instance, in 1838 he warned Richard Delafield, then superintendent, against making minor alterations in the curriculum lest he establish a precedent for proliferation which would result in "teaching a little of many things instead of much of a few."[7] Fifteen years later Thayer vented his spleen on Secretary of War Davis and Joseph Totten, the chief of engineers, for considering changes in the disciplinary system. In a letter to Capt. George W. Cullum, a fellow engineer officer who would become Thayer's principal apologist, the former superintendent excoriated the secretary of war as "a recreant and unnatural son who would have pleasure in giving his alma mater a kick and would disown her if he could." And Totten, in Thayer's eyes, was "perfectly pliable."[8] That Davis and Totten were two of the staunchest champions of the military academy carried no weight with Thayer. In contemplating a change to his system they had warranted damnation.

The lingering influence of Sylvanus Thayer was an important external force exerting pressure on the antebellum military academy, but there were others as well. Their positions in the chain of command entitled the president, the secretary of war, the commanding general of the army, and the chief of engineers to intervene in affairs at West Point as they saw fit. But whether each of these functionaries elected to exercise his prerogatives directly or merely accept decisions made at lower levels of the hierarchy was largely a matter of personal choice. Generally, the presidents and secretaries of war in the years between 1833 and 1854 restricted themselves to political and budgetary concerns. The commanding general seldom interfered with the operation of the academy but did perform an important symbolic function. Totten, as chief of engineers, on the other hand busied himself almost constantly with West Point. His duties as inspector of the military academy would have required considerable involvement in any case, but his temperament drove him to go far beyond the demands of his official responsibilities.

As commander in chief the president theoretically exercised almost absolute power over all military academy affairs. In practice, however, the pre–Civil War chief executives seldom intervened except to reinstate discharged cadets.

Andrew Jackson was undoubtedly the foremost of the presidential meddlers. The squabble with Thayer over the restoration of Cadet Ariel Norris apparently did not induce "Old Hickory" to consider the deleterious effects of his paternalism, for he continued the practice of restoring delinquent students. In September 1835 Jackson ordered that three boys who had been sent home the preceding June for academic failure be reexamined,[9] and in November of the same year he directed that Cadet Marcus M. Hammond, who had been dismissed by a court-martial, be permitted to return to the academy. In this instance Jackson, finally awake to the problems his indulgence was creating, delivered a stern warning to the corps: "I had hoped that a lenient system of administration would be found sufficient for the government of the Military Academy—But I have been disappointed; and it is now time to be more rigorous in enforcing its discipline. . . . Hereafter, therefore, the sentences of courts-martial will, when legal and regular, be confirmed."[10]

Jackson's change of heart was genuine. Never again did he interfere with internal discipline at West Point.

Old Hickory's concern for maintaining law and order at the military academy reflected a sincere interest in the welfare of the institution. In two annual messages to Congress the president took occasion to praise West

26

Point. In the first he said, "I recommend to your fostering care as one of our safest means of national defense the Military Academy. This institution has already exercised the happiest influence upon the moral and intellectual character of our army."[11]

And in 1835 he cited the academy for the services its graduates were rendering as custodians of government funds: "These diversified functions [public works, Indian affairs] embrace very heavy expenditures of public money and require fidelity, science, and business habits in their execution. . . . That this object has been in a great measure obtained by the Military Academy is shown by the state of the service and by the prompt accountability which has generally followed the necessary advances."[12]

Nor was Jackson's praise limited to public utterances. In a letter to his nephew Andrew Jackson Donelson, class of 1820, Old Hickory enthusiastically endorsed the military academy as the "best school in the world."[13]

Martin Van Buren, Jackson's protégé and successor, also saw fit to commend the institution in an annual message: "The Military Academy continues to answer all the purposes of its establishment, and not only furnishes well educated officers to the Army but serves to diffuse throughout the mass of our citizens, individuals possessed of military knowledge and the scientific attainments of civil and military engineering."[14]

By going on record in favor of West Point the two political leaders were running counter to the wishes of some of their supporters who advocated the abolition of the academy; however, neither president, regardless of his personal views, made any effort to restrain those Jacksonians who wanted to destroy the institution.

Van Buren, like his predecessor, had family ties with West Point, his son Abraham having graduated in 1827,[15] but unlike Jackson, the "Red Fox" did not intervene personally in affairs at the military academy; instead, he left such matters to his gifted Secretary of War Joel Poinsett.

With the exception of James K. Polk, all the presidents from William Henry Harrison through Franklin Pierce followed Van Buren's laissez-faire policy. Polk, however, interfered in several cases. Once he overruled a court-martial which had dismissed two cadets, using alleged irregularities in the trial proceedings as his pretext. Yet Polk, like Jackson, understood the difficulties executive clemency could create. In a message to the corps of cadets he first explained why lenience seemed the proper course in the case at hand but then admonished: "The cadets must not forget that they are supported and educated at public expense, and the nation is entitled to their best exertions. While so many meritorious youth are seeking admission to the Academy, there is no place for the idle or disobedient."[16]

A few months later the president demonstrated his new firmness. In 1848 he refused to mitigate a sentence of suspension despite the plea of a con-

27

gressman.[17] In 1849 Polk went even further, overruling a recommendation for clemency from a court which had sentenced two cadets to dismissal. Even though in this instance the superintendent of the military academy had seconded the court's entreaty, the president remained unmoved and ordered the sentences executed.[18]

Polk also intervened in another matter affecting the academy. In 1847 the adjutant general attempted to block the commissioning of civilians in the regular army, intending instead to fill the vacancies with West Point graduates. The president adamantly opposed this move and eventually carried the day.[19] Polk disclaimed any hostility toward the military academy, but did not subscribe to the belief that only West Pointers were fit to hold commissions.

As a New Hampshire congressman, Franklin Pierce had participated in the attacks on West Point in 1835 and 1836, going so far as to deliver a speech in the House on 30 June 1836 in which he resurrected Thomas Jefferson's old charge that the academy was unconstitutional. But firsthand knowledge of the performance of West Pointers in the Mexican War convinced Pierce he had been mistaken;[20] as president he supported the institution at least to the extent of giving Secretary of War Davis carte blanche to carry out his reforms.

As a rule, the chief executives from 1833 through 1854 refrained from exercising their authority over the military academy directly. Those who did intervene, particularly Jackson and Polk, limited their interest almost exclusively to the restoration of cadets. However, both of these activist presidents, politicians though they were, came to see the necessity for upholding disciplinary standards at West Point.

Similarly, the secretaries of war generally eschewed exercising their formidable power over the military academy, preferring instead to rely on the recommendations of others. The secretary's official responsibilities embraced appointing and discharging cadets, approving changes in the curriculum, reviewing the budget, and informing Congress and the president annually of the state of the institution. His advisor on such concerns was the chief of engineers under whose purview the academy fell. Most secretaries looked to that officer alone for advice on West Point matters, but one, Joel Poinsett, also maintained an unofficial line of communication with Professor Mahan in an effort to keep his finger on the pulse of the academy.

As was true of the presidents, some secretaries of war intervened more often and more actively than others. Usually, those who remained in office longest, such as Cass, Poinsett, and Davis, tended to be the most energetic interventionists.

In dealing with West Point Cass followed the lead of his chief Andrew Jackson. The secretary larded his reports with praise for the academy, claiming that because of it "the standards of acquirement for the military profession have been raised . . . and we have been better able to keep pace with the improvements which the nations of Europe have made." He also supported an endeavor to obtain professorial rank for the teacher of drawing and another to build a new chapel and barracks. On the other hand, the secretary, in true Jacksonian style, always stood ready to uphold the cause of the cadet, especially if he happened to come from a poor family. In 1835, for instance, Cass, in ordering the reinstatement of a destitute student, wrote the superintendent: "Poverty indeed cannot constitute of itself a claim to admission or retention at the Military Academy, but other things being equal, it may justly be taken into view in a decision which may determine for life the prospects of a young man who has no means of his own."[21]

The secretary of war did not limit his concern to indigents. He occasionally remitted the court-martial sentences of other cadets as well, particularly when the offender appeared before him in person to plead his case. Cass would invariably lecture the miscreant on the need for mending his ways and assure the authroities at West Point that he supported their struggle to maintain discipline, but this guarantee held good only until the next unfortunate student knocked on his door.[22]

These intercessions on behalf of delinquent cadets prompted the academic board to chide the secretary: "It may safely be affirmed that the leniency extended for the safety of one has, in the end, caused the destruction of many, who, without such a hope of escape held up before them, might have persevered in the correct course." Benjamin F. Butler, Cass's successor, heeded the board's warning and served notice on the corps of cadets that he intended to enforce discipline.[23] Butler was as good as his word, but since he held office for only a few months, his policy had no long-range effect.

Van Buren's secretary of war, Joel Poinsett, was a dedicated military innovator who took a keen interest in West Point. It was largely through his efforts that equitation, or horsemanship, was introduced into the curriculum, that the professorship of chemistry, mineralogy, and geology was established, and that the term of service for graduates was increased from three to four years. In addition, Poinsett pushed through a construction program which eventuated in a new barracks, a new academic building, a library, and an observatory.[24] The secretary also played an active role in selecting a superintendent and a chaplain, his choice for the latter post being one of Poinsett's few mistakes.[25]

The secretary firmly believed in upholding discipline at West Point and refused to reverse decisions without first ascertaining the facts in the case, a refreshing change from the habits of his predecessors. Yet Poinsett dis-

29

couraged the practice of dismissing cadets for minor offenses; in 1838 he specified that thenceforth dismissals would be approved by his office only if the offender were guilty of conduct that was "vicious, depraved, and dishonorable." The secretary made the commanding general responsible for reviewing all court-martial cases involving the discharge of cadets; this was the first time that officer had been assigned a direct role in matters pertaining to West Point. In January 1837, not long after the secretary of war had assumed his post, Lieutenant William W. Bliss, then stationed at West Point, wrote his classmate Henry Du Pont, "We expect everything from Mr. Poinsett." [26] The secretary did much during his term to fulfill those expectations.

John Bell and John McClean, who successively followed Poinsett, remained in office only a few months apiece. Neither made an appreciable impact on the academy except that Bell shut down the private line of communications Poinsett had established with Professor Mahan, insisting instead that from then on all correspondence from West Point flow through official channels. [27]

John C. Spencer, who replaced McClean at the War Department, became convinced by the board of visitors report of 1841 that cadets should study logic. The academic board balked, claiming that no time could be found for this subject in the overcrowded curriculum without reducing or eliminating some other course the professors considered more important. The secretary refused to yield, however, and eventually forced the board to comply with his desire. Spencer also supported the chief of engineers in an attempt to obtain the men and equipment to institute a course in practical military engineering. At the outset they achieved partial success, and a department was established at West Point to teach the subject; however, it was not until much later that the necessary resources became available to conduct instruction. [28]

James M. Porter, William Wilkins, William L. Marcy, and George W. Crawford, who followed Spencer in the order named, did little for the military academy, but they continued the practice of reinstating discharged cadets. This finally forced the superintendent in 1848 to request that the War Department desist, referring in his note to the dire consequences which had sprung from tampering with the disciplinary system. At the same time he proposed a specific remedy for one particularly troublesome offense—drinking. The superintendent suggested that in such cases the secretary of war immediately dismiss the culprit without trial, but nothing came of this recommendation. [29]

Most secretaries, except for the reformers, confined their interference in West Point affairs to the reinstatement of cadets who had been dismissed for misconduct; however, Charles M. Conrad took the additional step of challenging the academic board's findings of scholastic failure. The professors instantly protested this invasion of their province and took the secretary to task for demanding that the deficient cadets be reexamined. Thereupon, Conrad stingingly rebuked the board: "The Academy is placed by law under the direction of the President, who in this, as in all other military matters acts through the Secretary of War. In no portion of the duty thus imposed on him is the personal care and watchfulness of the Secretary more necessary than in regard to the rejection or dismissal of cadets. . . . Academic Boards are not infallible."[30]

In response the board declared its innocence of any intent to defy the secretary of war but repeated the claim that it was better equipped than any outsider to determine questions of academic proficiency. Nevertheless, the professors did offer to reexamine the cadets,[31] thus avoiding a showdown. Conrad, a man with a mind of his own, also intervened in another academic matter. He flatly vetoed a proposed five-year curriculum despite the fact that the measure had been advocated by boards of visitors for many years and was warmly endorsed by the chief of engineers.[32]

Jefferson Davis, Conrad's successor, did implement the five-year course, undoubtedly the most radical reform in the history of the antebellum military academy. In addition, Davis obtained funds for building a riding hall, enlarging the cavalry stables, improving the hospital, and installing a gaslight system. As secretary of war and later as a senator, Davis worked tirelessly for the welfare of his alma mater, Thayer's canard notwithstanding.

Examination of the roles of the secretaries of war brings to light a chronic problem which plagued the academy. Because of its dual status as a governmental agency and an educational institution, attempts to maintain high disciplinary and academic standards were sometimes thwarted by bureaucratic and political pressures beyond the control of the faculty. On occasion able secretaries, such as Poinsett and Davis, sensitive to the needs of the institution and willing to put principle ahead of expedience, not only cooperated but led the way in implementing needed changes and maintaining standards. All too often, however, politics rather than the pursuit of excellence was the determining factor.

The responsibilities of the secretary of war with respect to the military academy were clearly defined; those of the commanding general were not. In fact, the ambiguity attached to that office was as much in evidence at West Point as elsewhere in the army. So far as the evidence shows, Alexander Macomb, who held the post from 1828 to 1841, took no part whatsoever in affairs pertaining to the academy. Nor did his successor, Winfield Scott, play a much more active official role aside from serving on several boards of inspection and reviewing the cases of court-martialed cadets as directed by Secretary Poinsett.

31

Although not a graduate, Scott was an enthusiastic booster of the military academy;[33] in fact, the general and his family spent most of their summers at West Point where Scott, resplendent in full regalia, delighted in dazzling scores of visitors and several generations of cadets, including Ulysses S. Grant, who proclaimed him "the finest specimen of manhood my eyes have ever beheld and the most to be envied." Grant did not stand alone in his admiration; the writings of practically every other antebellum cadet also demonstrate clearly that "Old Fuss and Feathers" indelibly impressed the members of the corps. This, then, was Scott's role—father figure, living legend, walking inspiration[34]—but not an active participant in academy affairs.

In his capacity as inspector of the military academy the chief of engineers officially represented the institution in Washington. This function required a high degree of political acumen and an acute sense of timing together with a keen appreciation of the necessity for tempering idealistic aims in the face of reality. Moreover, the chief had to be adept at mediating between the Washington establishment and West Point authorities as well as refereeing between squabbling intramural factions at the academy. Furthermore, he had to be a wise, energetic administrator, able to stretch chronically thin resources to meet a host of diverse requirements, varying from the military academy at one extreme to western exploration at the other.

Charles Gratiot served as chief of engineers from 1828 until he was cashiered ten years later for refusing to relinquish funds in his possession. Thayer, in the erroneous belief that Gratiot had not sustained him in the quarrel with Andrew Jackson, complained that the chief of engineers would not stand up for the military academy, but the record indicated otherwise.[35] Although not a dynamic leader, Gratiot did try to bring about improvements at West Point. For example, he strongly supported the effort to build a new chapel and an additional barracks; he also assisted Secretary Poinsett in initiating the course in equitation, and he was instrumental in obtaining better classroom facilities for the departments of chemistry and natural philosophy.[36] Even though the credit for originating these improvements belonged to others, Gratiot at least deserved acknowledgment for diligently working to implement them.

Joseph G. Totten who succeeded Gratiot held office as chief of engineers and inspector of the military academy for twenty-five years. The nephew and ward of Jared Mansfield, first professor of mathematics at the academy, Totten had enrolled as a cadet in 1802 just a few months after West Point opened; he was not quite fifteen at the time. Following graduation in 1805 he spent two years exploring and surveying the Northwest Territory, then became assistant engineer for the harbor defenses in New York City and New Haven. At the outbreak of the War of 1812 Totten was appointed

Joseph G. Totten, class of 1805, Chief of Engineers, U.S. Army, 1838–1864.

chief engineer for the Niagara Frontier and later won a brevet promotion to lieutenant colonel for gallantry at the Battle of Plattsburg. Between the end of the war and 1838 he planned and supervised the construction of defenses along the Atlantic coast. In the same period Totten published *Essays on Hydraulic and Common Mortars and on Lime Burning* and also renewed his association with the military academy, serving on five boards of visitors during the period. On 7 December 1838 he was promoted to colonel and replaced Gratiot as chief of engineers. Totten headed the engineer bureau for the rest of his life. Without relinquishing his office as chief of engineers, he accompanied Winfield Scott in the invasion of Mexico. As a member of Scott's "Little Cabinet" Totten was instrumental in planning and conducting the siege of Vera Cruz, winning a brevet to brigadier general for his performance of duty.

After the war he resumed his post in Washington, but the heavy administrative load did not dull his innovative spirit. As a member of the lighthouse board he pioneered in the use of Fresnel lenses in beacons on the Atlantic seaboard, an accomplishment which ranked Totten as "one of the greatest engineers of the age," according to Maj. Gen. John G. Barnard, a fellow engineer officer. Totten made more direct contributions to military engineering as well. From 1855 to 1857 he conducted a series of experiments to determine the effects of firing heavy artillery pieces from casemates in permanent fortifications and related tests to evaluate the damage inflicted on the same casemates when struck by the various kinds of artillery projectiles.

Beginning in 1859 Totten made a two-year inspection tour of defenses on the Pacific coast to ascertain their state of readiness. During the Civil War he supervised the construction of the defenses around Washington and served on a board to standardize heavy artillery in addition to carrying out his duties as chief of engineers. Totten was engaged in those tasks when he died in 1864. The day before his death Congress cited him for fifty years of "faithful and eminent service."

Joseph G. Totten was more than a brilliant and imaginative engineer. As an amateur scientist he gained national recognition for his work in conchology and had two seashells named in his honor. In addition, he was an original regent of the Smithsonian Institution and a charter member of the National Academy of Sciences.[37] His stature as an engineer and scientist put Totten on the same intellectual plane as the professors at West Point. Moreover, his knowledge of and dedication to the institution, coupled with the even temper, inventiveness, energy, and political savoir faire that were his trademarks made him an ideal spokesman for the antebellum military academy.

Less than a month after taking office as chief of engineers in 1838 Totten began a campaign to improve professional training at West Point. After winning the backing of the secretary of war and carefully coordinating with the authorities at the academy,[38] the chief of engineers set about amassing the necessary personnel and resources to form a company of sappers, miners, and pontooneers. The unit was to be stationed at West Point where it would present instruction in practical military engineering, but because of limitations on funds and manpower it was not until May 1846 that the company was activated. The following October the unit sailed for Mexico. Totten's tenacity eventually bore fruit, however; at the conclusion of the Mexican War the company returned to the military academy, and instruction finally got underway.

The chief was also aware of other weaknesses in the curriculum, specifically, the inadequacy of instruction in English, history, geography, ethics, and law. Boards of visitors had recognized these defects as early as the 1830s and had often recommended a one-year extension to the course of study as a corrective. Convinced of the need for this measure, Totten commenced advocating it to secretaries of war in 1846,[39] but it was not until Jefferson Davis's administration that he won sufficient support to bring it about.

The chief also had to concern himself with more mundane matters such as settling disputes between the superintendent and the professors, and occasionally, arguments between cliques within the faculty.[40] This required considerable tact and patience, for Totten was dealing with strong-minded, hypersensitive men, each quick to bridle at any imagined slight. In addition, the chief of engineers reviewed every change in texts and proposed course revision before making recommendations to the secretary of war. Totten did not view this as a pro forma responsibility; he diligently studied every recommended change and refused to concur until satisfying himself that the innovation was desirable, even though it might involve nothing more than the substitution of one text in ethics for another.[41]

One of the chief's most important duties was representing the military academy in Washington. Among other things, this entailed haggling with the other staff bureau chiefs over the assignment and relief of instructors at the academy, determining the most equitable distribution of graduates to the corps and regiments, and obtaining sufficient funds to operate the institution.[42] The chief of engineers was also called on from time to time to soothe the ruffled feelings of dignitaries who felt they had been snubbed by authorities at West Point and to defend the actions of the academic board in discharging delinquent cadets against irate congressmen, secretaries of war, and once in awhile even presidents.[43]

Totten performed all these tasks well, indeed, probably better than any of his contemporaries could have; however, he was not without faults. Addicted to verbosity and circumlocution, the chief was sometimes vague and invariably tiresome in his long-winded preachments. Also, whenever possible he skirted rather than confronted controversial issues. Yet when forced to take a stand, Joseph Totten fought with courage, integrity, and wisdom. And if at times he enmeshed himself in trivia and indulged in over-supervision, just as often he displayed a breadth of vision beyond the ken of his peers.

The position of the chief of engineers and inspector of the military academy was, by its very nature, the single, most important element of external control. But Totten, spurred by his personality and his love for the academy, went beyond the official requirements and in so doing became a central figure in the history of antebellum West Point. On hearing of his death, Joseph Swift wrote, "Totten was a faithful servant of his country and worked himself to death under an idea of responsibility that in fact belonged to others."[44] Swift would have been more accurate as well as more charitable had he appended a list of Totten's accomplishments to the epitaph.

Taken together these components of the external hierarchy of control—Thayer's persistent influence, the presidents, secretaries of war, commanding generals, and chiefs of engineers—constituted a powerful force working to shape the pre–Civil War academy, but by no means was it the only or even necessarily the most significant one. Like any other bureaucratic institution, the academy was molded by internal as well as external pressures. Thus, it was as much a matter of what men on the Hudson did as what those on the Potomac wanted that made antebellum West Point what it was.

The Men Who Governed at West Point

In his history of the military academy Stephen Ambrose introduces Thayer's administration with the assertion that "In the nineteenth century the most important single element in the life of any American college was the president. He dominated all. The success or failure of an institution depended directly upon him."[1]

This is an inaccurate description of the role of the superintendent of the military academy in the antebellum era. Though titular head of the institution, he was by no means "the most important single element" in its life; nor did he "dominate all." Above him stood chiefs of engineers, secretaries of war, and presidents who could overrule him at will or, for that matter, curtail his career, as Thayer learned in 1833 and others would later. Even at West Point the superintendent's authority was limited except in purely military affairs.

Until 1866 the superintendent invariably came from the corps of engineers; usually he was a captain or at most a major. Engineer officers did not consider the post a particularly desirable one. Some, like Joseph Totten, begged off when offered the appointment; others accepted it but sought early relief; and those who served full terms seemed happy when the time came to leave.[2] The pressure of having to assume heavy responsibilities without sufficient resources or authority to carry them out was too great, and the financial compensation was too small. Furthermore, the essentially bureaucratic nature of the office kept it from being as exciting or professionally rewarding as other engineer assignments such as river and harbor work, fortress construction, or exploring. Nor was the superintendency a necessary stepping stone for advancement in the corps of engineers. Of the

Richard Delafield, class of 1818, Superintendent, U.S. Military Academy, 1838–1845, 1856–1861, 28 January–1 March 1861; Chief of Engineers, U.S. Army, 1864–1866.

ten men who occupied the office between 1833 and 1866 only Richard Delafield ever became chief of the bureau.[3]

Its limitations notwithstanding, the position was an important one. As
commander of the garrison at West Point the superintendent was responsible for the welfare and conduct of all the enlisted men, officers, civilians,
and dependents who worked or lived there. He was also accountable for all
government property on the reservation, that is, everything from muskets
and cavalry horses to wharves and public buildings. In addition to these
obligations, common to all post commanders, the superintendent also had
to provide for the comfort and safety of large numbers of visitors: official
dignitaries, friends and relatives of cadets, and ordinary tourists.

Maintaining discipline in the corps of cadets was another of the superintendent's important functions. Although he had other officers to assist in
the routine aspects, such as inspecting the barracks and punishing minor
infractions of regulations, the superintendent alone was responsible for
handling serious cases. This entailed time-consuming administrative
chores: appointing an officer to investigate the matter, reviewing evidence,
and when appropriate arranging for a court-martial. Then, in instances
involving heavy penalties, such as dismissal or suspension, the superintendent frequently had to spend even more time trying to justify the sentence to irate parents, congressmen, and secretaries of war.

In carrying out his educational duties the superintendent found himself
in a unique position for a military commander. He was president of the
academic board but had only one vote and no veto. The board reached
decisions by majority rule, and the superintendent was bound to forward
its views to the chief of engineers whether or not he concurred. As a
member of the board he could participate in discussions and make recommendations on academic as well as military matters; in fact, however, only
once in the period between 1833 and the coming of the Civil War did a
superintendent propose an academic reform, and the professors tabled
that.[4]

The academic staff and the superintendent seldom clashed openly in the
antebellum era, and then only when the latter insisted on exact compliance
with what the professors considered discretionary regulations governing
faculty conduct. As a general rule superintendents avoided antagonizing
the teachers; in fact it was futile to do otherwise, for even in the rare instance when a superintendent did impose an unpopular policy, his victory
was only temporary. The professors merely had to wait until he left and a
more sympathetic successor took over.

Between 1833 and 1861 Maj. Rene De Russy, Maj. Richard Delafield,
Capt. Henry Brewerton, Bvt. Col. Robert E. Lee, and Capt. John G. Bar-

nard served as superintendents of the military academy.[5] Richard Delafield was the only officer of this group who made a persistent effort to assert his authority to the extent that Thayer had. Delafield, who held office three times during the period, failed in his endeavor but not because he lacked energy or determination.

Born into a prominent New York City family in 1798, Richard Delafield had matriculated at West Point when he was sixteen, becoming a member of the first class to pursue a four-year curriculum. Graduating at the head of his class in 1818, he received a commission in the corps of engineers and was assigned to duty constructing permanent fortifications, a field that was to become his specialty. After tours at Hampton Roads, Virginia, and along the Mississippi River near New Orleans, he assumed the superintendency at West Point in 1838. On completion of this assignment in 1845 he returned to constructing coastal defenses. Delafield was engaged in that activity when Secretary of War Davis appointed him to a military commission to observe the Crimean War. While in the Crimea Delafield carefully studied siege operations against permanent fortifications; his analysis of those operations had a direct bearing on the American coastal defense system and thus constituted an important part of the commission's report.

After returning to the United States in 1856 Delafield went back to West Point as superintendent. He remained on duty there until January 1861 when Bvt. Maj. Pierre G. T. Beauregard replaced him. However, the secretary of war relieved Beauregard almost immediately on suspicion of disloyalty and ordered Delafield to resume temporarily the post he had just relinquished. Two months later he turned the command over to Maj. Alexander H. Bowman and took a staff appointment, organizing New York State troops and inspecting the defenses around New York Harbor. In 1864 Delafield was promoted to brigadier general and named chief of engineers, remaining in that office until he retired in 1866.[6]

Richard Delafield's first term as superintendent began in 1838 when he relieved Maj. Rene De Russy. The new incumbent immediately set about restoring the disciplinary standards his popular but lax predecessor had allowed to slip. According to a contemporary student, Delafield not only punished every infraction of the rules with a heavy hand but "deprived cadets of all the amusements and recreation he possibly could." Specifically, the superintendent scheduled fire drills on Saturday afternoons in what had previously been free time, ended De Russy's practice of permitting students to attend officers' parties, and forced cadets to answer self-incriminating questions.[7]

Delafield's zeal in enforcing conduct regulations was matched by a passion for keeping cadets free of indebtedness to the government, especially when they were in imminent danger of being discharged for academic deficiencies. In keeping with this policy he denied new plebes (freshmen) permission to replace worn-out clothing by buying garments on credit at the cadet store, suggesting instead that the youngsters mend their old clothing. The superintendent also refused to let plebes purchase overcoats until they had passed the January examinations no matter how cold the weather might turn before then. Delafield's parsimony was motivated in part by the desire to protect government funds, but it had another purpose as well. The superintendent knew that some cadets traded their clothing to civilians for whiskey or tobacco, then purchased replacement items on credit from the cadet store. In order to curb this practice he had to scrutinize each request to buy clothing with great care. Most cadets disliked Delafield, and so did other members of the garrison. As an Irish janitor put it when the superintendent departed on a river boat at the end of his first term, "there was many a dry eye at the dock."[8] But Delafield occasionally displayed a better nature, at least in his dealings with cadets. John Tidball, later to become a distinguished Union horse artilleryman, claimed that Delafield had saved him from dismissal on learning that the charges against him had been made by an unfair and vindictive tactical officer. And E. P. Alexander, who subsequently commanded Confederate batteries, found that Delafield, unlike most officers at West Point, was not bound by custom and would act on any reasonable suggestion for improvement. At Alexander's request he lengthened the period between parade and supper so cadets would have time to bathe and also ordered that both tea and coffee be served in the mess hall every night. Up until then coffee had been served one night and tea the next, regardless of which the cadets preferred.[9]

Delafield broke with tradition in other ways too. During his first administration he replaced the side-button trousers which the cadets wore with fly-fronts, much to the embarrassment of Mrs. Delafield and the other ladies of the post. In his second term he lengthened the tails of the cadet officers' coats, an idea he had borrowed from the European armies he had observed in Russia. Also, in the winter of 1859 the superintendent, aware that the cadets needed an outlet for pent-up energies, had the soldiers of the cavalry detachment hitch their horses to large sleighs and take the entire corps for rides along the roads to Buttermilk Falls and Fort Montgomery, two nearby villages.[10] No other superintendent ever took such an unorthodox approach to the problem of winter boredom. But occasional thoughtfulness and innovation were not enough to soften Delafield's image in the minds of students. Even those who appreciated his good points looked on him as a tyrant.[11]

The same characteristics which angered cadets provoked open resistance among the faculty. Paragraph forty-five of the academic regulations specified that professors would carry a full teaching load in addition to serving

41

as department chairmen. Although some professors complied fully, others ignored the directive or taught only one section, arguing that a greater teaching burden would prevent them from adequately supervising the instructors in their departments. His predecessor had winked at these violations of the rules, but not Delafield. Soon after taking office in 1838 he directed the professors and their assistants to exchange sections occasionally so the department heads could determine their subordinates' competence in the classroom. Delafield's edict clearly implied that if the professors were not teaching, they should be; at the same time it neatly destroyed their contention that they must be free to supervise—the superintendent had provided a way for them to teach and check on their instructors at the same time. When his order failed to produce the desired results, Delafield resorted to stronger action, demanding a written explanation for every violation he detected. The professors grudgingly conformed with the order to submit excuses to the superintendent but did not mend their ways in other respects.[12] This dispute touched on an issue larger than the prerogatives of command. Had the professors been willing to shoulder a greater share of the instructional burden, it would have reduced or perhaps have eliminated the necessity for detailing upperclassmen to teach freshmen and sophomores, an evil which plagued the military academy for most of the antebellum era.

With equal determination the superintendent attempted to dragoon all of the professors and army officers into attending Sunday services at the cadet chapel as required by regulations. To encourage obedience he again turned to administrative harassment, requiring a written explanation each Monday morning from everyone who had missed chapel the day before.[13] For the time being the officers and professors acquiesced, but when Capt. Henry Brewerton, Delafield's successor, tried to maintain the policy, several officers rebelled. Lt. Simon Bolivar Buckner, Bvt. Capt. George B. McClellan, and Lt. George Deshon stood on consitutional grounds and refused to attend chapel services or submit excuses. Eventually, the secretary of war solved the problem by transferring the recalcitrants to frontier posts where church attendance was not required.[14]

When Delafield first became superintendent, Professor Mahan had commended him to Secretary of War Poinsett as an officer possessing "clearsightedness, promptitude . . . and a determination to examine everything with his own eyes."[15] Even though his enthusiasm soon cooled, Mahan's initial estimate of Delafield was correct. Nevertheless, the superintendent's energy, persistence, and willingness to discard tradition had no lasting effect on the academy. He served a total of twelve years in office, but aside from earning a reputation as an able administrator and a strict disciplinarian, together with making minor alterations in the uniform and daily routine, he had accomplished little. In that respect Delafield personified the antebellum superintendency. Obviously, the power associated with the office in Thayer's day now resided elsewhere.

The agency which came closest to achieving autonomy was the academic board. This body, created by Thayer, consisted of the superintendent, the heads of the instructional departments, and during examinations, the instructors of the cadets being tested. The superintendent presided at meetings and the adjutant served as non-voting secretary. Even though the board made its decisions by majority vote, dissenting minorities could forward their views to Washington.[16] In practice, however, this was a futile gesture; rarely did the secretary of war or the chief of engineers side with the dissidents.

The board controlled every phase of the academic operation at West Point. Its routine functions included designing instructional programs, selecting texts, and considering curriculum changes, as well as examining cadets, determining order of merit standings, recommending graduates for branches of the army, and deciding whether students found deficient at the semiannual examinations should be allowed to continue with their class, be turned back to a lower one, or discharged from the academy.[17]

From time to time the board had to defend the exacting standards it imposed on cadets from critics higher in the chain of command. For instance, after observing the examinations in June 1835 the board of visitors concluded that two cadets had been failed unjustly and urged the academic board to reexamine them. To avoid the appearance of insubordination the academic board agreed to test the students again, but only to satisfy the board of visitors. According to the professors, the reexaminations would not affect the original findings of deficiency, for "no doubts are entertained by the [academic] board as to the propriety of their decision on this subject." At that point the board of visitors elected to drop the matter.[18]

A year later the board remonstrated with Secretary of War Cass for ignoring its recommendations and restoring deficient cadets, pointing out that "Reinstatements of discharged cadets have, but in very few cases, proved of no benefit to the individuals themselves, whilst on the mass the examples of such exceptions to the regulations have produced effects the most unfortunate."[19]

In 1839, having lost faith in the efficacy of appeals, the board sought to strengthen its position by resolving that no cadet separated from the academy would be reinstated "under any circumstances unless the same be recommended by the academic board."[20] Secretary Poinsett respected this policy, but the board's victory was merely temporary. Poinsett's successors generally paid little attention to the resolution.

Occasionally the academic board also had to justify the scientific orientation of the curriculum, the heavy emphasis on mathematics in particular. In 1843 a board of officers headed by Winfield Scott took issue with the undue stress on that subject, and other groups voiced similar complaints in later years. To refute these charges the board built a stylized rejoinder based on the premises that all officers needed a knowledge of mathematics, science, and engineering, that only cadets in the upper sections went beyond the scope of courses taught in civilian colleges, and that mathematical training developed mental discipline.[21] Although founded on unproven assumptions, the argument usually disarmed critics and enabled the board to retain the basic coloration of the academic program.

One of the most worrisome chores of the academic board was curriculum revision, a time-consuming, complicated task. The regulations specified that no more than ten hours daily be devoted to academics, including both classroom time and study periods; each department, of course, fully utilized every minute of its allocation. Military formations and duties occupied much of the remaining time, leaving cadets with just a little more than two hours a day for recreation.[22] Because the schedule was so crowded a new course could be introduced only by shortening or eliminating an existing one. Thus, even a slight modification of the curriculum required painstaking study, planning, and interdepartmental haggling. Even though the desire to maintain the supremacy of mathematics, science, and engineering was the major factor discouraging curriculum revision, the sheer complexity of the task was an important consideration too.

As a rule the academic board united against outside pressures, but this did not mean it was free of internal strains and divisions. Not only did Delafield and later superintendents sometimes quarrel with other members of the board, the professors clashed with each other. One extended dispute concerned whether the semiannual examinations should be conducted by the board as a whole or by committees. Both methods were tried from time to time, and each had its staunch partisans. Nor did the board exclude internal departmental matters from its jurisdiction. In one instance Professor Mahan sharply criticized a colleague from another department for adopting a text Mahan considered too elementary for cadets. Also, the necessity for adding new subjects to the curriculum prompted heated debates over which subjects in the existing program should remain untouched and which should be sacrificed.[23] The board, then, was not a monolith but a forum where men who shared a common commitment felt free to argue over the best means of meeting it.

The academic board set the intellectual tone for the military academy, or more precisely, the professors who dominated the board did. And even within that small group some men exerted far more influence than others. The leaders, both with respect to prestige and the weight attached to their

Dennis Hart Mahan, class of 1824, Professor of Civil and Military Engineering and the Art [later Science] of War, 1833–1871.

William H. C. Bartlett, class of 1826, Professor of Natural and Experimental Philosophy, 1836–1871.

Albert E. Church, class of 1828, Professor of Mathematics, 1837–1878.

Jacob W. Bailey, class of 1832, Professor of Chemistry, Mineralogy, and Geology, 1838–1857.

courses, were: Dennis Hart Mahan, head of the Department of Civil and Military Engineering and the Art of War; William H. C. Bartlett, professor of natural and experimental philosophy; Albert E. Church, professor of mathematics; Jacob W. Bailey, chairman of the Department of Chemistry, Mineralogy, and Geology, and his successor Henry Kendrick.[24]

Other permanent members of the board were the professors of drawing and French and the professor of ethics who also doubled as garrison chaplain. The courses these professors were responsible for counted less in determining order of merit standings than mathematics, science, and engineering. Then too, the three professors seldom took the lead in board discussions or chaired important committees; rather they customarily deferred to the heads of the more prestigious departments.[25]

The instructors of practical military engineering and infantry, artillery, and cavalry tactics also served on the academic board. They were regular army officers assigned to the academy for three- or four-year terms.[26] The short tenures of these officers limited their influence on the board, but as disciplinarians, teachers of professional subjects, and representatives of the active army, they significantly affected the attitudes of cadets.

The ubiquitous and talented Dennis Hart Mahan stood preeminent among the professors and instructors. The son of Irish immigrants, Mahan had been born in New York City but spent his boyhood in Norfolk, Virginia. While studying medicine in Richmond he developed an interest in drawing. Not finding a suitable teacher in the local area, he obtained an appointment to West Point in order to pursue the subject there. Mahan graduated first in his class in 1824 and received a commission in the corps of engineers. Thayer retained him at the academy first as an assistant professor of mathematics and subsequently as an assistant professor of engineering. Then on Thayer's recommendation Mahan was sent to France where he studied at the School of Application for Artillerists and Engineers at Metz. Returning to the academy in 1829, he was appointed acting professor of engineering and assumed the chair permanently in 1832.

Throughout his long tenure as a professor Mahan used his brilliant intellect and facile pen to add lustre to the military academy to an extent his colleagues never matched. It was Mahan who defended West Point in the press, Mahan who acted as confidential advisor to prominent public figures and who exploited those connections to protect what he perceived to be the best interests of the academy, and it was Mahan who published articles on military affairs in the leading journals of the day. It was also Mahan who, by virtue of his seniority, prestige, and force of personality guided the academic board for four decades.[27]

Mahan's contributions to scholarship were truly impressive. At the be-

Henry L. Kendrick, class of 1835, Professor of Chemistry, Mineralogy, and Geology, 1857–1880.

Robert W. Weir, Professor of Drawing, 1846–1876.

Hyacinth R. Agnel, Professor of French, 1848–1871.

Patrice de Janon, Professor of Spanish, 1857–1882.

ginning of his teaching career he lithographed notes on architecture and engineering for cadets since there were no suitable texts available. Later, he published books on engineering, field and permanent fortifications, industrial drawing and the application of descriptive geometry to fortification drawing. His text on field fortifications was used as a manual by officers in the Mexican and Civil Wars. Mahan's best known work, *An Elementary Treatise on Advanced-Guard, Outpost, and Detachment Service of Troops, With the Essential Principles of Strategy and Grand Tactics,* first published in 1847 and later revised, was so esteemed the Confederates printed a pirated edition for their officers. Indeed, *Outpost* still ranks as one of the foremost American contributions to the study of war.[28]

Mahan was aloof and relentlessly demanding in his dealings with cadets. Sloppy thinking and careless attitudes toward duty were anathema to him. As a teacher he required a thorough grounding in basic principles, precision of thought, and common sense; these essentials, Mahan believed, would serve as springboards for students capable of thinking creatively and as adequate guidelines for those with more pedestrian minds. In keeping with that philosophy the professor brusquely corrected every deviation from academic or disciplinary standards he detected. If, for instance, he saw a cadet slouching, he would order him to "Attention," noting that when the body was in that position so was the mind. When a student handed in an exercise in fortification drawing which did not suit him, Mahan would make the delinquent do it over on a weekend, depriving him of the little time he had for recreation. Moreover, any youngster who failed to answer a question with sufficient accuracy could expect to feel the sting of the professor's sarcasm.

His personality prevented Mahan from winning the affection of cadets; they saw him as a man to be respected and perhaps feared, but not loved. Later in their lives a few graduates did come to appreciate what he had done for them and the academy, but this was only after considerable experience and reflection. Mahan's inability to relate to students may have stemmed from boredom. In a letter to fellow graduate and former colleague Alexander D. Bache, a prominent antebellum physicist, the West Point professor complained, "Nothing can present a more dreary blank than the years I have passed in my present occupation. . . . One day is much like another; such is the history of this sadly monotonous existence." Frail health aggravated by a chronic nasal infection may also have affected his disposition.[29] Regardless of the reasons, the man whom historians rightly acknowledge as a seminal personage in the evolution of American military thought and professionalism never enjoyed popularity with his students.

Another of Thayer's protégés, William H. C. Bartlett, professor of natural and experimental philosophy, was Mahan's closest rival in notability.

49

Bartlett had been born in Lancaster County, Pennsylvania, but grew up in Missouri. With only a backwoods education he entered West Point in 1822 and finished at the top of his class four years later. Thayer kept Bartlett on at the academy as an instructor after graduation as he had Mahan. But after two years teaching engineering Bartlett was transferred to the office of the chief of engineers. In 1834 he returned to West Point as acting professor of natural and experimental philosophy, receiving a permanent appointment as head of the department in 1836.

Although there were similarities in their backgrounds, Bartlett and Mahan differed in important respects. The squabble which arose over a proposed textbook is one indicator of this divergence. In 1852 Bartlett sought the approval of the academic board for a text on acoustics and optics he had written. Mahan, however, opposed the work on the grounds that it did not require cadets to use their knowledge of calculus and thus was not sufficiently rigorous.[30]

Bartlett's interests were also narrower than Mahan's. The professor of natural and experimental philosophy concentrated on his own discipline, especially mechanics and astronomy, without venturing into other academic areas. Neither did he write articles for newspapers or cultivate relationships with political figures. Bartlett did achieve distinction in natural and experimental philosophy. His *Elements of Analytical Mechanics,* first published in 1853, went through nine editions and was widely used in American colleges. In that work he demonstrated that the algebraic formulae for expressing mechanical phenomena could all be derived from a single mathematical statement of the law of conservation of energy, thereby enabling students to see the theory of mechanics as an interconnected whole rather than a series of unrelated principles. The West Point professor was the first American ever to formulate this concept. He also wrote texts in optics and astronomy which were used at the military academy for fifty years. In addition, Bartlett published several articles in scientific journals on experiments he had conducted in mechanics.[31]

The professor gained recognition as an astronomer too. On returning from a visit to several European observatories in 1840 he supervised the construction of one at West Point. From there he observed the comet of 1843 and presented a report of his findings at a meeting of the American Philosophical Society. Bartlett photographed the eclipse of 1854 from the same site and made astronomical measurements from the picture, becoming the first astronomer in the United States to use photography for this purpose.[32]

Cadets liked Bartlett better than Mahan. For one thing, they found his physical appearance intriguing. Bartlett's constantly darting eyes, long, sharp nose, pointed chin, and shock of unmanageable hair gave him an elfish look. Also he had a nervous habit of violently jerking his head from side to side as though snapping at his collar or trying to bite an ear. Even though he liked to sneak into the section room and catch unwary students at play and would sometimes lose patience with dullards, cadets did not resent him. His warm, engaging personality won their affection, and his ability to make complicated subjects more understandable earned their admiration. Bartlett went out of his way to interest students in what he was teaching. From time to time he would assemble the entire class in a lecture hall and put on illustrative demonstrations with laboratory apparatus. Then too, he would depart from the standard textbook-recitation method on occasion and through skillful questioning lead students to see the subject from a completely new perspective. This stimulating approach was highly unorthodox at antebellum West Point, and the brighter cadets appreciated it. As Edward S. Holden, one of Bartlett's students and a distinguished astronomer and teacher in his own right, stated: "It was always easy to see he was able, but it was on such exceptional occasions that we knew he was great."[33]

Albert E. Church, professor of mathematics from 1837 until 1878, resembled Bartlett in devotion to a single academic discipline but lacked his colleague's ability to stimulate the interest of students. A native of Connecticut, Church had entered the academy when he was sixteen and graduated at the head of the class of 1828. There were no vacancies in the corps of engineers that year, so he accepted a commission in the artillery. On Thayer's request Church remained at the academy after graduation to teach mathematics. In 1832 he left to join his artillery regiment but returned to West Point two years later and resumed his duties as assistant professor of mathematics. He became the head of the department in 1837, a position he held for the rest of his life. By the time he died in 1878 Church had completed forty-eight years of teaching mathematics at the military academy.[34]

The professor gained scholarly recognition with a series of texts which were used in civilian colleges as well as at the academy. His publications included *Elements of Differential and Integral Calculus, Elements of Analytical Geometry, Elements of Analytical Trigonometry,* and *Elements of Descriptive Geometry.* Florian Cajori, in his history of mathematics, acknowledges Church's influence on the way the subject was taught in the United States and in that regard faults the West Point professor for reinforcing the existing trend among college teachers of concentrating on the purely mechanical aspects at the expense of the philosophical and thus dulling the interest of students.[35]

Church was not a dynamic classroom teacher. Morris Schaff, a graduate who wrote a chronicle of antebellum West Point, caricatured the professor as "an old mathematical cinder, bereft of all natural feeling" and Cadet Arthur Hardy, later to become prominent as a mathematician at Dartmouth, complained "He did not inspire me—he had no magnetism—was as dry as dust, as his textbooks." Hardy also evaluated the quality of mathematics instruction during Church's tenure. "The mathematical recitation was a drill room. In my opinion the result was a soldier who knew the maneuvers, but it did not give an independent, self-reliant grasp of the methods of research. In descriptive geometry the academy had a magnificent collection of models, but they were shown to us after the study was finished—in other words, mental discipline was the object—practical helps and aims were secondary."[36]

On the other hand, future generals David S. Stanley and John C. Tidball found Church to be a kindly, patient teacher, willing to work with a struggling student as long as there was the faintest hope of success. And William F. Smith, who taught at the academy under Church before winning fame in the Civil War, claimed that the professor agonized over the large number of cadets who failed mathematics each term. Church was indeed embarrassed by the disproportionate percentage of academic casualties his department inflicted; however, the solution, as he saw it, was not to reduce the content of mathematics courses or dilute standards but to eliminate more of the non-scientific subjects from the curriculum so that cadets could devote three or four hours a day to mathematics.[37]

Since his program supported engineering and natural and experimental philosophy, Church could count on Mahan and Bartlett to assist him in resisting attempts to modify it. He always succeeded. In none of the periodic revisions which took place during the antebellum era did the Department of Mathematics curtail a single subject or lose an hour of allocated time. Furthermore, even though the relative weights assigned different subjects in computing order of merit varied on occasion, mathematics never lost its place as a prime determinant.

Chemistry, mineralogy, and geology had been taught at West Point since 1820; it was not until 1838, however, that a permanent professorship was established. Jacob W. Bailey, the first incumbent, held office until his death in 1857. Bailey had been born in Massachusetts but left home at the age of twelve to work in a bookstore in Providence, Rhode Island. There the secretary of Brown University befriended the boy and helped him study Latin and French in his spare time. Bailey entered the military academy in 1828 intending to leave the army and pursue a career in railroading as soon as he completed his obligatory term of service following graduation. Finishing fifth in the class of 1832, he accepted an appointment as a second lieutenant of artillery and spent two years on active duty with that branch. In 1834 he returned to West Point as an instructor in chemistry, and a year later became acting professor of chemistry, mineralogy, and geology, holding that position until the professorship was made permanent.[38]

Although the head of a department which taught chemistry, mineralogy, and geology, Bailey earned his scholarly reputation in botany. He pioneered in the use of the microscope in that field and won international recognition for his studies of freshwater algae. Using the microscope, he became the first American to detect these organisms in the fossil state; he also discovered crystal formations in plants and traces of vegetable fossils in anthracite coal.

Unlike Mahan, Bartlett, and Church, the professor of chemistry, mineralogy, and geology did not write textbooks but made substantial contributions to scholarship nonetheless. Bailey published a series of reports on the characteristics of harbor bottoms on the Atlantic and Gulf Coasts for the U.S. Coastal Survey as well as articles on botany in *Silliman's Journal, Smithsonian Contributions,* and *The Journal of Microscopic Science.* In addition, graduates of the academy sent him numerous mineralogical and geological specimens from the frontier which Bailey used to create one of the largest collections in the country. The professor's achievements in science were acknowledged in Europe as well as in the United States. In 1853 he was elected to the Society of Natural Sciences of Cherbourg, and at the time of his death he was serving as president of the American Association for the Advancement of Science.[39]

In 1852 Bailey's wife and daughter died in a steamboat fire, but neither this tragedy nor the burden of caring for an invalid son embittered his relations with cadets. Whenever they mentioned him in letters or memoirs, it was always with affection and respect. A kindly, gentle man, the professor never failed a student if there were a way to avoid doing so. Also, like Bartlett, he knew how to stimulate interest by departing sometimes from the routine. On such occasions Bailey would give lectures and demonstrations to show how chemistry could be applied to technology, particularly in the military field, and in his classes on mineralogy and geology he would attempt to relate those subjects directly to the practical conditions graduates were likely to encounter in their service. The professor's diffident and gentle manner masked an unbending will. Though the son of a minister, he rejected organized religion, and neither Superintendent Delafield's administrative harassment nor the chaplain's public denunciations from the pulpit could coerce him into attending Sunday chapel services.[40]

When Bailey died in 1857, Henry L. Kendrick, a former assistant professor of chemistry, became head of the department. Although equally popular with cadets, Kendrick differed markedly from his predecessor in background and interests. A native of New Hampshire, he had graduated from

West Point in 1835, standing in the upper third of his class but nowhere near the top. After graduation Kendrick taught chemistry at the academy until 1847, then joined his artillery regiment. He saw action in the Mexican War, winning a brevet promotion to major for gallantry in the defense of Puebla. After the war Kendrick served on the frontier for a number of years. In 1849 he commanded the protective escort for the Sitgreaves Expedition which was exploring the Southwest. While crossing the desert the party not only ran out of water and lost its pack mules, but was attacked by Yuma Indians. Kendrick saved the day by organizing a Fabian defense which held off the enemy until help arrived. Subsequently, he remained on the frontier until recalled to West Point in 1857.[41] Kendrick's extensive field experience set him apart from the other permanent professors, none of whom had seen combat or even served on active duty for more than a couple of years.

Kendrick was undoubtedly a good teacher but not a scholar. In his thirty-five year career as an academician he never published an article, wrote a text, or conducted an experiment. In this respect he was a precursor of the post–Civil War West Point professor: an officer with military experience but no scholarly interest in his academic discipline beyond the requirements of the classroom.

Compassion, a keen sense of humor, and a theatrical demeanor combined to make Kendrick a favorite of cadets, and over the years he became one of those legendary figures about whom anecdotes abound. For example, a tablet on the wall of the cadet chapel bore an inscription from Proverbs, "Righteousness exalteth a nation, but sin is a reproach to any people." Since the letters were Roman sytle, the u's resembled v's. Kendrick delighted in reading aloud the latter portion of the maxim as "brevet [bvt] sin is a reproach to any people," adding that brevets were indeed a sin that had reproached armies since the days of the prophets. He would also invite cadets who were pledged to abstain from whiskey to his quarters on Saturday afternoons and serve them spiced peaches heavily laced with brandy to ease the pain of forced abstinence. He was equally considerate in class. If a student gave a wrong answer, the professor, instead of marking him down, would continue to ask leading questions until the cadet eventually was able to guess the right response and obtain a passing grade. In this regard Kendrick shared Bailey's conviction that no youngster who was otherwise qualified should be denied a commission in the army for failing to comprehend the finer points of chemistry, mineralogy, or geology.[42]

When Robert W. Weir accepted an appointment as teacher of drawing at West Point in the summer of 1833, he became the second American to occupy the position. Drawing had been included in the original curriculum, and since no suitable instructor could be found in the United States, a

Frenchman had been recruited to teach it; he had been followed in turn by a Swiss and another Frenchman. Charles A. Leslie, the first American to hold the position, had found the military atmosphere uncongenial and had quit after only a few months. Weir, his successor, experienced no such difficulty; he remained at the academy for forty-two years.[43]

Even though drawing had been taught ever since West Point opened, it remained secondary to mathematics, natural and experimental philosophy, and engineering in the eyes of the academic board. Not only did drawing count less than these other subjects in determining order of merit standings, no professorship was established until 1838. Those in mathematics, natural and experimental philosophy, and engineering, on the other hand, dated back to 1812.[44]

Weir, who became the first professor, was a native of New Rochelle, New York. He had not attended the military academy but had studied art in Italy for three years. On returning to the United States he opened a studio in New York City and was working there when he obtained the appointment to the West Point faculty. An illustrator, portraitist, and landscape painter, Weir was judged by contemporary critics to be an accomplished technician rather than a creative artist. Before moving to the academy he had established a reputation for competence if not brilliance with a work titled, "Paul Preaching at Athens" and had been elected to the American Academy of Design. While at West Point Weir painted the "Embarkation of the Pilgrims" which hangs in the rotunda of the national Capitol, "War and Peace," an allegorical work in the cadet chapel, portraits of Winfield Scott, and Red Jacket, last chief of the Senecas, and landscapes of the Hudson highlands. Moreover, he designed the Episcopal Church of the Holy Innocents and donated the proceeds from some of his paintings to help build it in the village of Buttermilk [Highland] Falls just outside West Point.[45]

Firmly committed to having cadets learn by doing, the professor did not lecture or conduct demonstrations in class but set students to work sketching human figures or landscapes as soon as they entered the drawing academy while he strolled around, palette in hand, making corrections on the cadets' sketches. This habit led to the confrontation so popular among chroniclers of West Point between the professor and James M. Whistler who even as a cadet took great pride in his artistic ability. Seeing that Weir was about to touch up one of his drawings, Whistler stopped him with "Don't, Sir, you'll spoil it!" Fortunately for the future artist the professor shrugged off the incident and did not report him for disrespect. Weir was also indulgent toward less talented students; any boy who made an honest effort could pass the course even though the professor might have difficulty distinguishing the "cows" from the "trees" in his drawings. In addition,

Weir frequently invited cadets to his quarters to view his paintings. Even students with no interest in or talent for art appreciated the professor's forbearance and hospitality; without exception cadets and graduates who mentioned him in letters and memoirs did so with affection.[46]

At the time of his death in 1848 Claudius Berard, professor of French, was the senior member of the academic board in length of service, but by no means did he enjoy equivalent influence. Berard, who had joined the faculty in 1815, was the last of the Frenchmen who had been hired as instructors in the early days of the institution. After fleeing France to avoid the draft in the Napoleonic era, he had taught for a short while at Dickenson College, Carlisle, Pennsylvania, before coming to the military academy. When the professorships of drawing and French were created in 1846, Berard was named to the latter. Two years later Hyacinth R. Agnel, a former assistant in the department, became professor on the death of Berard. Agnel, who was the first native-born American to hold the post, remained in office until 1871.[47]

Although cadets strongly disliked some of the instructors who taught French, the two professors do not seem to have impressed their pupils either positively or negatively to any great extent. Both were courteous and conscientious but not overly demanding, and neither associated with cadets outside the classroom. The combination of blandness and detachment probably explains why Berard and Agnel receive so little attention in cadet letters and memoirs.

While teaching at West Point Berard wrote two books on French grammar which were used at the academy for many years. Agnel designed a text which displayed verb endings, prepositions, idioms, and other parts of speech in a tabular arrangement. During classroom recitations cadets had to write the tables on the blackboard from memory.[48]

French, like drawing, was considered less important than mathematics, natural and experimental philosophy, and engineering. It received relatively little weight in determining order of merit, and the professorship was established long after the others. Even so, the Department of French under Berard and Agnel did a competent job of teaching cadets to translate. The engineering and scientific treatises, tactical studies, and weapons manuals which antebellum West Pointers rendered from French into English attest to the fact.

The professors of drawing and French, if of little consequence in the governing councils of antebellum West Point, at least enjoyed lifetime sinecures. The same could not be said for their colleagues who occupied the chair of ethics. Between 1833 and the coming of the Civil War five Protestant clergymen filled that office and the affiliated post of garrison chaplain. Three of the five resigned under pressure or were dismissed; one left voluntarily, and only one remained in office until he died; no other academic department experienced such a high rate of turnover.

Thomas Warner, who had taken the position in 1828, resigned ten years later after having charged the post surgeon with negligence in the death of a cadet. A court of inquiry, convened because of the chaplain's allegation, cleared the surgeon but chastised Warner for poor judgment in acting on unsubstantiated rumors. He resigned soon afterwards. Jasper Adams, Warner's successor, habitually preached two-hour sermons, condemning the cadets to a cold lunch each Sunday. One Sunday in May 1839 while he was still in the pulpit the drum beat "Mess Call." On hearing the signal Cadet Michael Culbertson, the first captain, stood up and commanded, "A Company, rise!" Cadet Henry W. Halleck, the captain of B Company followed Culbertson's lead, as did the other two company commanders, and the corps began trooping out of the chapel. Enraged at having his congregation march off while he was in the midst of a homily, Adams fired a broadside, charging the entire student body with profanity, drunkenness, and insubordination. This resulted in another court of inquiry. Winfield Scott, who presided, refused to punish the cadets but suggested to the chaplain that he might be happier in a civilian parish. Adams took the hint and left. Martin P. Parks, a graduate of the academy, followed Adams. Because of his military background Parks got along well with the authorities and the students. He organized the cadet chapel choir and successfully proselytized among the corps on behalf of the Episcopal Church. After six years at West Point Parks resigned voluntarily to take a parish in New York City. William T. Sprole, the next incumbent, was a Presbyterian. Some cadets considered Sprole an inspiring preacher and an effective teacher who enlivened his classes in ethics with personal anecdotes and touches of humor. But the professor's denomination tainted him as far as the largely Episcopal faculty was concerned. It also conflicted with the principle laid down by Superintendent Joseph G. Swift in 1813 that the chaplains at West Point should be Episcopalians. Several professors, including William H. C. Bartlett, who rarely concerned himself with such matters, let friends in Washington know that they disapproved of Sprole. At about the same time Secretary of War Davis decided to replace the chaplain with an Episcopal friend. Sprole, however, refused to relinquish the post voluntarily and had to be fired. John W. French, the next chaplain and professor of ethics, continued in office until his death in 1871. A gifted preacher, French was not particularly effective in the classroom largely because he failed to make the courses he taught interesting or relevant to cadets. The professor did win the gratitude of some students when, to relieve the monotony of mess hall fare, he invited them to his quarters for dinners of smoked Virginia ham.[49]

Ostensibly, the chair of ethics was as permanent as any of the other professorships, but its tie to the chaplaincy rendered the position more vulnerable to bias and manipulation. This, together with the inability of several of the incumbents to adjust to the West Point environment, accounted for the high rate of attrition. It is also apparent that the subjects the department offered, English grammar and literature, rhetoric, law, and ethics, were considered as more ornamental than essential by the majority of the academic board. Not only did this group of courses count for little in computing order of merit, it provided the readiest candidates for sacrifice whenever new subjects were added to the curriculum.

The academic board was not the only intramural body which contributed to the shaping of antebellum West Point. The large group of regular army officers who taught in the academic and military departments also helped give the academy its distinctive character. These officers came into daily contact with the cadets, not only in the section room, but in the barracks, on the parade ground, and in the summer encampment. Short tours of duty and low rank prevented them from seriously affecting official policies; however, they exerted a powerful influence on the corps of cadets. Indeed, as professional soldiers they probably did more to fix students' attitudes toward the calling they were preparing for than the professors who, after all, were remote from the active army and the world of the cadet. In addition, the officers played an important antithetical role as described by Peter S. Michie, a professor of the postwar generation.

> These two bodies [professors and army officers] are in some degree antagonistic. The former are from the nature of their duties conservative; the latter, by the varied service experienced in a small army, scattered over a widely extended country, are radical and highly critical, if not iconoclastic. The healthy attack and defense of a system in which both are mutually interested results in slow, gradual, but permanently beneficial changes acquiesced in by all parties . . . . If the academy were governed alone by the academic board, there would be a danger of too great extension toward mere theoretical excellence; while, if controlled by officers of the active list of the army, the practical would be unduly developed at the expense of the solidly theoretical.[50]

Michie may have exaggerated the positive effects of the synthesis, but he was correct in asserting that the periodic infusion of fresh ideas from the field helped retard the growth of intellectual atrophy at the academy.

In his complaint that the service had fallen on evil days when soldiers abandoned the "high and noble duties of their profession to become schoolmasters at West Point," Quartermaster General Thomas S. Jesup undoubtedly spoke for his fellow staff bureau chiefs and line commanders too. Faced with chronic personnel shortages aggravated by ever increasing requirements, Jesup and his peers understandably resented having to provide officers for the military academy. Yet the records show that they resisted what must have been a strong temptation to send the less competent and keep the best for their own organizations. General Jesup's "schoolmasters" for the most part turned out to be well qualified professionals, many of whom later won accolades in the Civil War. Among such officers were: William Hardee, John Gibbon, George B. McClellan, Edmund Kirby Smith, Robert Anderson, John Schofield, James B. Fry, Cadmus Wilcox, O. O. Howard, John F. Reynolds, Dabney H. Maury, Fitzhugh Lee, Joseph J. Reynolds, Simon B. Buckner, James M. Hawes, Charles W. Field, Fitz-John Porter, William S. Rosecrans, Robert S. Garnett, Delos B. Sacket, and Henry Clitz.[51] Given the competing requirements and the haphazard assignment methods of the time, it is remarkable that the active army did so well in meeting its obligations to the military academy.

Close analysis reveals that of the several groups which participated in shaping antebellum West Point, the permanent professors, acting through the academic board, were the most important. Presidents, secretaries of war, chiefs of engineers, superintendents, and active duty officers could bring pressure to bear, but they could effect consequential change only when their aims coincided with those of the professors. The evidence also strongly suggests that Mahan, and to a lesser extent Bartlett and Church, dominated the board and therefore determined the intellectual tone of the military academy. Several facts substantiate this conclusion. The academic board did much of its work by committees, and one of the three chaired every important committee from 1833 until the end of the Civil War. Furthermore, the subjects taught by their departments carried more weight than any of the others in determining order of merit throughout the era, notwithstanding criticisms of this emphasis by boards of visitors and the eventual imposition of a curriculum specifically designed to reduce the stress on mathematics, science, and engineering. In this regard it is also significant that Mahan, Bartlett, and Church led the successful campaign to abolish the reform after a short and inconclusive trial period.[52]

The power of the three professors derived to some extent from their long, uninterrupted tenure. This endowed them with sufficient stature to overwhelm some critics and sufficient time to outlast others. The three also enjoyed several advantages over their colleagues on the academic board. The professorships of mathematics, natural and experimental philosophy, and engineering antedated those in the other departments, and seniority was important in a rigidly hierarchical institution. Moreover, tradition favored Mahan, Bartlett, and Church. In earlier periods of West Point history the teachers of drawing and French and the chaplains who taught ethics customarily yielded to the professors of mathematics, science, and

59

engineering in matters pertaining to curriculum and governance. Personalities also played a part. Bailey, Kendrick, Weir, Berard, and Agnel either were too unassertive by nature or too absorbed in their own interests to become leaders on the academic board. As for the professors of ethics, they were temperamentally unsuited for leadership, but even had the case been otherwise, the instability of their position would have precluded a more active role.

Mahan, Bartlett, and Church did not operate as a cabal, imposing their will on a hostile majority; in fact, as the textbook controversy demonstrated, they did not always agree among themsleves. Also, in most cases the other members of the board willingly followed their lead. Thus, there was nothing sinister or secretive about the dominance of the three. Not only did everyone in the chain of command understand that Mahan, Bartlett, and Church steered the academic board which, in turn, governed West Point, they usually accepted the arrangement without question.

In the final analysis politicians, bureaucrats, soldiers, and faculties comprised but half the forces working to mold antebellum West Point. Equally important were those generated by the corps of cadets, that body of young men who gave the military academy its reason for existence.

The Corps
of Cadets: Socioeconomic
Composition and the
Military Environment

★

In the years preceding the Civil War critics of West Point charged it with being a bastion of aristocracy and privilege.[1] Defenders parried these thrusts by maintaining that the academy was open to all youth regardless of family circumstances,[2] and in order to substantiate that claim the chief of engineers had the superintendent record the financial status and occupation of the father of each cadet, together with a statement indicating whether the boy came from a rural or an urban background. The compilation began in 1842 and continued until 1879; it confirmed that the military academy was indeed open to youngsters of all classes.[3] More importantly for the historian, the statistics reveal significant clues to the socioeconomic composition of the antebellum corps of cadets.

An extract of data from the source document, "Circumstances of Parents of Cadets, 1842–1879," appears in appendix 1. It shows that of the more than a thousand students who entered in the antebellum era, approximately 1.9 percent classified their families as being in "Indigent Circumstances," 10.7 percent in "Reduced," 86.1 percent in "Moderate," and 4.2 percent in "Affluent." Of the same group 38.2 percent reported that they came from the "Country," 38.8 percent from "Towns," and 23 percent from the "City."[4] Although these categories are imprecise, they show clearly that a large majority of the corps was of middle class origin with more of a rural-small town than an urban orientation. Even so, fewer cadets came from farms than might be expected, considering the distribution of the population of the United States at the time.

Of the large number of parents' occupations listed in the "Circumstan-ces" ledger eleven comprised 1 percent or more of the total and are there-fore statistically meaningful. In order of magnitude they were: farmers, 24.8 percent; merchants, 12.4 percent; lawyers, 12.2 percent; physicians, 7.8 percent; army officers, 5.4 percent; planters, 4.4 percent; mechanics, 2.1 percent; clergy, 1.9 percent; editors, 1.7 percent; manufacturers, 1.2 per-cent; and naval officers, 1 percent. These figures take on added meaning when compared with the percentages of the same occupations in the general population as revealed by federal census reports. Thus, farmers, even though they enjoyed the greatest representation in the corps of cadets of any single occupational group, were actually underrepresented in terms of their percentage of the entire population by 19.2 percent, since they made up 44 percent of the total work force. Similarly, merchants fell short by 6.4 percent, planters by 0.6 percent, clergy by 3 percent, and mechanics by 0.8 percent. Lawyers, on the other hand, were overrepresented by 7.7 percent, army officers by 5.3 percent, editors by 1.3 percent, naval officers by 0.9 percent and manufacturers by 0.8 percent. Obviously, the critics had a point. The institution may have admitted poor boys, but the sons of men in certain occupational groups, namely, those with governmental connections or political influence, obtained more than their fair share of the appointments.

The statistics reinforce an impression gained from studying the *Register of Graduates,* other biographical material, and primary sources. Notwith-standing that most of the youngsters came from families with access to political influence—indeed, the appointment system guaranteed that—they were not members of the American aristocracy. To be sure, a sprin-kling of Lees, Heberts, Du Ponts, McAlesters, and even a Bonaparte, as well as members of other prominent families, occasionally graced the stu-dent body. But the greatest dynasties seldom sent their sons to West Point. There were no Byrds, Randolphs, Carters, Boylstons, Peabodys, Win-throps, De Lanceys, De Peysters, Schuylers, or others of their status in the antebellum corps of cadets. Therefore, the academy cannot with accuracy be accused of catering to bluebloods.

Not only were the critics careless in defining the terms of their allega-tions, they also evaded the central issue. If there were a socioeconomic imbalance in the corps of cadets, it could not be blamed on the military academy. Neither the chief of engineers nor the authorities at West Point had any say in selecting the nominees for cadetships; this was purely a matter of congressional and presidential patronage over which the military had no control. Every congressional district, each territory, and the Dis-trict of Columbia was allotted one appointment apiece. Members of the House of Representatives nominated candidates from their districts. The president named those from the District of Columbia and territories; in addition, he could appoint ten cadets "At Large," that is, without regard to residence. Traditionally, the sons of army and naval officers received preference in awarding "At Large" appointments, with first priority given to boys whose fathers had died on active duty.[5] This practice of having politicians choose the candidates for cadetships went as far back as 1828 and was regularized by law in 1843. All the West Point authorities could do was examine the nominees for fitness. Any boy who had an appointment and could meet the standards for admission had to be accepted.

Certainly the entrance requirements were not designed to exclude. Candidates had to be in good physical condition and demonstrate rudimentary proficiency in reading, writing, and basic arithmetic. Furthermore, each boy received free tutoring prior to taking the examinations, and anyone who failed the first time in June could try again in August, provided his congressman had not named another candidate in the interim.[6] As a result of this leniency 93.1 percent of the antebellum nominees were accepted as cadets,[7] yet more than a quarter of those admitted failed to graduate because of academic deficiencies.[8] Clearly, the entrance requirements were ineffective screening devices.

This defect did not pass unnoticed at the time; boards of visitors commented on it in several annual reports. The academic board and the chief of engineers also realized the standards were too low, but feared that raising them would "eliminate many, particularly, those from the poorer classes," thereby exposing the institution to more charges of elitism.[9] Eventually, in 1854, Joseph Totten and Secretary of War Davis tried a different approach to the problem of inadequate preparation by instituting a five-year curriculum, but this experiment was abandoned in 1861. It was not until five years later that the entrance requirements were finally raised. Another solution, competitive examinations, was also advocated from time to time. In 1841, for example, Representative Henry Wise of Virginia announced that he would thenceforth make appointments on the basis of merit, presumably ascertained by some sort of test. In 1862 M. F. Colell of Brooklyn employed competitive examinations to fill the vacancy in his congressional district. At about the same time Congress decided to name Union soldiers to the cadetships left vacant by the seceded states. The field commanders who were given responsibility for selecting the candidates ordered boards of officers to test the applicants and rank them according to merit. The men at the top of the list received the appointments. After the war the push continued, with the *Army and Navy Journal, The New York Times,* boards of visitors, the faculty, and even Sylvanus Thayer lobbying for the reform. Congress debated the issue but balked at mandating a requirement for competitive examinations since this would necessitate surrendering a cherished political plum. Some experienced officers also opposed the concept but for other reasons. David S. Stanley felt that the cadets who had won appointments by competitive examinations during the Civil War "had lowered the gentlemanly tone of the corps," and John C. Tidball feared that "youthful phenomena and hot-house plants" would "carry off the prize" rather than the boys who would make the best officers.[10]

Plans for inducting new cadets began in May annually when the superintendent designated the professors of mathematics and ethics to oversee the preparatory instruction of the candidates. In turn, the two professors chose the cadets who would conduct this instruction. At the same time the commandant selected other upperclassmen to give the new men basic military training and set aside rooms in the barracks for quartering them.[11]

The largest groups of aspirants reported in June and September, but others straggled in throughout the summer since unreliable transporation made it almost impossible to comply with an exact reporting date. For some candidates the trip took a considerable length of time. John Tidball, later to become a distinguished Union horse artilleryman and military reformer, described his journey from Ohio in the summer of 1844: "My introduction to military life was when, about ten o'clock of the seventh of June 1844, I landed from a North River Steamer on the wharf at West Point. . . . After a week's travel up the Ohio, then by stage across the Alleghenies, and by canal to Harrisburg—at this time the westward terminus of the railroads—and thence by rail to New York City . . . I arrived at the end of, not only my journey, but of my life as a civilian. . . . This was the first time I had been east of the Alleghenies or had seen cities like those of the Atlantic Seaboard, and all was of astonishing newness to me."[12] Sherman, Grant, Thomas "Stonewall" Jackson, George Crook, and Sheridan, who entered during the same period, did not record their initial experiences in such detail, but they were undoubtedly similar.

After putting his baggage on a horsedrawn cart the candidate followed it on foot up the long hill from the dock to the Plain, where, if he arrived at the right time of day, he could see the old cadets at drill or parade. The new boy's first stop was the adjutant's office where he verified his identity and signed the register. Next, he visited the treasurer who relieved him of all his money. From then on he could not have cash in his possession as long as he remained at West Point.[13] Having reported for duty and turned in his money, the candidate found the room to which he had been assigned and presented himself to the upperclassman who had been detailed to teach him how to be a soldier. At this juncture the novice became an "Animal" or "Plebe,"[14] the lowest of the low in the West Point social order.

Next, the prospective cadet reported to the quartermaster to draw the minimal furniture and equipment he would need for his stay in barracks before taking the entrance examinations. This consisted of a pair of blankets, a chair, an arithmetic text, a slate, a bucket, a tin or coconut dipper, a tin washbasin, a lump of soap, a candlestick, a tallow candle, and a supply of stationery. The candidate didn't realize it at the time, but the blankets he had just received were about to pervade him with a distinctive aroma. The manufacturer habitually neglected to clean the blankets properly; hence, after sleeping on them the plebes reeked of rancid lanolin. To make matters worse, the odor lingered for several weeks.[15]

In the interval between his arrival and the entrance examinations the recruit divided his time between the classroom where, for four hours daily, cadet instructors tutored him in arithmetic and grammar, and the parade ground where student drillmasters taught him the fundamental military skills. These educational and training programs began even before the candidate had been fitted for a uniform. The first formation of a group of novitiates, still in civilian clothes, made a curious spectacle. As John Tidball described it, "There were about sixty of us—increased in a few days to ninety by the new arrivals—as we marched, or tried to march, there was a constant losing of step, occasioning the most ludicrous, and to us, the most vexatious shuffling, stumbling, and kicking of heels. . . . Coming from every section and quarter of the country, [we] represent[ed] every degree of provincialism. . . . Some were arrayed in straw hats while others sweltered in fur caps; some sported long-tailed coats . . . the great majority were painfully rustic in homemade clothes, while a few were foppish with city fashions."[16]

George C. Strong, who would later die of wounds received while fighting for the Union at Fort Wagner, gave a similar picture of his class at its first formation in June 1853. "The beating of drums at one o'clock P.M. was the signal for repairing to the parade ground for dinner roll call . . . a motley looking crowd it was. The pale-faced, taciturn youth of the city, the weather-beaten heroes of the plough . . . We were forced by dint of much pulling and pushing on the part of our instructors, into ranks. . . . The roll was called, and we started for the mess hall . . . losing the step, of course, and tumbling over each other . . . at the same time receiving bitter rebukes for our inattention."[17]

The tutoring and drilling temporarily ceased around the twentieth of June while the new cadets took their physical and mental examinations. For the former, medical personnel weighed, measured, and checked each boy for skeletal and dental deformities. Visual acuity was tested by having the aspirant tell whether a dime, held up fourteen feet away, was "heads" or "tails." In later years this test was replaced by one requiring the candidate to read coarse print on the wall. Only 7.5 percent of all those tested were rejected for physical defects.[18]

65

The mental examinations conducted by the academic board were not very discriminating either. For the arithmetic portion the candidate had to solve a problem at the blackboard, then answer several questions put to him by the professor of mathematics. Next, the professor of ethics required every man to read aloud from a book; also, as a test of spelling, punctuation, and penmanship the candidate had to transcribe a paragraph dictated by the professor. After passing the examinations the novices were assigned to companies according to height and marched to the Plain where they joined the cadet encampment already in progress.[19]

Beginning with their arrival at West Point and continuing for the rest of the summer, the new boys underwent hazing, or "devilment" as they called it, at the hands of the upper classes. These initiation rites consisted mainly of practical jokes and personal service, such as cleaning muskets, pitching tents, and hauling buckets of water for old cadets.[20] Thus, the hazing characteristic of antebellum West Point differed both in nature and duration from the year-long, sometimes sadistic, ordeals of later periods in the history of the academy. Occasionally, however, even in the era before the Civil War, the practice resulted in serious injuries. In the summer of 1844, for instance, a group of third classmen (sophomores) so tormented a plebe sentinel that he lost his temper and hurled his musket, bayonet foremost, into the crowd. The bayonet gashed Cadet Henry Heth's thigh, incapacitating him for several weeks.[21] In June two years later a group of upperclassmen set upon Candidate Thomas Seabury during his first night at West Point and spread-eagled him, face down, on the ground. While Seabury was pinioned in this position the old cadets poured turpentine on his buttocks and tied a string so tightly around his testicles that it caused severe swelling and pain.[22]

Vicious treatment and serious injuries were the exception, however. Most of the hazing resulted in nothing more painful than the loss of a plebe's dignity. Typical of this kind of devilment was the mock trial in which a novice was hauled before a court of upperclassmen, charged with and convicted of some heinous crime, and sentenced to a terrible punishment which, of course, was never executed. Late one night in the summer of 1844, for example, Jesse Valentine, a plebe from Buncombe County, North Carolina, had to stand trial before a court of third classmen. Henry Heth, one of the participants, described the scene: "A room in the 'cockloft' [attic] of old North Barracks was prepared for Jesse's trial. The windows of the room had blankets tacked up to prevent any passing officer of the army from seeing the light. A long table, covered with green baize, was improvised. [Ambrose] Burnside, personating the president of the court, sat at the head of the table, and on his right and left were arranged twelve cadets, dressed in blue coats such as cadets wear on furlough."

66

Valentine was brought before the court and charged with violating the regulations against marriage. He explained, "Gentlemen, before God I am not married; I suppose the mistake occurred in my being engaged to be married, and I would have been married, but my mule died and I could not make a crop." When the court asked the name of his girl, Jesse replied, "Nancy Hicks."

This response evoked cries of "Bigamy! Bigamy of the worst kind!" from the jurors, and that offense was added to Jesse's crimes. Soon afterwards the court convicted him and ordered that he be shot at sunrise. On hearing the sentence the condemned man fell to his knees and sobbed, "Oh, my God! Shall I never again see my mother or sisters? Oh, if my mule had not died!"

Jesse's anguished lament moved the tribunal to soften the punishment, and "president" Burnside informed the prisoner of his good fortune: "Plebe Valentine, you are a great sinner and deserve to die, but as Christian soldiers we cannot send you, with all your sins, to eternity. You must be given time for repentance, and instead of being shot tomorrow, we grant you a respite; you will stand with your head in a mortar until tomorrow morning." Heth, the prisoner's guard, then led Jesse out to the Plain and made him stick his head down the tube of a mortar. The next morning a passing officer found him still in that position.[23]

Another favorite trick was to camouflage a barracks room as a barbershop and lure unwitting novices inside for a haircut. Such a stratagem enabled Heth to get Thomas F. McLean, a new cadet from Missouri, seated in a chair for a trim by "barber" Burnside. McLean had just arrived at the academy and still wore the flowing red mane and shaggy beard that had earned him the nickname "Bison" the first time the upperclassmen had seen him shambling across the Plain. Burnside applied scissors and razor with a will, and by a masterpiece of timing managed to have shorn exactly half the Bison's head and beard when the signal for parade sounded. At that instant the two old cadets dashed out of the room and fell into ranks, leaving McLean to explain his weird appearance to an irate superintendent as best he could.[24]

Not even in the classroom were candidates safe from devilment. When officers were not present, cadet tutors and their friends sometimes hazed the new boys by asking loaded questions and giving impossible assignments. George Strong recounted the following personal experience in 1853. A tutor inquired about his politics; Strong replied that he was an "Administration man." "Just as I thought, Sir," the tutor snapped, "It's evident you have mistaken your calling. You should have known ere this that an officer of the army has nothing to do with politics."

Asked if his father were a politician, Strong answered, "No, Sir, a farmer." The tutor scolded, "Contumacy, Sir, and you shall be punished for it. I asked you, Sir, if your father were a politician, and you have entered gratuitously upon the subject of agriculture." The tutor then ordered Strong to go to the blackboard and make a topographical sketch of "your father's farm on a scale of one ten-millionth, with a plan of all the buildings, and give the tilled and unbroken land a fair evaluation, as well as the buildings, stock, etc., including all the money at interest, at the same time discounting for all outstanding debts. . . . To make your sketch more complete I wish you to draw a vertical projection of your grandfather on receiving the intelligence of the Battle of New Orleans."[25]

Other traditional hazing techniques included attempting to confuse and disarm plebe sentinels, administering doses of foul-tasting "remedies" to cure horrendous ailments diagnosed by make-believe doctors, tossing plebes in blankets, pulling tents down on new cadets at night and dragging them out of bed.[26] All forms of devilment were forbidden, and each year the authorities issued stern warnings against it; moreover, if caught, offenders faced serious punishment. John Schofield, who in later years won the Medal of Honor at Wilson's Creek and went on to become superintendent of the military academy and eventually commanding general of the army, was dismissed in July 1852 for permitting classmates to haze candidates he was supposed to be tutoring in arithmetic. Senator Stephen A. Douglas had Schofield reinstated, but others, less fortunate, lost their places permanently.[27] However, even such draconian measures did not abate the practice.

The efficacy of the pre–Civil War style of devilment was retrospectively debated by some of the participants. From the vantage point of forty years of service, including a short term as commandant of cadets, John Tidball viewed the hazing of his days in the corps "more as beneficial than otherwise, a weaning of the new cadets from boyhood to manhood." Similarly, David S. Stanley believed the custom "promoted fun; it quickened the wits of the new cadet, made him alert." On the other hand, Phil Sheridan, Stanley's classmate, branded it "a senseless custom which an improved civilization has now [1888] about eradicated." James H. Wilson, who achieved fame as a Union cavalryman and subsequently as commander of the China Relief Expedition in 1901, characterized the devilment he had endured in 1855 as "good-natured, but at times rather rough play between old and new cadets which, so far as I could see, did no harm but much good to all. It sharpened our observation, stimulated our vigilance, and excited our curiosity. It may have discouraged the homesick and weak-hearted, but it certainly did no injury whatever to such as met it with good-natured resistance and were fit for the life they had chosen."[28]

Finally, George Strong, in his *Cadet Life at West Point,* published in 1860 three years after he had graduated, defended the practice as "a thorough breaking in . . . conducive to the best interests of all concerned. It teaches the 'Plebes' never to be surprised at anything, to meet future difficulties with greater fortitude, and to make their reliance a reliance upon themselves."[29]

On balance the hazing of the antebellum period probably did more good than evil. In the first place, it identified the most obvious misfits, those psychologically incapable of adjusting to discipline. Secondly, the practice helped create a close-knit band of plebe brothers, united against the upper classes, thus solidifying at an early stage the class spirit so dear to West Pointers. Also, by occupying so much of the novice's time and attention, hazing may have softened the pangs of homesickness. Moreover, the practice forced the new cadet to respond quickly in unusual situations. On the debit side, deviling encouraged blind obedience to instructions, no matter how absurd they might be—a different thing altogether from the prompt and wholehearted, but reasoned, response to lawful orders, universally recognized as a military virtue.

Though hazing preoccupied the plebes and their tormenters alike, it was by no means the most important summertime activity. During the encampment both old and new cadets pursued the practical phases of their professional training, performing the duties of privates, noncommissioned, and commissioned officers under the supervision of the officers of the Department of Tactics. The fourth (plebe) class learned the functions of privates, the third (sophomore) class those of noncommissioned officers, and the first (senior) class those of lieutenants and captains. The second (junior) class spent the summer on furlough, the only extended leave of absence granted cadets in their entire stay at the academy.[30]

The summer schedule was a busy one. Drills began at 5:30 A.M. and continued until 5:00 P.M. During the day cadets took instruction in riding, dismounted drill, infantry tactics, musketry, artillery drill and firing, and fencing. In addition, the boys walked guard, served on fatigue details, and, of course, paraded. Moreover, the first class devoted a part of the summer to making rockets, grenades, powder bags, and other munitions in the ordnance laboratory.[31]

Despite the crowded agenda, cadets were able to gain a respite from study and classroom recitations. In their free time they could swim in the Hudson, hike through the hills, and, if they wished, read and learn how to dance. Prospective third classman W. T. Sherman recounted how his class arranged the two last-named activities: "Our class have been debating how to spend the encampment in the most enjoyable manner. They have concluded to spend it in the usual manner, that is, buy a library and have a dancing school . . . I was put on the library committee—will have nothing to do with dancing."[32]

The visits of relatives, friends, and the general public also enlivened the summer. West Point was a favorite spot for tourists, and the cadets were the main attraction. Each Saturday night and occasionally during the week the upper classes organized dances to which all the pretty girls in the vicinity, as well as the guests of cadets, comely or otherwise, were invited.[33]

The major social event of the season was the Fourth of July celebration. Festivities began at dawn when the cadet battery fired a thirteen-gun federal salute. From then until "Retreat" at sunset all official duties were suspended. Around eleven in the morning a procession consisting of the band, the colors, the corps of cadets, a student orator, officers of the staff, and visitors, formed and marched to the chapel. There, after one cadet read the Declaration of Independence, the orator delivered a patriotic address. At the conclusion of the chapel observance the cadet battery fired a national salute, one gun for each state in the Union. This was followed by a holiday dinner and a ball later in the evening.[34]

Meanwhile, temporarily free of restraint, the second class passed its furlough, at times in ways which shocked the more prudish members of the faculty. In 1838, for example, Professor Mahan complained to Secretary of War Poinsett: "Last summer, visiting New York after the examinations, I was struck with the need of some regulations regarding cadet furloughs. I found about sixty in the American Hotel, half in uniform, smoking, drinking at the bar, and committing various excesses in Public."[35]

Ten years later Henry Brewerton, then superintendent, found it necessary to change the regulations governing the furlough uniform. Up to that time cadets had worn the standard officer's blue coat without epaulets while on leave. But some youngsters, according to Brewerton, were modifying the coats illegally by attaching officer's insignia—one going so far as to put on shoulder straps "appropriate to a major-general." Whatever the uniform, the furlough class exploited every minute of liberty to the fullest. In 1851 Professor Weir commented on the "ungentlemanly conduct" of second classmen returning to West Point on the riverboat because of "The excited state they were in from the use of *spirits* and *tobacco* and the exhibition of themselves in all parts of the boat; puffing their smoke among the ladies and using the most boisterous and profane language. . . ."[36]

The frustrated anticipation of similar frivolities prompted Sherman, on learning that his stepmother had contrived to have him accompany the straightlaced daughter of a family friend home, to protest, "Now is this not provoking, after having made arrangements with about a dozen classmates

70

to go as far as Wheeling all together and, of course, to cut up and enjoy ourselves?"[37]

The summer season ended with a ball on the night of 30 August. The next day the second class returned from furlough while the remainder of the corps broke camp and marched back to barracks. The academic grind was about to begin.

On returning to barracks cadets were assigned to quarters according to company, but they could choose their roommates. In sharp contrast to modern custom members of different classes could live together. When Sherman was a second classman, for instance, he roomed with a plebe and two first classmen. The authorities reserved the right to transfer roommates whenever the boys' own choices proved troublesome. The exercise of this prerogative brought two future Civil War generals, Heth and Burnside, together when both were plebes. Heth had originally roomed with Gus Seward, whose father would one day become Lincoln's secretary of state, and the two youngsters had quickly acquired a formidable number of demerits. Superintendent Delafield mistakenly assumed that Seward was leading Heth astray so he ordered Heth to move in with Burnside who, Delafield thought, would act as a stabilizing influence on the Virginian[38]— surely one of the grossest military miscalculations since Waterloo!

Barracks life was Spartan. Cadets lived in crowded quarters; sometimes four or five boys occupied a twelve-by-twelve, poorly ventilated room, hot in summer, cold in winter. Boards of visitors, military surgeons, and boards of officers frequently noted these unsatisfactory conditions, but there was no improvement until new barracks were built in 1850.[39] Overcrowding was not the only inconvenience. An old-fashioned well with a wooden pump was the only source of water. Cadets had to carry water to their rooms in buckets, and there were no facilities for heating it. This was eventually rectified when a bathroom, complete with hot water, was installed in the new barracks. Thereafter, bathing became a matter for military regulation; each boy had to take a bath once a week, but not oftener without special permission from the superintendent.[40]

The opening of the new barracks in 1850 also marked the advent of steam heat. Until then coal-burning grates had been used; these provided little warmth but did give off enough light to permit Thomas J. Jackson, and doubtlessly many others, to study after the lights went out at taps. It was not until 1857 that gaslight was installed. Previously, illumination had come from candles and whale-oil lamps which John Tidball remembered as giving off an odor similar to that Jonah must have smelled from inside the whale.[41] Room appointments carried out the Spartan theme. The furniture was neither decorative nor comfortable. In fact, until 1839 cadets slept on

71

mattresses on the floor; iron bedsteads were introduced in March of that year. Moreover, the boys were not permitted to beautify their quarters in any way.[42]

Inside his room or elsewhere, the student could seldom escape observation. Officers inspected quarters several times daily and nightly, and they scrutinized the cadets in ranks almost as often. In addition, the corps marched to meals, classes, and chapel, always under the supervision of officers or fellow cadets. Privacy was perhaps the rarest of luxuries at antebellum West Point.

Partly to enhance control and surveillance and partly to afford practice in command, the corps of cadets was organized as a battalion of infantry, consisting of four companies. The officers, that is, the lieutenants and captains, came from the first class, sergeants from the second class, and corporals from the third. A cadet captain commanded each company; the senior of the four student officers was the "First Captain." He was responsible for maintaining discipline throughout the entire corps as well as in his own unit.[43] The first ranking cadet lieutenant was the adjutant; his duties included publishing the orders of the day, detailing cadets for guard duty, and making room assignments. Next below the adjutant ranked the quartermaster, also a lieutenant, who was responsible for issuing supplies and military equipment to the corps. Twelve cadet lieutenants, three per company, were the lowest ranking officers. They assisted the company commanders, inspected divisions in the barracks, and commanded platoons at drills. The remaining first classmen wore "clean sleeves," that is, they held no rank, but in deference to their status as seniors they were termed "High Privates" in cadet parlance.[44]

The senior ranking second classman was the sergeant major who assisted the adjutant in his duties; likewise, the second ranking junior, the quartermaster sergeant, aided the quartermaster. Below him ranked the four first, or orderly, sergeants, one in each company; they were responsible for assembling their units, calling the rolls at formations, keeping the company guard roster, and overseeing discipline in the ranks. The color bearer, also a sergeant, ranked just below the first sergeants. The lowest ranking noncommissioned officers of the second class were the twelve sergeants, three per company, who acted as guides and file closers. All other second classmen were privates. From the third class came the sixteen corporals, four in each company; they acted as squad leaders, drillmasters, and "carvers" at tables in the mess hall. Two other members of the same class served as color corporals, guarding the flag at ceremonies. The remainder of the third class and all plebes were privates.[45]

According to regulations, the criteria for selecting cadet officers and noncommissioned officers were "soldier-like performance of duties, and

. . . exemplary . . . general conduct." Academic standing did not affect selection except to the extent that cadets holding rank had to be proficient in their studies.[46] The historical record suggests that there was little, if any, correlation between cadet rank and subsequent success on the battlefield. For example, Henry Halleck, J. E. B. Stuart, P. G. T. Beauregard, E. P. Alexander, John Sedgewick, Braxton Bragg, and, incredibly, Ambrose Burnside, were all cadet officers; also, James B. McPherson, the hero of Atlanta, and Patrick H. O'Rorke, who died fighting gallantly for the Union at Gettysburg, were "First Captains." On the other hand, Grant, Sherman, Sheridan, Tidball, John C. Pemberton, Emory Upton, G. K. Warren, and "Stonewall" Jackson graduated as "High Privates."[47]

Military duties consumed a relatively small fraction of the cadet's time during the course of the academic year. After reveille roll call at dawn each man spent the next half hour cleaning his room; then, he studied until seven o'clock. Breakfast was from seven to seven-thirty. A half hour of recreation followed. The rest of the morning, from eight until one in the afternoon, was devoted to classroom recitations and study periods. Dinner, from one to two o'clock, was followed by afternoon classes until four. The period from then until sunset was taken up with drills, parades, and recreation. Supper began at sunset and lasted half an hour. Fifteen minutes later cadets had to repair to their rooms where they studied until nine-thirty. Another half-hour period of recreation followed. Every student had to be in bed at taps which sounded at ten o'clock. All told, the boys spent between nine and ten hours daily in class or studying, approximately three hours in military exercises, two hours in recreation, and two hours at meals.[48]

The authorities relied on an intricate and comprehensive system of punishments and demerits to enforce discipline. Demerits, although closely associated with chastisement, were actually assessments against the cadet's grade in conduct, whereas punishments entailed loss of priviliges, confinement, extra duty, and expulsion. Offenses were divided into eight categories depending on the degree of seriousness. Those of the "First Grade," such as mutinous conduct or unauthorized absence, were worth ten demerits while those of the "Eighth Grade," for example, late to roll call or improperly blacked shoes, were valued at only one or two demerits. A cadet who accumulated two hundred or more demerits in a calendar year was declared deficient in conduct and recommended for discharge by the academic board even though all his offenses may have been minor ones.[49] On the other hand, a student who committed a single grave crime, such as drinking or consorting with prostitutes, faced dismissal by court-martial regardless of his previous conduct record. Lesser penalties, graded like demerits according to the gravity of the offense, included suspension from the academy, confinement in "Light" or "Dark" prison (barracks rooms with the windows covered by blankets or uncovered), restriction to quarters, extra tours of guard duty, reduction in rank, and denial of privileges—for example, being prohibited from walking "on the public lands" during recreation periods.[50]

Every evening at parade the adjutant announced the delinquencies which had been recorded for the day. The offender then had twenty-four hours to submit a written excuse to the commandant. If the explanation was accepted the offense was expunged; if not, the miscreant received an appropriate number of demerits and penalties. Some cadets believed writing excuses was futile. As George M. Wharton pointed out to the commandant in 1842, "I have denied certain reports most firmly—denials which I would repeat on my deathbed—and yet they are recorded against me as though I had said nothing whatsoever. Methinks it is but mockery to grant one liberty of speech and still pay no attention to his words."[51]

Possibly, Wharton was too skeptical. The records indicate that in most cases the authorities did accept reasonable excuses, particularly if the boy was on the verge of being deficient in conduct. Then too, at least one commandant of the era could be manipulated. John Tidball, a contemporary of Wharton, maintained that a cadet could insure acceptance of his excuse by filling it with grammatical errors. The commandant at the time, J. Addison Thomas, had formerly taught English at the academy, and could not resist correcting mistakes in the students' papers. On receipt of a poorly written explanation he would call the offender in and help him redraft it. Having thus made the excuse more satisfactory, Thomas could not very well refuse to approve it without denying his own grammatical ability and the force of his own logic.[52]

In any event cadets could appeal a decision they considered unjust to the secretary of war who, as often as not, ruled in the youngsters' favor.[53] Because of the varied means by which a student could avail himself of a fair hearing it is safe to assume that the disciplinary code, though harsh and demanding, was reasonably just. The system can be faulted on other grounds, however. It rewarded alibiing, docility, and punctilious obedience to a set of minutely detailed rules. Also, the code did not reward—in fact, it attempted to discourage—initiative. Had the regulations been literally and unthinkingly applied, West Point could only have produced automatons. That it did not was due less to the system itself than to the more humane and broad-minded members of the staff who refrained from pushing the code to its limits and to the stouthearted young men who refused to surrender their individuality regardless of the pressures for conformity.

The Corps
of Cadets:
Activities,
Honor,
and Religion
★

Cadets could temporarily escape the pervasive military environment by several officially approved means: debating and literary exercises, sports, reading, and occasional entertainments. In addition, some students, not content with sanctioned activities, engaged in illegal enterprises which, if nothing else, added zest to what was otherwise a drab existence.

The oldest authorized extracurricular organizations were the several literary and debating clubs which traced their origins to the Amosophic Society founded in 1816. These eventually merged into one body, the Dialectic Society, in 1837.[1] Plebes were ineligible for membership, and upperclassmen could join only by invitation. The society met on Saturday nights to read and critique members' papers and to debate topics which had been approved by the superintendent. Among the issues argued during the antebellum era were: "Does the United States owe a greater debt to Thomas Jefferson or Alexander Hamilton?"; "Should Capital Punishment Be Abolished?"; "Ought Females To Receive a First-Rate Education?"; "Should Nations Go To War To Preserve the Balance of Power?"; "Whether Universal Suffrage Should Be Allowed"; "Has a State The Right to Secede from the Union?"; and "Have Republics more of that in them which will tend to their Decay than to their Preservation?" The single recorded instance of official interference took place in March 1843 when Superintendent Richard Delafield vetoed the topic, "Has a State under any circumstances the Right to Nullify an Act of Congress?"[2] In addition to serving as an outlet for forensic and writing activities the Dialectic Society also provided the orator and the reader of the Declaration of Independence for the annual Fourth of July celebrations.[3]

Even though the club afforded cadets an opportunity to expand their speaking and literary skills beyond the narrow scope of the curriculum in those areas, the academic staff gave it scant support. The professors believed that Dialectic Society functions took too much time away from the members' studies and that some boys joined merely to escape from barracks on Saturday nights. Because of these misgivings the authorities permitted the organization to exist but firmly resisted all proposals to establish similar groups.[4]

Intercollegiate athletics were unknown at the pre–Civil War military academy. Cadets did engage in competitive sports among themselves but only on an informal, voluntary basis. Football—apparently a form of soccer—was popular. Cricket, on the other hand, never caught on despite the efforts of the superintendent to stimulate an interest in it. Cadets could also swim in the Hudson during the summer and skate on it in winter, as well as ride, hike, and sleigh in the hills surrounding the post.[5] Furthermore, the military program required considerable physical activity, with classes in equitation, fencing, and, after a gymnasium was established in 1846, calisthenics.[6] Then too, each youngster inevitably obtained exercise in the course of his daily routine: drilling, parading, and marching back and forth to the mess hall, classrooms, and the barracks. Therefore, the typical cadet remained in good physical condition throughout his stay at the academy.

Students could use the library for recreational reading, but under strictures which inhibited enjoyment. Even in the reading room a cadet had to keep his uniform buttoned to the chin. Moreover, fiction and other volumes not pertaining directly to course work could be withdrawn only on Saturday afternoon and had to be returned the following Monday.[7] Selections available for recreational reading leaned heavily toward devotional material, military history, heroic novels, and biographies of the "Great Captains." Sherman, for example, read Bourrienne's *Napoleon;* Beauregard withdrew Chateauneuf's *Grands Capitaines,* together with a volume of Montesquieu's works; while J. E. B. Stuart took out a book on chivalry, Sully's *Memoirs,* and a volume on ancient history. Grant—something of an exception to the general rule—read more fiction than anything else, completing, according to his autobiography, "all of Bulwer's . . . Cooper's, Marryat's, Scott's, Irving's, and Lever's novels"; the official records show that he also read volume two of Livy and some of Swift's works. Stonewall Jackson, however, avoided romances, concentrating instead on a biography of Napoleon, a military dictionary, and a chemistry text. Phil Sheridan

76

who came to the academy with a poor preparatory background and who, according to his classmate David S. Stanley, was "ignorant of the world" and "totally unqualified with books," apparently tried to make up for these deficiencies by reading extensively while a cadet. He withdrew a biography of Samuel Johnson, four studies on Napoleon and his campaigns, a biography of Byron, another of Mohammed, geographies of Ireland, Greenland, Oregon, and California, the Waverly novels, and some of Irving's works. John Schofield, like Stuart, read a book on ancient history; he also took out the Waverly novels, collections of Tennyson's and Scott's poetry, and a work on ethics. Two cadets who never withdrew books from the library, as far as the records show, were Heth and Burnside.[8] Also, students whose accounts were solvent could subscribe to one periodical of their choice and, with the superintendent's approval, receive newspapers and magazines from home.[9]

Christmas and New Year's were the only holidays of the academic year. Both occasions were celebrated by suspension of classes for the day and a feast in the mess hall. The chaplain conducted services on Christmas Day, but attendance was optional. Also, Lee, when superintendent, held parties for cadets during the holiday season; furthermore, the other officers of the garrison, in keeping with military tradition, received calls from members of the first class.[10] Students with satisfactory grades who lived close enough to West Point could go home for a day or two during the holidays, but most came from areas too distant to qualify for this indulgence.[11] The authorized holiday activities were sedate and nonalcoholic; however, sometimes cadets managed to obtain whisky and hold their own celebrations after taps. One such Bacchanalia got so out of hand that a group of boys pelted several army officers with lumps of coal.[12]

Except for holidays, Saturday nights were the only periods of the week when cadets could attend authorized entertainments. In the main, such activities included the Dialectic Society exercises, plays put on by cadets, and band concerts. Occasionally, variations were offered; these included Professor Weir's exhibitions of his paintings, a display featuring the fossilized remains of a mastodon, and a demonstration of phrenology.[13]

If the officially sponsored entertainments had a bland and monotonous flavor, the same was true of the food in the cadet mess. The daily diet was heavy on bread, potatoes, and meat, especially beef, veal, and mutton, but skimpy on green vegetables and sweets. Breakfast and midday dinner were the large meals, each consisting of meat, potatoes, bread, and butter; supper or "tea" was limited to coffee, tea, milk, bread, and butter, supplemented occasionally by cornbread and molasses. The menu changed every day but repeated itself weekly. As nearly as can be determined, no one went hungry, but complimentary remarks about the mess are almost nonexistent. The main complaints were that the food was poorly prepared, that students had to wolf down their meals in order to finish on time, and that the fare was boring. As John Buford, who was to become a distinguished Union cavalry officer, put it, "The fare of the mess hall is miserable—bull beef and bread and bread and bull beef continually—it would be quite a luxury to miss a meal."[14]

A dozen or so cadets were allowed to eat at a boarding house operated by Mrs. Alexander R. Thompson, the widow of an officer who had been killed in Florida. This cherished privilege was passed on by each graduating boarder to a successor of his choice, though the superintendent could revoke it at any time for misconduct. The main attraction of eating at "Mammy" Thompson's was less the food than the relaxed atmosphere. Another pensioner ran a "soda shop" in the basement of the barracks where cadets with sufficient money in their "Treasurer's Accounts" could buy a dollar's worth of sundries monthly, mainly cakes, cookies, candy, and pickles.[15]

The tame diversions approved by the authorities did not suffice for the bolder and more imaginative boys. Drinking, smoking, absence without leave, fighting, and cooking in barracks rooms were the principal illegal means cadets used to relieve the tedium.

Drinking, possessing, or introducing alcohol onto the reservation, and visiting taverns were offenses warranting dismissal, but this did not deter the likes of Grant, Sherman, Heth, Warren, Strong, Burnside, Bragg, Fitz Lee, George Custer,[16] and undoubtedly many others as well. Cadets could obtain liquor from several sources. The most notorious of these was Benny Havens's tavern in nearby Buttermilk (Highland) Falls. For decades the proprietor foiled the efforts of West Point authorities to close his establishment, all the while managing to provide several generations of pre–Civil War students with food, beer, and whisky. Indeed, the tavern was so popular it was eventually immortalized by the ditty, "Benny Havens's O!" In addition, Havens, as well as other local civilians, sometimes smuggled liquor onto the post via the river, landing at a secluded cove below the Plain under cover of darkness. Drummer boys of the band would also sneak whisky inside the gates and sell it to cadets, and students would bring bottles back with them from furlough. Certainly the most original method of slaking thirst was demonstrated by Cadet George Custer, if one of his biographers can be believed. Whenever his class was scheduled to make a mounted march beyond the limits of the reservation, Custer and his friend, future Confederate cavalryman Tom Rosser, would arrange to be at the tail of the column. As the group rode past a tavern not far from the post, the pair would peel off, unseen by the officer at the head of the column, tether their mounts in a concealed spot, enter the tavern and drink until the class returned. Then, on a signal from the rear guard, they would resume their places in the formation, with the instructor being none the wiser.[17]

A cadet found guilty of drinking or trafficking in alcohol faced dismissal; however, if all the members of his class pledged to abstain from strong drink as long as they remained at the academy, the offender was usually reinstated. Despite the severity of these terms, there is no recorded instance of students failing to rescue a hapless classmate. Although pledging was voluntary, the evidence suggests that the tactical staff took every occasion to encourage it in order to lighten their workload. Obviously this was the case early in 1861. In February of that year a fire broke out in the nearby Cozzens Hotel, and the entire corps of cadets was ordered out to help extinguish the blaze. The plebe class, the only one not on pledge at the time, received the mission of removing the contents of the wine cellar. The inevitable happened, and before nightfall two plebes were arrested for drunkenness. Their classmates took the pledge, so for the remainder of the year the tactical officers could relax their vigilance a bit, secure in the knowledge that teetotalism was in force throughout the corps.[18]

Another dismissal offense was unauthorized absence from the military reservation, a crime frequently associated with drinking. Benny Havens's tavern was a powerful magnet, pulling cadets away from their authorized haunts, but it was not the only one. Girls and other attractions occasionally induced students to stray also. Moreover, according to John Tidball and James H. Wilson, some youngsters went off limits for the sheer thrill of "running it," that is, pulling off a daring escapade under the very noses of the authorities. No doubt it was this spirit that goaded John Schofield to ride a riverboat to New York City and back between two roll calls in one day.[19]

Smoking, though prohibited, was not a dismissal offense. For years the authorities went to great lengths trying to stamp it out, even going to the extent of punishing the cadet in charge of a room if the odor of tobacco could be detected. But the crusade proved hopeless, and in 1857 the superintendent abandoned the struggle. From then on cadets were permitted to smoke in their rooms and in a few other areas if they obtained parental consent.[20]

Fighting was a popular pastime too. The antebellum cadet was pugnacious; his sense of honor was prickly, and an insult or injustice almost invariably provoked a scuffle. In all probability students also fought in order to release pent-up energy and to entertain and impress their comrades as well. Usually, the altercations were simple fist fights, resulting only in bloody noses and black eyes, but occasionally the combatants resorted to weapons with intent to do bodily harm. In such affrays they used clubs, knives, bayonets, and sabers. Sometimes boys would receive serious injuries in these contests, but no one was ever killed. Although fighting was prohibited, the officers generally looked the other way. As Richard Delafield explained, ignoring minor scuffles between students was "far better than driving them to a more serious mode by pistols, swords, etc. that would inevitably be the case if severer measures were taken."[21] When a cadet assaulted another who was acting in an official capacity, however, the case was too serious to overlook. Phil Sheridan, for instance, was suspended for a year after he assaulted a cadet sergeant in 1851, and similar instances in other times were handled with equal severity.[22] Ambrose Burnside also found himself in serious trouble because of a fracas between a cadet private and a noncommissioned officer. Burnside was not a principal; his offense consisted of preventing others from stopping the fight, insisting that it was a fair one even though the private was hitting the corporal with a club. This and a related incident almost cost Burnside his military career, prompting Superintendent Delafield to endorse the commandant's report of the incident with the comment: "Recommend that Burnside . . . be at once separated from the academy as the greatest act of mercy and clemency to the Corps of Cadets."[23] Fortunately for Burnside, if not for the Union troops at Fredericksburg in December 1862, Delafield subsequently relented and withdrew his recommendation.

In contrast, Cadet First Sergeant James E. B. Stuart received a light penalty for striking Cadet Private John L. Grattan in front of the barracks after breakfast one morning. Fighting in such a public place made punishment obligatory, but the authorities were lenient with Stuart because Grattan had assaulted him in the mess hall earlier while he, Stuart, was performing his duties. Besides, neither of the boys had suffered any injury.

Other future cavalrymen also ran afoul of the regulations against fighting. Tom Rosser, later to serve under Stuart, was a well-known hellion earning official notoriety and near dismissal, for leading a saber-swinging melee in the summer of 1857. Rosser's companion George Custer also came to grief over an altercation even though he, like Burnside, had not been a participant. Just before graduation in June 1861 Custer, while on duty as officer of the guard, observed two plebes fighting, but instead of breaking up the brawl as the regulations required, he egged the boys on. Custer was punished for this dereliction by being held in confinement until after his class had graduated. In fact, he probably would have been dismissed if the need for officers had not been so urgent. As it was Custer received his diploma and commission several weeks behind his classmates.

Still another fight, one relished by academy chroniclers because of its sectional implications, took place between Wade Hampton Gibbes, a South Carolinian who later became a cavalryman and later still a Confederate participant in the attack on Fort Sumter, and Emory Upton of New York. The fight occurred in 1859, soon after the hanging of John Brown, an event which had raised regional sentiments in the corps to fever pitch. During a discussion of the Brown incident, Gibbes claimed that Upton had enjoyed the favors of Negro girls while attending Oberlin College. The New Yorker had not been present when the remark was made, but on learning of it, called Gibbes out. The South Carolinian gladly obliged, and a bloody encounter took place.[24]

A more peaceable pursuit, making "hash" over the coal fires in cadet rooms, was also a common illicit activity. The youngsters obtained the ingredients for their hashes in several ways. They smuggled bread and butter from the mess hall under their caps, stole poultry from officers' barnyards (Major Delafield inadvertently contributing two ducks on one occasion), and robbed convenient fruit orchards. One of the most daring of these foraging expeditions was carried out by Henry Heth and several confederates who, by combining stealth and speed, successfully made off with a complete holiday dinner from the officers' mess. An equally imaginative

West Point comrades in 1853. Cadet Philip H. Sheridan is flanked by recent graduates Bvt. Second Lieutenant George Crook, left, and Bvt. Second Lieutenant John Nugen. Sheridan missed graduating with his friends because of misconduct resulting in a year's suspension from the academy. First classmen (seniors) were sometimes permitted to grow mustaches before graduation.

group of first classmen (seniors) persuaded a group of plebes to make a midnight raid on a nearby apple orchard. While the plebes were carrying out their mission the old cadets put on blue furlough coats and hid in the bushes beside a path the foragers would have to take to get back to their quarters. When the plebes with their pillowcases full of apples passed the ambush point, the upperclassmen sprang out and chased them. The foragers, thinking they were being pursued by officers, dropped the pillowcases and ran, leaving the spoils to the seniors.

Having obtained the provisions, the hash-makers covered the windows of their rooms with blankets to prevent light from showing through, bribed the sentinel on post with the promise of a share of the hash, and then cooked up the mess in a makeshift container. When done, the meal was served to as many guests as could crowd into the room, not forgetting the sentinel. After eating, those who were smokers lit their pipes, and a merry evening followed unless the officer in charge interrupted the festivities. For the most part, students successfully evaded the authorities when it came to foraging and hash-making. More surprisingly, in light of what went into the hashes, the boys also seemed to avoid gastric troubles.

Hash-making almost disappeared in the early fifties when steam heat replaced the coal grates in barracks rooms, but the installation of gaslight evoked a renaissance. However, cadet tastes had changed in the interim; the favorite concoction of the new generation was taffy made from butter and sugar smuggled from the mess hall and cooked over the gas jets.[25]

In comparison to hash-making, smoking, drinking, and fighting, few students indulged in sexual activity insofar as the records show. In the summer of 1840 the surgeon detected symptoms of veneral disease in three cadets; the culprits were confined to camp and prohibited from "attending any of the cotillion parties or other assemblies of ladies."[26] Also, in 1847 and again in 1849 students brought prostitutes onto the post; the two who came in 1847 spent the night in barracks. In both instances the offending cadets were dismissed.[27] Otherwise, the official records make no mention of sexual conduct and, naturally, letters and memoirs are silent on the subject. Perhaps more members of the corps engaged in such illicit ventures than the records reflect, but the lack of evidence probably means more or less what it implies; sexual activity was infrequent if for no other reason than lack of opportunity.

The highly legalistic, minutely regulated, and carefully supervised honor system of present-day West Point was unknown in the antebellum era. The cadet of that day, like his officer counterpart, was expected not to steal or make false official statements and, if found guilty of either of these offenses, could be dismissed. As the drinking pledges demonstrate, the authorities trusted cadets, and the latter, for their part, upheld that trust.

Another illustration of this mutual faith was the use of the term "All Right." An officer or cadet inspector checking the barracks to ascertain that all the occupants were present would inquire "All Right?" at the doorway of each room without entering or looking inside. The response, "All Right" from within signified that everyone was present or in some authorized place. A cadet illegally absent when the inquiry was made had to turn himself in. Similarly, the authorities accepted roll calls and other official accountings from cadets without question. On other matters, however, students interpreted honor in the narrowest way imaginable. A cadet undergoing official interrogation about the misbehavior of a comrade would testify only to what he had literally seen. For instance, no matter how drunk a boy might have been, his fellows would not state that he was inebriated unless they had actually observed him taking a drink of whisky. Moreover, a cadet serving as officer of the day or in some other official capacity which required him to report violations of regulations risked the opprobrium of his peers if he apprised the authorities of an infraction he had not witnessed with his own eyes, no matter how compelling the circumstantial evidence might have been.[28]

Stealing was likewise a dismissal offense.[29] Instances of theft were fairly rare. Between 1833 and 1861, for example, only three cases were reported, and two of these turned out to be nothing more than careless borrowing. In the Civil War years three more incidents occurred; these revealed a new tendency in the corps—vigilante justice. The first manifestation of this innovation took place in connection with the theft of a case of drawing instruments by a third classman. The superintendent, anticipating trouble, advised the thief to leave the academy immediately without awaiting formal action; he also placed the boy in protective custody and had him escorted under guard to the riverboat wharf, but a large group of cadets brushed the escort aside and seized the offender. They were preparing to tar and feather him when the officer of the day intervened to restore order. In the second case a group of cadets called on a boy whom they suspected of stealing and conducted an informal hearing on the spot. The suspect, after confessing, promised to resign immediately, so he was permitted to leave the academy in peace. The third instance involved a student caught by his classmates with marked money in his possession following a rash of burglaries in the barracks. The four cadet captains and the adjutant stripped the culprit of his uniform and forced him to don civilian clothes. He was then marched before the assembled corps and ordered to leave the post forthwith. The cadet vigilantes had to pay a penalty for their unwarranted assumption of authority in these instances, but the relative mildness of their punishments indicates that West Point officials tacitly approved their aims if not the methods they used.[30]

83

The Civil War era witnessed the advent of yet another recognizable feature of the modern honor system. Not only did the students occasionally enforce the code themselves, the authorities sometimes used the cadet concept of honor as a tool to prevent violation of academy regulations. Beginning on the eve of the war, hazing took a vicious turn with plebes being subjected to injurious pranks, such as "smoking out." This consisted of confining a new boy in a closed tent and blowing tobacco smoke in his face until he became ill. Then, in 1862 an upperclassman stabbed a plebe sentinel with a bayonet. The following year the superintendent felt compelled to call the attention of the chief of engineers to several brutal hazing incidents. In the summer of 1864 a third classman poured hartshorn into the nostrils of a sleeping new cadet, and the next summer another plebe complained that after having been dragged from his tent during the night, he had been flung into a ditch where he had struck his head on a rock. In 1866 a New York congressman informed the superintendent that he had received numerous complaints about hazing, including incidents "so infamous and revolting that I should not hesitate to put anyone to death who attempted to perpetrate them on me." In desperation Alexander Bowman, the superintendent, turned to the device which had long been used to control drinking. In the summer of 1863 he pardoned several third classmen who had been charged with hazing after receiving pledges from their classmates that they would refrain from pulling the plebes out of bed and harassing them as they walked guard. The wording of this promise proved too restrictive, however, with the upperclassmen discovering ways to get around it. At that juncture Bowman decided to extract pledges covering all forms of hazing from the entire third class, threatening them with deprivation of leave unless they signed. In July 1864 the superintendent further expanded the pledge to include all upperclassmen and to embrace all leaves and passes.[31] Bowman's use of coercion in these instances stood in sharp contrast to the earlier drinking pledges which cadets had taken of their own volition.

Contrary to later views at West Point, cheating was not considered a serious breech of morality in the antebellum era, and detection did not bring expulsion at the hands of officers or fellow cadets. The most prevalent forms of cribbing were smuggling another student's drawings into the classroom and passing them off as one's own, surreptitiously copying from a book or from a neighbor while working at the blackboard, and writing unauthorized notations in texts. The authorities frowned on all of these, but the penalties were usually mild: a few demerits, a zero on the lesson, and several extra tours of guard duty. In fact, a bit of glamour attached itself to several cadets who stole copies of the French examination in 1861, and Custer, according to his roommate, lost no status in the eyes of the corps when he attempted a similar feat. Standing dangerously low in the ethics course and knowing that the approaching examinations might be disastrous, Custer decided to risk all on one daring maneuver. He managed to gain admission to the quarters of his instructor while the latter was absent. Finding a copy of the examination, Custer was busy copying it when he heard footsteps approach. Without thinking the cadet tore the questions out of the instructor's notebook, stuffed them in his pocket, and ran. The teacher, on entering the room and seeing his notebook, quickly realized that some student had stolen the test. Consequently, Custer appeared before the examiners only to find himself confronted with a set of questions he could not answer. "Yellow Hair's" proverbial luck held, however, for the secretary of war permitted him to continue on with his class despite the poor showing on the examination.[32]

West Point authorities did not rely solely on negative measures to instill the principles of ethical behavior. Those principles, along with the other tenets of Protestant Christianity, were expounded from the pulpit of the chapel every Sunday morning. Attendance was mandatory for all cadets. Catholics and Episcopalians could go to the services peculiar to their faiths, but the others, including Jews and atheists, had to attend the rites at the Cadet Chapel.[33] Students who desired could also participate in several other religious activities, such as the chapel choir, Sunday school, and Bible classes. For most of the antebellum period statistics showing the extent of cadet involvement in these activities do not exist. There is evidence which indicates that fifteen or twenty students met with Lieutenant O. O. Howard of the mathematics department for Bible study on Monday nights, during the late fifties,[34] but whether this figure is representative of other periods cannot be determined.

It is equally difficult to gauge the effectiveness of religious training at the academy, but the records suggest that it was usually insignificant or negative. Most references to the spiritual atmosphere in cadet letters are derogatory in some way or other. Grant, for example, felt that compulsory chapel was not "republican," and he resented the Episcopal tone of the ostensibly nondenominational services. Schofield took umbrage at Chaplain Sprole's barb, "God-hating geologists," which the cleric hurled at the absent Professor Bailey in the midst of a sermon. Cadet O. O. Howard opined, "The influences here are not of the healthiest kind as far as concerns the moral character."[35] The less priggish Sherman agreed. According to him, Sunday was not observed with proper reverence at the academy "where the only religious duties consist in attending the Episcopal service . . . a service in which but a few take interest, much less join in heartfelt devotion." Similarly, Emory Upton found that among the corps "few scoff at it [religion], yet a great majority totally ignore it." In a different vein John Tidball noted the soporific effects of the sermons and complained of the uncomfortable chapel furniture.[36] Other letters and reminiscences generally are silent on the subject, leading to the conclusion that the religious aspects of West Point did not make much of an impression on the writers. Also, the corps of cadets remained largely unaffected by the waves of revivalism, mass conversions, and other manifestations of religious enthusiasm which swept the country in the antebellum era. Moreover, the temperance movement, though encouraged from the pulpit and by tracts distributed in the barracks,[37] clearly made little headway at the academy. Thus, except for introducing some cadets to Episcopalianism, West Point probably changed prior attitudes toward religion little if any. But after all, the institution was a military academy, not a seminary.

The Academic Environment, 1833–1854

★

A basic feature of the Thayer legacy was the evaluation of student performance in each subject virtually every day. This was accomplished through an instructional device appropriately called the "recitation": the cadet's diligence in preparing his lessons and his ability to remember accurately what he had read in a text were tested orally, on paper, or at the blackboard. The teacher merely asked questions or assigned problems and graded the responses.

In keeping with the sacrosanct academy notion that human failure and achievement could be measured with mathematical precision, a comprehensive grading scheme ranging from 3.0 to zero was used. A mark between 2.6 and 3.0 signified a "Thorough" or "The Best" recitation; the spread between 2.5 and 2.1 was reserved for a "Good" performance, while 2.0 stood for "Fair," and the span between 1.9 and 1.1 for "Tolerable." A "Bad" or "Very Incomplete" recitation called for a mark between 1.0 and 0.1 and a "Complete Failure" or "The Worst" got zero. At the end of the week each instructor reported the daily grades of his students to the superintendent. The latter forwarded a consolidated monthly report to the chief of engineers who sent extracts to each boy's parents.[1]

Cadets not only recited daily, they stood general examinations in each subject twice a year, in January before the academic board and in June before the same body meeting jointly with the board of visitors. His performance on the January examinations determined a student's relative standing in each subject taken during the fall term; this, in conjunction with the results of the June test, fixed his general order of merit ranking for the year. Daily grades did not directly affect standings, but the academic board did consider them in deciding the disposition of delinquent cadets and in breaking ties on examination grades since no two students could hold the same order of merit ranking in a course.[2]

Each subject had a weighted value in determining general order of merit, or class standing. Fourth class mathematics, for example, counted two; third class French counted one; second class natural and experimental philosophy counted three, and so on.[3] To facilitate computation these weights were converted to three-digit numbers, mathematics becoming two hundred, French one hundred, and natural and experimental philosophy three hundred. The student who stood first in a given subject at the examinations received the total number of points for that subject. The best cadet in fourth class mathematics, for instance, got two hundred while the one who stood highest in French obtained one hundred. The last man still deemed proficient received one-third of the total number of points, 66.67 in mathematics and 33.33 in French. Each student between the extremes was awarded a portion of the total number of points corresponding to his relative ranking in the course.[4] The annual general order of merit grade was the sum of the scores in the various subjects taken during the year.

Graduation order of merit, or final class standing, was computed by adding all of the cadet's annual order of merit grades. This was the most important ranking a student received, for it determined the branch of service he could enter on graduation and his place on the promotion list as well.[5] Obviously, both factors crucially affected an officer's career, particularly in a day when seniority rather than merit was the essential criterion for advancement.

The examinations not only decided class standings, in some cases they determined whether a cadet could remain at the academy. Any boy who failed a subject in June forfeited his place and was either turned back to a lower class or discharged. Prior to 1849 only fourth classmen were dropped for failures in January, but in that year, the secretary of war, at the request of the academic board, amended the regulations to permit the dismissal of upperclassmen in January also. The purpose of this provision was to spur those old cadets who had neglected to prepare for the January examinations, knowing that with a little extra effort they could pass in June.[6]

Another cornerstone of the Thayer System was the division of each class into academically homogeneous sections of a dozen or so cadets. The initial sectioning for plebes in September was alphabetical since they had not yet had a chance to demonstrate their academic prowess, but afterwards they, like the upperclassmen, were sectioned according to merit in each subject.

The arrangement of upper class sections at the beginning of the fall term was based on standings in a related course the preceding June, or according to general order of merit if there were no cognate subject. For example, the original sectionings for first class engineering in September were made up according to final class standings in second class natural and experimental philosophy. Chemistry sections, on the other hand, were based on third class General Order of Merit, there being no sophomore subject which correlated directly with second class chemistry.[7] About two weeks after the beginning of the fall term, and periodically thereafter, sections were rearranged according to current performance in each subject; therefore, a student could move up to a higher section or down to a lower one at intervals throughout the semester in accordance with his performance in the classroom.

A few cadets questioned the objectivity of the mechanistic, mathematically precise grading system. John Tidball, for instance, claimed that after struggling three years to improve his standing, he reached the first section in ethics only to discover that it was not composed of an intellectual elite as he had supposed, but merely of youngsters whose superior preparatory education had enabled them to excel early in their cadetships and who subsequently retained their places largely through bluff. Similarly, William Harris wrote his father, "There is nothing like a reputation here . . . to everyone who hath, to him shall be given, etc." Henry A. Du Pont went even further, accusing Professor Church of rank favoritism and insisting that a cadet's performance in mathematics so prejudiced the academic board it affected his standings in completely unrelated subjects such as French. And Edward Anderson detected a strong connection between receiving high grades in Lieutenant O. O. Howard's mathematics section and attending the pious teacher's Bible classes.[8] As any experienced instructor knows, the degree of truth in these classic complaints and excuses can never be ascertained satisfactorily. It is clear, however, that the marking and sectioning systems at antebellum West Point came about as close to eliminating human bias as possible.

Usually the department heads taught the first sections in their courses; assistant professors, including cadets detailed to instructional duty, taught the other sections, each teacher taking one or two, depending on the size of the class.[9] The thought behind assigning instructors in this manner was that the professors, being the most experienced teachers, were uniquely qualified to push the first sections at an accelerated pace. Although the arrangement provided expert guidance for the advanced groups, it also entailed putting the less competent cadets under the tutelage of inexperienced teachers; however, the faculty did not consider this a significant drawback.

Since classroom recitations were based on material from textbooks, there was no necessity and little incentive for cadets to use the library. Although students could gain access to it under certain conditions, the

89

primary purpose of the book collection was to support the faculty. Therefore, the holdings leaned heavily toward science, mathematics, engineering, and military affairs. In 1830 the collection included 123 works on military engineering, 308 on civil engineering, 366 on mathematics, 187 on natural philosophy, 182 on chemistry, mineralogy, and geology, 273 on strategy and tactics, and 235 on military history, compared to 317 which were classified as "miscellaneous literature." However, the library did subscribe to several literary journals: *The Edinburgh Review, The London Quarterly Review, The Literary Magazine and American Register*, and *The North American Review*.[10]

The collection had numbered 3,000 volumes in 1830. By 1844 it had grown to 14,564, but despite an increase in the "miscellaneous literature" category, almost four-fifths of the holdings remained in the engineering, science, and military fields. By 1852 the collection had increased to 15,500 volumes,[11] yet the ratio between categories stayed at about the same level it had been in 1844.

As a rule, Congress appropriated one thousand dollars annually to purchase and repair books, but from 1846 through 1848 no funds were voted because of an economy drive.[12] The library was not completely dependent on public largesse. Private donors, colleges, and church groups also gave books to the academy; in addition, the West Point library participated in an exchange scheme with several other government agencies and with educational institutions in France, trading duplicate copies of some volumes for others the military academy collection did not contain.[13]

A faculty member acted as librarian in addition to his other duties. His assistant, an enlisted man, worked full time at the library, carrying out the day-to-day tasks. The building was open between eight o'clock and noon and from one o'clock to sunset daily. The assistant was present during all these periods, but the librarian attended only between four o'clock and sunset. Faculty members were admitted whenever the library was open; however, cadets could visit it only between four o'clock and closing time.[14]

The surviving records are too fragmentary to permit an exact estimate of the use students made of the library, but they do show that the corps took out between one thousand and three thousand volumes annually. There were approximately 250 cadets at the academy in any given year between 1833 and 1854 so the average annual usage was from four to eight volumes per student. This figure is simply a mathematical mean; some cadets took out considerably more; others never withdrew any. In 1852 the librarian reported that twelve thousand volumes had circulated in the previous twelve months.[15] Taking this as a typical year and assuming the general validity of the estimate of cadet usage, the faculty must have withdrawn between nine thousand and twelve thousand of the total number of books.

That is, between three-fourths and eleven-twelfths of the books circulated were taken out by the teachers.

The decided mathematical, scientific, and engineering tinge which characterized the library collection was even more evident in the allocation of instructional time to the various subjects and in the relative weights accorded them in calculating order of merit rankings. For instance, in 1833, at the beginning of the period, 71 percent of the total classroom hours in the four-year curriculum went to mathematics, natural and experimental philosophy, chemistry, topographical drawing, engineering, mineraology, and geology, while 29 percent went to French, drawing of the human figure, moral and political science, rhetoric, and tactics. In determining order of merit at that time 55 percent of the total score depended on performance in engineering, mathematical, and scientific courses; 17 percent on French, rhetoric, moral and political science, and drawing of the human figure; 14 percent on tactics; and 14 percent on conduct.[16] By 1854, on the eve of the five-year program, several subjects had been added to the curriculum, yet the same general ratio still obtained with respect to classroom time: 71 percent to mathematics, science, and engineering, with 29 percent to all the others. Similarly, the general order of merit weights varied only slightly from what they had been in 1833: 54 percent of the total went to mathematics, science, and engineering; 20 percent to ethics, drawing of the human figure, French, moral and political philosophy, and English grammar; with 13 percent each to tactics and conduct.[17] Yet even though mathematics, science, and engineering enjoyed greater emphasis than the humanities, the latter carried more weight than tactics. At least the academic board was not guilty of letting the "military tail wag the academic dog."

For each of his first two years at West Point every cadet attended recitations in mathematics for an hour and a half daily, six days a week. As appendix II illustrates, the course included algebra, plane and solid geometry, plane and spherical trigonometry, analytical geometry, descriptive geometry, shades, shadows and perspectives (the application of geometric principles to architectural drawing), differential and integral calculus, and surveying.[18]

From ten to twelve cadets comprised a section in mathematics. The first section studied the entire text for each course, with the last section carrying about half that load, and the intermediate groups going at a pace somewhere between the first and last. All sections attended class in morning periods during both years of the course. On rare occasions Professor Church lectured, but usually cadets spent the periods working problems at the blackboard and explaining their work to the instructor. Also, from time to time Church visited each classroom and asked searching questions of the students, a practice which terrified the "Immortals" (cadets on the verge of deficiency) of the last section. Cadet John Pemberton, who had attended the University of Pennsylvania before coming to West Point, maintained that he had learned more in six months of fourth class mathematics than he would have in six years at college.[19] The future Confederate commander exaggerated only slightly. The scope of the mathematics program was impressive indeed. But the attempt to cover so much ground in such a short period exacted a heavy toll. Mathematics produced far more academic casualties than any other single subject.

The Department of French also taught both third and fourth classmen. Until the early 1840s both classes recited one hour daily throughout the academic year, but subsequently the recitations were reduced to an hour every other day in order to provide time for English grammar and geography.[20] In this regard it is significant that these subjects were introduced into the curriculum at the expense of French rather than one of the mathematics, science, or engineering courses. Recitations in French classes focused on grammar and translation. In a typical section room some cadets would write sentences and conjugate verbs at the blackboard while others would read aloud from a French text and translate passages into English. In addition, the first two sections of the third and fourth classes occasionally practiced speaking, and the first section of the third class translated portions of an English reader into French.[21] The stress on translation stemmed from the fact that the primary purpose of the course was to provide cadets with a foundation which would enable them to read scientific and military works in French; proficiency in speaking was much less important.

The Department of Ethics, chaired by the chaplain, presented a hodgepodge of courses at various times to the first, third, and fourth classes. The subjects taught were rhetoric, political philosophy, ethics (sometimes called moral science or moral philosophy), international law, English grammar, geography, and possibly some history, though the record is not clear on that point.

The course in English grammar included spelling, punctuation, and syntax; geography covered national boundaries, natural resources, commercial, naval, and military strengths, and the use of globes and maps. Rhetoric embraced the rise, structure, and philosophy of language, writing style, and the history of eloquence. Logic comprised the different mental operations employed in argument, the nature of terms, fallacies, and the "Discovery of Truth." Ethics concerned the duties of man, the relation of man to God, and the moral principles and practices of the professions. Political science covered American constitutional law, Supreme Court decisions, and international law, with emphasis on the laws of war.[22]

Classes taught by the Department of Ethics were one hour in length;

sections met three times a week either in the morning or afternoon. Some subjects, such as grammar and geography, were limited to blackboard recitations, while others—ethics and law, for example—consisted mainly of lectures followed by question periods. In addition, cadets wrote themes in the composition segments of the course. Few students or graduates bothered to comment on the substance of the ethics curriculum. One who did, John Tidball, thought that the text used for rhetoric was too advanced for most of his contemporaries and that one devoted to basic English usage would have been more appropriate.[23] Certainly, the uninhibited spelling and punctuation found in the writings of Tidball and some of his comrades lend credence to this charge.

The Department of Drawing instructed both the second and third classes, the former for two hours daily and the latter for two hours every other day.[24] Moreover, cadets received additional training in drawing in conjunction with their mathematics and engineering courses.

The drawing curriculum included lettering, topographical drawing, signs and symbols, the human figure, landscape drawing, painting, and water colors. For the most part students sketched models in the drawing academy, but in the landscape portion, they went outside and made actual terrain sketches. The aim of the program was utilitarian, not aesthetic. It existed to give cadets an underpinning for their engineering courses and to equip them with the skills they would need as officers in the field, where some ability to map and sketch was required.[25]

The Department of Chemistry, Mineralogy, and Geology presented courses to cadets in each of their last two years at the academy. Second classmen studied chemistry for the entire year, but the seniors took mineralogy and geology in the spring term only.[26]

The second class course consisted of inorganic, organic, and applied chemistry together with several subjects which today would be considered more appropriate to physics—namely, gravity, the properties of light and heat, and electricity. Chemistry sections met every other day for one hour in the morning throughout the entire academic year. These sessions consisted mainly of blackboard recitations; students did not work in the laboratory.[27]

Even though chemistry was a science and directly related to military technology, the authorities considered it of secondary importance, in the same category as ethics and French. The reply of Superintendent Richard Delafield to Professor Bailey's protest against taking time away from chemistry in order to introduce a program in equitation was indicative of the official attitude. "Chemistry," wrote Delafield, "I consider a valuable auxiliary, yet not to compare to the courses of Engineering, [Natural and Experimental] Philosophy, and Mathematics." The superintendent re-

93

flected the views of the rest of the hierarchy; chemistry counted one (later one and a half) in determining general order of merit, whereas mathematics, natural and experimental philosophy, and engineering counted three each.[28]

The department also taught mineralogy and geology to the first class. Cadets not only found these courses interesting but useful as well. Graduates exploring the West were able to render accurate reports of the geological formations and the mineral deposits they found; commanders of frontier garrisons could pick the best plots for post gardens and determine the most suitable fruits and vegetables to plant; and even more importantly, West Pointers could draw on their knowledge to help them in selecting the likeliest sites for finding water. Thus, the offerings of the Department of Chemistry, Mineralogy, and Geology had an applicability that transcended the narrow limits of military technology.

Natural and experimental philosophy was a combination of what today would be called physics, mechanics, and astronomy. It included electricity and magnetism, accoustics, mechanics, optics, and astronomy. Cadets studied these topics in one-hour blocs each weekday morning during the academic year.[29]

In compliance with accepted practice at West Point, the Department of Natural and Experimental Philosophy relied chiefly on the daily recitation as a teaching device. Cadets did not conduct experiments, but they did make observations with the barometer, sextant, and other measuring instruments. Also, each student learned to use the zenith telescope mounted in the observatory. Although cadets found Bartlett amusing and enjoyed using the telescope, they viewed the course in natural and experimental philosophy with apprehension since it demanded almost total recall of mathematical techniques they had learned earlier but had half-forgotten by the time they became juniors.[30]

The capstone of the academic program was Dennis Hart Mahan's military and civil engineering and the science (sometimes called art) of war, which first classmen took daily. The major portion of the fall term was devoted to civil engineering; this was followed by architecture and stone-cutting together with a large bloc of engineering drawing. Military engineering, which occupied most of the spring semester, consisted primarily of permanent and field fortifications and fortification drawing. A six-lesson (nine-hour) course titled "The Science of War" was sandwiched between the field fortification segment and drawing.[31]

Instruction in permanent fortifications was designed primarily to serve potential engineer officers who would be responsible for constructing and maintaining defenses along the water frontiers. A knowledge of field fortifications, on the other hand, was necessary for officers of all arms. This latter course dealt with such topics as the selection and trace of field positions, the construction of batteries and entrenchments, and the use of materials at hand to erect fortifications and obstacles, as well as ways of channeling enemy attacks onto unfavorable terrain. Mahan drew extensively on the French experience in both courses. Even so, he taught the application of principles in the light of common sense, not blind adherence to textbook rules. In fact, the professor preached the use of reason in military matters so vehemently and so frequently, the students nicknamed him "Old Cobbon Sense" in deference to the effect a chronic nasal infection had on Mahan's pronunciation of his favorite dictum.[32]

The six-lesson course entitled "The Science of War" followed fortifications. This too, Mahan taught largely by historical example, mainly French. The science of war included the composition and organization of

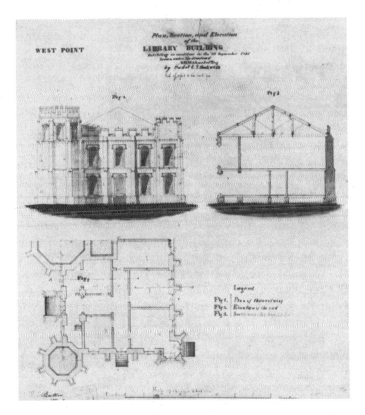

A drawing of the USMA Library made by Cadet Edward G. Beckwith, class of 1842, in his engineering course. Beckwith, as an artillery officer, explored the route between Utah and California later followed by the first transcontinental railroad.

armies, order of battle, castrametation, reconnaissance, outpost duties, attack, and defense, together with the elements of grand tactics and strategy.[33]

Historians have often speculated about the extent to which Mahan's thought, and hence, the content of his course, was influenced by the writings of Antoine Jomini, the Swiss military theorist who derived a set of operational principles from his analyses of Frederick the Great and Napoleon. David Donald, T. Harry Williams, and others have gone so far as to suggest that the alleged preoccupation with Jominian concepts reflected in the thoughts and actions of some Civil War commanders can be traced to the teachings of Mahan.[34] At the risk of further muddying murky waters it is necessary to mention several factors which plead for the application of "Cobbon Sense" to this sweeping generalization. To begin with, it seems incredible that one short course would so influence a student that it would continue to govern his thinking years later, overriding such subsequent experiences as the Mexican War and Indian fighting. Conversely, the rare cadet capable of such retention would surely have remembered his old professor's caveat regarding the use of judgment, not to mention Jomini's similar caution against slavish obedience to abstract rules. It is also significant that in their writings cadets and graduates almost never referred to Jomini or his teachings, and on the few occasions when they mentioned Mahan, it was usually in connection with his engineering courses, not strategy. The same evidence reveals that Napoleon seemed to fascinate the writers, as did Winfield Scott, but mainly as heroic figures rather than exemplars of strategic principles. Moreover, though it may be true that some officers—Beauregard, Halleck, McClellan, and possibly Lee, for example—continued their professional studies after graduation and thus gained a deeper appreciation of Jomini, the same cannot be said for the vast majority of their contemporaries. Most antebellum regular officers had neither the opportunity nor the inclination to study.[35] In fact, the idea of men like Heth, A. P. Hill, Joseph Hooker, Custer, Pope, Burnside, George Pickett, and John Bell Hood charging into battle "with a sword in one hand and Jomini's *Summary of the Art of War* in the other" is almost as ludicrous taken figuratively as literally. It is true that cadets studied Mahan's *Outpost* in some detail and that the same book served as a popular primer for officers trying to learn their trade during the Civil War. But a comparison of Mahan's volume with the *Precis* shows clearly that the West Point professor was not an unalloyed Jominian. This is not to say that the military academy experience had no bearing on the way the war was planned and fought but to suggest that the influences exerted by the academy worked in a more subtle and complex manner than the inculcation of abstract strategic principles through a brief sub-course.

A related thesis asserts that the Jominian-minded Confederates, after a string of early victories, eventually met defeat at the hands of those inadvertent, sometime Clausewitzians, Grant and Sherman.[36] This thesis condemns Mahan at least by implication, for not having abandoned Jomini in favor of the Prussian philosopher of war. The notion has the virtue of simplicity. But its questionable association of the two Union commanders with such concepts aside, the thesis suffers from an even graver defect, anachronism. French military thought had held sway over the West ever since the Napoleonic era, and continued to do so until after the Civil War when Sadowa and Sedan forced recognition of the rising Prussian star and drew attention to the technological and strategic developments which undergirded that rise. Perhaps Mahan should have anticipated the change, but prescience has seldom characterized American military thought, in this instance not even Mahan's.

Taking a different tack, Robert Utley in his *Frontiersmen in Blue* claims: "It [the academy] did not teach a prospective officer how to fight Indians. The incisive lectures of old Professor Dennis Hart Mahan probed the nature and art of war and laid down the principles by which his students would conduct the coming Civil War, but his teachings remained barren of guidance on how to employ a company of dragoons against the only enemy any of them could see in their future. West Point . . . sent them forth to learn Indian fighting by hard experience."[37]

Other scholars have repeated this charge. It is essentially correct with respect to Indian warfare. The tactics instructors who should have dealt with the subject ignored it. Yet the techniques of Indian fighting were not neglected altogether. Somehow, Mahan found time to squeeze a general discussion of the problem into his crowded curriculum, advising cadets to employ tactics which would capitalize on the white man's firepower and which, whenever possible, would drive a hostile tribe into conflict with its traditional Indian enemies so as to economize on the expenditure of white soldiers.[38] This was pitifully little, considering the magnitude of the army's pacification mission and the high degree of likelihood that most graduates at some time in their careers would be called on to assist in carrying it out.

Each student took about 192 hours of drawing during the courses in engineering and permanent fortifications.[39] Previously, he had spent almost five hundred hours on drawing in his second and third class years. Thus, the new graduate may have been ignorant of the techniques of Indian warfare and only dimly aware of the principles of strategy, but he should have been an accomplished draftsman.

Mahan's engineering courses were purely theoretical. After 1851, however, cadets learned the practical side as well. In that year Joseph Totten's efforts bore fruit with the establishment of a course in practical military engineering. At first, instruction was limited to having cadets observe the drills of the company of engineers, but later first classmen actively participated in these exercises.[40] The course, under the auspices of the Department of Practical Military Engineering, consisted of surveying positions, making route itineraries using the compass and odometer, laying out field works, supervising work parties, constructing scale models of field fortifications, and building military bridges. Cadets performed these tasks under the supervision of officers from the engineer company. Since there were no classroom recitations, the students did not receive grades.

The seniors learned practical military engineering during drill periods in the academic year and in summer camp also; there were a total of sixty such drills each calender year. The Department of Practical Military Engineering was not under Mahan's purview. An officer of the corps of engineers chaired the department and served as a member of the academic board in his own right.[41]

In addition to practical military engineering, cadets also received training in other professional subjects, specifically infantry, artillery, and cavalry tactics, equitation, and the sword exercise, or fencing. Like practical military engineering, these topics were taught during the academic year and in summer camp, but in contrast to practical military engineering, portions of these courses consisted of graded recitations and therefore counted in determining order of merit.

Artillery and infantry tactics, together with the sword exercise, were all taught before 1833. In the fall of 1839 horses were procured, and equitation became a regular feature of the curriculum. In the beginning only first classmen rode, but in 1846 a course was added for juniors and in 1851 for the third class also.[42] Equitation, a program designed to improve the cadets' horsemanship, imparted a skill required by officers of all branches. Cavalry tactics, that is, the methods of employing horse units in the field, was not presented until 1849. This course grew out of the dedicated efforts of Lieutenant James M. Hawes, Second Dragoons, who on his own initiative began to teach cavalry tactics as part of the equitation program.[43]

Counting summer camp and the academic year, the first class attended a total of thirty-two one-hour recitations in artillery, and fifteen apiece in cavalry and infantry tactics. Infantry and artillery each counted one and a half in computing order of merit while cavalry tactics counted three-fourths.

Only the first class received classroom instruction in tactics, but all cadets participated in drills. These exercises took place in the fall and spring after classes had ended for the day and in both morning and afternoon hours in summer camp.

The total number of artillery, cavalry, and infantry drills in the four-year program came to 204 for artillery, 268 for equitation, and 540 for infantry. In addition, there were 108 half-hour periods devoted to fencing. Until 1852 this instruction was limited to seniors, but from then on the fourth class took fencing too.[44]

Infantry instruction began with the school of the soldier and progressed through the company and battalion to "evolution of the line," a series of maneuvers for regiments and brigades. From the 1850s onward cadets also drilled as light infantry, deploying from line of battle into skirmishers and moving to the front and flanks in open order.

Artillery instruction also followed a logical progression from the school of the individual crewman to the maneuver of units. The course began with the school of the gunner; next came the school of the piece which covered the duties of the members of a gun crew, and finally, the school of the battery, a topic dealing with the movements of that unit on the battlefield. In addition, cadets studied the technical and theoretical aspects of artillery, including the manufacture of powder and projectiles, the construction, testing, and inspection of weapons, and the characteristics of various artillery pieces and ammunition. Students also learned firing theory, aiming and firing grape shot, Congreve rockets, and grenades, night firing, the effects of rifling, the composition of siege trains, the construction of siege batteries, counter-battery techniques, and the employment of coastal artillery.[45]

The course in equitation included bridling and saddling, mounting and dismounting, moving at the several gaits, and jumping low obstacles. Also, cadets practiced using the cavalry saber while mounted, slashing and thrusting at straw-filled dummies at the gallop. In the more advanced phases of instruction students made road and cross-country marches and learned the rudiments of stable management.[46]

Cavalry tactics began with the school of the trooper. Next in progression came the school of the company and squadron, covering maneuvers from line into column and vice versa, moving to the flanks, passing through friendly lines, and charging in line and in column. The final segment was the school of the regiment in which students practiced similar maneuvers with that unit.[47] The formations and movements taught in cavalry tactics at West Point were derived from European concepts; in fact, Hawes, the first instructor, was a graduate of Saumur. Because of this orientation the mounted tactics learned at the academy had limited applicability to the dragoon-style warfare which characterized many American cavalry actions. But inasmuch as the cadets did obtain a thorough grounding in infantry tactics, they were probably better prepared to serve as dragoon officers than might appear to be the case. If Lieutenant Hawes and the officers who succeeded him as instructors of cavalry tactics neglected the Amer-

99

ican side of their subject, they at least made a serious effort to identify and train potential leaders for mounted units. At about the same time he created the course in cavalry tactics Hawes initiated two practices which continued for the remainder of the antebellum period. Before each class graduated the instructor of cavalry tactics furnished the academic board with a list of seniors who had demonstrated particular aptitude for cavalry service. Although not binding, these recommendations were considered by the board in deciding what branches a graduate was qualified to enter. In addition, Hawes and his successors designated certain cadets to act as corporals, sergeants, and officers during equitation classes and cavalry drills; these appointemnts were made on the bases of horsemanship and leadership capacity. Among those chosen were Cadets Kenner Garrard, George Bayard, Fitzhugh Lee, James E. B. Stuart, David Mc. Gregg, and William Averill,[48] men whose subsequent records as horse soldiers demonstrated that the instructors of cavalry tactics were highly competent in judging aptitude for mounted service.

Thorough though it was, professional military training at pre–Civil War West Point fell short in some respects. On several occasions boards of visitors and, more significantly, boards of officers found that cadets were drilling on obsolete artillery pieces. Also, commanders of mounted regiments complained that some of the lieutenants who joined their units fresh from the academy were deficient in horsemanship and tactics—a charge which prompted Hawes's innovation. Then too, until the mid-1850s cadets rode the same horses for cavalry and artillery training despite the fact that in the field the two services used animals of different size and conformation. Furthermore, students had to ride on out-dated, ill-fitting saddles. Nor can a related deficiency be overlooked. The first regiment of dragoons was activated in 1833, but it was not until sixteen years later that a course in cavalry tactics was introduced at West Point. Also, instruction in the use of cavalry against Indians was ignored.

Then too, military training was sometimes presented in a manner which alienated cadets. In 1832 Jacob W. Bailey grumbled, "Artillery and Infantry Tactics are disgusting. I would as soon commit to memory a table of logarithms as some of the lessons in these studies." Sherman also found infantry tactics dull, and John Tidball recalled that in his day infantry instructors had been dogmatic, refusing to permit the slightest deviation from the drill manual. In 1843 a board of officers noted that tactical instruction was limited to the mechanics of the subject, that cadets were not taught to consider terrain or enemy dispositions in planning maneuvers, and that students were not encouraged to reflect on tactical concepts.[49]

It may seem anomalous that professional training at the military academy was inferior in quality to other portions of the curriculum, but the explanation is simple. The men who controlled the institution viewed its mission as being the production of engineers who could also function as soldiers rather than the reverse.

The quantitative impact of the academic environment at the academy in the years between 1833 and the advent of the five-year program is best illustrated by comparing the number of students who graduated with the number who failed academically. Appendix III displays a detailed compilation of the academic deficiencies by class and by subject. In summary, 25 percent of the more than two thousand matriculates in that twenty-one year span failed one or more subjects and were recommended for discharge by the academic board. The great majority of these failures, 69.7 percent, occurred during the fourth class year, with the next largest increment, 18.6 percent in the third class year. Another 9.6 percent failed in the second class year, and an additional 1.9 percent in the first class year.

Mathematics was by far the leading producer of academic casualties. By itself that subject accounted for 43.1 percent of all failures; in conjunction with one or more others mathematics added another 35 percent to the deficiency list, or, to put it differently, 78.1 percent of all academic failures were attributable wholly or in part to mathematics.

The failures in mathematics were concentrated in the fourth and third classes, but the baleful influence of that subject did not end there. Among the junior courses natural and experimental philosophy, which relied heavily upon applied mathematics, caused the largest number of academic fatalities. Of the total number of second classmen declared deficient, 47 percent failed natural and experimental philosophy only, and another 17.6 percent failed that subject plus one or more others. Similarly, 70 percent of the first class deficiencies came from engineering, a subject with substantial mathematical requirements. Thus, about 85.6 percent of all academic deficiencies can be attributed to one of the following: mathematics alone, mathematics along with some other subject, or a course requiring mathematical ability. In contrast, not a single cadet failed tactics between 1833 and 1854. These figures show conclusively that a facility with mathematics was the sine qua non for graduating from West Point and gaining admission to the officer corps of the antebellum regular army.

The Military
Academy
in Its
Educational Context
★

Considering the ties between West Point and European military educational institutions, particularly those in France, one might logically expect the academy to have evolved into an Americanized version of L'École Polytechnique. Indeed, as appendix XII, "Contemporary Foreign Military Schools," illustrates, there were striking similarities between certain features of West Point and those of its European counterparts. The American, British, and French military academies emphasized mathematics, science, and engineering. Moreover, the schools in all three countries ranked cadets in order of merit for the purpose of assigning graduates to the various branches. Then too, British, French, and American students wore the uniform and lived in a military atmosphere. In addition, the systems of governance employed at the academies of all three nations, including the use of collegial boards to make policy and oversee academic affairs, were remarkably similar.

These resemblances notwithstanding, the differences between West Point and its European counterparts were even more significant. The British and the French separated infantry and cavalry cadets from those destined for the scientific corps and each group followed a different curriculum. Furthermore, in both countries the cadet was expected to have acquired most of his general education prior to entering; therefore, the program at the academy—be it Sandhurst, St. Cyr-L'École, or Woolwich—was more professional in orientation than was the case at West Point. Similarly, Great Britain and France demanded a higher degree of preparatory attainment for admission to the academies than did the United States, as the entrance requirements set forth in appendix XII attest. The higher standards, together with early specialization, enabled the British and French institutions to produce junior officers in half the time West Point required. This was the most critical difference of all.

East of the Rhine the concept of preparatory military education differed even more radically from that of the United States. In Prussia, the lesser German states, Austria, and Russia a multilevel system of cadet schools was used. The lower institutions, located in the provinces, were open to boys eleven or twelve years old. These schools provided a general secondary education and some military training within the framework of a four- or five-year curriculum. On graduation students who desired military commissions entered the upper-level cadet school located at or near the national capital. Here they remained two or three years, devoting all of their time to military subjects. Most cadets left the upper-level academy at the end of the second year and entered the army as aspirant-lieutenants. While serving on active duty they studied at regimental and division schools until passing the qualifying examinations for a commission. The top members of each second-year class, on the other hand, remained at the cadet school for a third year, becoming officers on graduation.

Dependent for support on a people who disdained the profession of arms, who begrudged military expenditures, and who prided themselves on a contempt for intellectual and social elitism, the United States Military Academy could not restrict its intake to a homogeneous group; nor could it afford the luxury of branch specialization. Moreover, the primitive state of secondary education in much of the country precluded the imposition of strict entrance requirements, for this would discriminate against some sections and thus alienate powerful politicians.

Historical inertia, always a major force in shaping military institutions, also helped make West Point distinctive. Even though some of the European military schools were founded at roughly the same time as the academy, the traditions which lay behind them were quite dissimilar. In the pre-Napoleonic era line officers in Europe had come from different backgrounds and pursued different training from those in the technical branches, and this concept of separateness carried over into the nineteenth century. In fact, the same tradition influenced the thinking of Alexander Hamilton and other early advocates of an American military educational system. But West Point did not follow that path. Instead, from the very first it sent officers into the infantry and artillery as well as the engineers. By the early 1830s the practice of commissioning graduates in all the arms and services had become so sanctified by tradition that not even the most radical reformers questioned it.

Because of its distinctiveness comparisons between the military academy and European military schools aid in fixing the place of West Point as an

103

educational institution, but only to a limited extent. The academy must also be examined as an American college, for despite its special purpose, West Point resembled its civilian compatriots as much as if not more than it did the British or continental military schools.

The first quarter of the nineteenth century was an era of ferment and attempted reform in American higher education. The traditional classical curriculum was brought into question, and the elective concept was explored. A few radical institutions even experimented with a scientific course of study, that is, one featuring the natural sciences and modern languages rather than the classics. Reformers also scrutinized such time-worn pedagogical devices as the daily, graded recitation and the related idea that the requisite amount of knowledge could, and in fact must be, gained from one authoritative book instead of wide reading in the field.

Eventually the reformers' efforts bore fruit, but this initial precursor of change aborted in the face of conservative opposition, and it was not until the last quarter of the century that the traditionalists were forced to give ground. There were, of course, exceptions—both Rensselaer and the University of Virginia adopted more liberal programs before the Civil War—but even in those institutions some of the classical teaching techniques, if not the curriculum, continued to hold sway.[1]

In 1828 the Yale faculty wrote a report aimed at stemming the tide of reform. This document ably articulated the views of the traditionalists, and thus represented the dominant voice of American higher education at the time. After denying charges of reaction the paper launched into a spirited defense of mental discipline, daily recitations, the fixed curriculum, and the role of the college in loco parentis:

> The two great points to be gained in intellectual culture are the *discipline* and the *furniture* of the mind; expanding its powers, and storing it with knowledge. The former of these is, perhaps, the more important of the two. A commanding object, therefore, in a collegiate course, should be, to call into daily and vigorous exercise the faculties of the students. . . . All this is not to be effected by a light and hasty course of study; by reading a few books, hearing a few lectures, and spending some months at a literary institution. The habits of thinking are to be formed by long continued and close application. . . .
>
> In laying the foundation of a thorough education it is necessary that *all* the important mental faculties be brought into exercise. It is not sufficient that one or two be cultivated while others are neglected. . . . As the bodily frame is brought to its highest perfection, not by one simple and uniform motion, but by a variety of exercises; so the mental faculties are expanded and invigorated, and adopted to each other, by familiarity with different departments of science.
>
> A most important feature in the colleges of this country is, that students are generally of an age which requires that a substitute be provided for *parental*

superintendence. When removed from under the roof of their parents and exposed to the untried scenes of temptation, it is necessary that some faithful and affectionate guardian take them by the hand and guide their steps. . . .

. . . But why, it is asked, should *all* students in a college be required to tread in the same steps? Why should not each one be allowed to select those branches of study which are best adapted to his peculiar talents, and which are most nearly connected with his intended profession? To this we answer that our prescribed course contains those subjects only which ought to be understood, as we think, by every one who aims at a thorough education.[2]

This "Conservative Manifesto" could as well have been datelined "West Point" as "New Haven." Some fifteen years later, in fact, the academic board, responding to the board of visitors' charges that mathematics and the sciences received undue emphasis in the curriculum, that infantry and cavalry officers needed less training in these subjects than engineers and artillerymen, and that military discipline was too severe, issued its own manifesto, one remarkably similar in tone to the Yale report of 1828. According to the West Point professors:

The Academic Board believe that one of the most important objects of the Academy is to subject each cadet . . . to a thorough course of mental as well as military discipline . . . to teach him to reason accurately, and readily to apply right principles to cases of daily occurrence in the life of a soldier. They are satisfied that a strict sense of mathematical and philosophical study . . . is by far the best calculated to bring about this end and that the present scientific course at the Academy—the result of the experience of many years, is, in its main features, such a course. They are aware that many of the cadets will have little occasion to make practical applications of the many mathematical formulae with which they meet, and that they may have passed over many particular problems without thoroughly understanding their meaning in all their points—still, if the course has been carefully taught, the reasoning powers will have been strongly exercised and disciplined, and a system and habit of thought acquired, which are invaluable in the pursuit of any profession, and as desirable for the infantry or dragoon officer as for any other officer in service. . . . The officer whose mind has been thus disciplined . . . will acquire facts and information in whatever station the interests of the service may place him. . . .

In looking at the restrictions [imposed] by the regulations the Academic Board would observe, that, the Institution holds the place of legal guardian with respect to the cadets, and in this position is under the highest moral obligation to surround them with every safeguard against immorality. Not the least of the purposes subserved by these restrictions to which the cadets are now subjected is their withdrawal from the temptation to irregularity which all experience shows, cannot be placed within reach of the young and inexperienced when thrown together in considerable numbers, beyond the control and influence of the parental roof, without inevitable ill consequences.[3]

The views of both the Yale and military academy faculties represented the norm. Professors at Harvard, Columbia, and Princeton, as well as a host of lesser colleges, viewed themselves as character-builders and disciplinarians of the mind first, and purveyors of knowledge second.[4] They were not anti-intellectual in the sense that applied to the mass of their compatriots. It was simply that, judged by standards of later times, they held extremely rigid views on the purpose and scope of higher education.

This intellectual climate was not the only characteristic common to West Point and its civilian contemporaries. Rates of student attrition were high in many colleges. At the University of Virginia, for instance, of the total number of students who enrolled between 1825 and 1850, about one-third remained longer than the first year; less than a fourth stayed two years, and only 10 percent completed three or more years. At Virginia, unlike most colleges at the time, a student could take electives and could choose the department with which he wanted to study, but apparently this freedom did not reduce academic casualty rates. In the same time span only one-sixteenth of those who began the course under the Department of Mathematics graduated, one out of six in natural philosophy, one out of eight in chemistry, one-eleventh of those in ancient languages, and one out of four in moral philosophy.[5] At Pennsylvania (Gettysburg) College, which did not permit student options, 38.2 percent of the matriculates between 1834 and 1854 graduated. At the College of Charleston the attrition rate was 44.8 percent between 1837 and 1854. At Rensselaer, where science and engineering were emphasized, approximately 45 percent of the matriculates who entered between 1824 and 1860 graduated. Amherst seems to have enjoyed the highest rate of success with about 73 percent of those who entered between 1833 and 1854 completing the course. On the other hand, Union Institute, the antecedent of Duke University, held the dubious distinction of graduating the lowest number of students, only 18.3 percent of those who entered between 1839 and 1854.[6]

The private and state military colleges, together with the naval academy at Annapolis, operated under conditions closely approximating those at West Point; thus, their attrition rates are particularly relevant. Of the cadets who entered Norwich, a military college in Vermont, between 1836 and 1854, 57.9 percent graduated. At V.M.I. 64.9 percent of the matriculates between 1842 and 1854 successfully completed the course. The Citadel, a military college in South Carolina, graduated 49 percent of the students who entered between 1842 and 1854. In contrast, the United States Naval Academy, which opened in 1845, granted diplomas to 77.4 percent of those who entered between that date and 1854. The graduation rate at West Point for the years between 1833 and 1854 was 48.1 percent,[7] a figure lower than the other military schools but on a par with or higher than the civilian colleges mentioned above. Being gross estimates which do not allow for important variables such as the different reasons students failed to graduate or variations in entrance requirements, not to mention academic standards, it would be foolish to rely on these statistics for a detailed comparative analysis; however, they do show that the attrition rate at the military academy, the allegations of its critics to the contrary, was not abnormally high in comparison to those of contemporary institutions.

Nor was West Point alone in its concern for student behavior. Practically every college in the country published a set of disciplinary regulations, and most employed a system of graduated punishments as well.[8] About the only distinctive features of the academy in this regard were that the tactical officers probably displayed more zeal and efficiency in enforcing the rules than their civilian counterparts, the tutors and proctors, and that punishments at West Point—extra guard tours, reduction in rank, and the like— were military in nature.

As for the sins these disciplinary systems were designed to curb, they too were pretty well standardized, and aside from purely military offenses, none were peculiar to West Point. Cadets were somewhat more circumspect than their civilian brethren at Virginia and Harvard when it came to overt defiance of authority, but in other respects there was little difference. Drinking, fighting, staying out after hours, and card playing were universally condemned by the authorities and enjoyed by the students whether in cadet grey or civilian attire.[9]

The positive concomitant of the collegiate disciplinary system was a dedication to spiritual uplift, reflected in the requirement for chapel attendance. Most institutions, sectarian or not, demanded that their students attend daily prayer services in addition to church on Sunday, and some went so far as to require faculty attendance as well. At Columbia, for example, both the professors and the students had to go to chapel until 1865.[10] Measured against such rigorous standards, the military academy was downright libertarian. This may explain, at least in part, why the corps remained almost impervious to the waves of religious enthusiasm and temperance crusades which swept other campuses in the antebellum era.[11]

With respect to the daily routine, the West Point schedule was not atypical except for its military aspects. As a general rule, the weekday on a college campus began soon after sunrise with mandatory prayers in the chapel. Immediately after breakfast, which followed the morning devotionals, students reported to their first class. For the rest of the day they attended recitations or studied in their rooms, the only break being a one- or two-hour lunch period. Classes continued until late in the afternoon; then came supper, followed by mandatory study in the dormitory until "lights out" at nine or ten o'clock. Proctors or tutors usually patrolled the dormitories during study hours and made periodic inspections of rooms after lights out.

There were other similarities. The food served in college dining halls was notoriously poor, or at least the students thought so; dormitory furnishings were austere, and rooms were crowded and uncomfortable. Furthermore, the college campus was not only intellectually but geographically isolated. Usually, founders chose rural sites for their institutions in order to insulate student bodies from urban temptations.[12] Columbia and the University of Pennsylvania were exceptions to this general rule, but West Point manifestly was not.

Had Cadets Heth, Burnside, Tidball, Stuart, Bayard, and the others transferred to Pennsylvania College, Rutgers, the College of Charleston, or to some other liberal arts institution they probably would have experienced little difficulty in making the transition. The struggles would have been with Greek and Latin rather than engineering, and the teachers would have been clerics, not soldiers, but otherwise cadets would have found much to make them feel at home. Stuart and Bayard, for instance, could have participated in civilian versions of the "Dialectic Society" and perhaps have made Fourth of July orations. Sherman, Heth, and Burnside could have exercised their culinary skills after lights out and endeared themselves to their civilian classmates if not to the college authorities. Also, those who desired could have taken dancing lessons, fenced, skated, and played "skinny," for all these diversions were as common on other campuses as they were at West Point. Moreover, had they enrolled at William and Mary, the University of Virginia, or V.M.I. they would have found codes of honor which, though unofficial, were as exacting as the one at the military academy.[13]

The marked similarity between some aspects of West Point and those of her civilian sisters did not extend to institutional government. On the surface the controlling elements of the military academy hierarchy may have resembled closely those which governed the typical civilian college, but in actuality the centers of power were quite different.

Customarily, a president or chancellor presided over the antebellum college. Above him stood an external supervisory body, in some cases the state legislature, in others a board of overseers, a board of trustees, a corporation, or a board of visitors. These supervisory bodies exercised surveillance over college presidents in all institutional matters, ranging from the budget to student discipline, and they exerted tremendous influence because of their political and financial power over the institution. The president, in turn, could bend the faculty to his will. He could, for example, secure the discharge of a recalcitrant professor without much difficulty, there being no such thing as tenure. This power alone was sufficient to give him tremendous leverage vis-à-vis the faculty. While it is true that the corps of professors usually managed to exert influence through a faculty senate or similar body, this was always subject to the dictates of the president and the extramural supervisory group.[14]

At West Point, on the other hand, the structure of real power was different. The superintendent could not control the academic board, nor could he discharge the professors since their appointments were approved by the president and endorsed by Congress. More importantly, the superintendent, unlike his civilian counterparts, was a temporary rather than a permanent institutional official, whereas the professors, his ostensible subordinates, enjoyed de facto tenure. Also, except on rare occasions, the boards of visitors at West Point acted as mere sounding boards and "rubber stamps" with little say in academic affairs. The real sources of external power in the governance of the military academy were the chief of engineers and the secretary of war, not the board of visitors.

Another difference between the academy and the civilian colleges was the makeup of the faculty. Professors at the latter were for the most part ministers of the gospel without formal postgraduate training in their particular academic disciplines. In fact, so little emphasis was placed on academic specialization that in some cases professors were transferred from one department to another in an unrelated field. Below the professors in the pedagogical hierarchy stood the instructors, variously called tutors or proctors. These young men, just out of college themselves, shared the instructional loads with the professors, but generally were not considered permanent members of the academic community and usually moved on to some other line of work after a year or two of teaching. It was during the antebellum era that these men began the evolutionary process that eventually transformed them into professional teachers, but this metamorphosis was not completed until the last quarter of the century.[15]

When it came to professional preparation, the instructional staff at the military academy certainly did not suffer by comparison with its civilian peers. Both Mahan and Bartlett, for example, had studied and traveled in Europe to prepare for teaching their academic specialties, and the other professors at West Point were at least as well-qualified with respect to undergraduate education and scholarly achievements as their civilian colleagues. Moreover, aside from the cadets who served as teachers from time to time, the majority of the instructors at the military academy, those selected from the active army after several years of service, were undoubtedly as competent as the tutors in civilian colleges; certainly, they were better disciplinarians. Likewise, the officers who taught tactics came to that task armed with practical experience and sometimes training at a school of application as well. Indeed, two, Hardee and Hawes, were graduates of the French cavalry school at Saumur.

In its teaching methods the military academy closely followed the contemporary pattern. The daily graded recitation was a near-universal practice at the antebellum American college. As Samuel Eliot Morison put it in his history of Harvard, "The faculty were not there to teach, but to see that boys got their lessons; to explain difficulties or elucidate a text would have seemed improper."[16] Even when professors lectured, they usually held recitations afterwards. In scientific courses students seldom worked with the apparatus or performed experiments themselves. The general practice was, as at West Point, for the professor to give an illustrative demonstration. Only Rensselaer departed from tradition to the extent of permitting students to work in the laboratory.[17]

Not only did classroom procedures and daily grading at West Point fit the general pattern, the practice of holding public oral examinations at the end of the academic year was also common in American higher education; however, the civilian colleges gradually abandoned the custom of announcing class standings because of student protests.[18]

One annual spring rite on the civilian college campus was not found at West Point. This was the commencement exercises featuring speeches by distinguished visitors and students and culminating with the presentation of diplomas to the graduates in public ceremonies.[19] It was not until the eve of the Civil War that this custom took hold at the military academy. Up to that time the only official acknowledgments of the end of the course for the graduates were a sermon in their honor and the publication of an order relieving them from duty. As often as not diplomas were not presented at graduation but were mailed later. Sometimes, the senior cadets celebrated the approaching end of their servitude by the unauthorized practice of kicking their hats into the air at the end of the last parade, but this was the only festive part of the commencement proceedings.[20]

The size of the library collection at West Point was not out of line with its civilian contemporaries. The holdings at the academy grew from about eight thousand to more than fifteen thousand volumes between 1830 and 1852. In approximately the same period the University of Viriginia collection expanded from eight thousand to twenty-five thousand. Yale's holdings went from ten thousand volumes in 1835 to twenty-one thousand in 1850. Harvard listed forty-one thousand titles in 1841; Brown, ten thousand in 1843; Rutgers, five thousand in 1845; and Union College, about five thousand in the early 1840s. Williams, on the other hand, had only five thousand volumes as late as 1860, and the collection at the University of Georgia in the same year numbered thirteen thousand, while as late as 1874 the University of Wisconsin library boasted only four thousand titles.[21]

No doubt the scientific, engineering, and military cant of the academy collection was distinctive, but the concept behind it—that the primary purpose of the library was to support the faculty—was not. Such was the typical view at the time. Books for leisure reading and for broadening the student's cultural outlook usually made up only a small fraction of the institutional holdings, so students, both at West Point and elsewhere, had to rely on the libraries of the debating societies or their own resources more than the college collection for recreational literature.[22] Nor were restrictions on library use peculiar to the military academy. Most college libraries remained open only a few hours a day or a few days a week for students, and the number of books a student could withdraw at one time was limited to two or three.[23] These regulations reflected the prevalent pedagogical concept that a student learned by assiduously studying a text, not by browsing in the library.

The many similarities between West Point and her civilian sisters cannot obscure certain fundamental philosophical differences. The typical antebellum college considered its mission to be the general education of "gentlemen." This entailed administering heavy doses of Greek and Latin, some mathematics, literature, and natural science, and a capstone course in ethics or moral philosophy taught by the president of the college to the senior class. As a general rule, utilitarian courses, except in law and medicine, were scorned, particularly in the first half of the century.[24] The military academy, on the other hand, existed solely for the purpose of producing professional soldiers, or more accurately, engineers capable of functioning as soldiers, and despite the fact that the academic aspects were emphasized over the military at West Point, the curriculum was basically utilitarian, not classical. This point was vividly exemplified by the fact that engineering rather than moral philosophy was considered by cadets and faculty alike to be the most important course at the military academy.

By virtue of its stress on science and engineering West Point, without intending to do so, placed itself in the vanguard of educational reform in the antebellum era. For in spite of the efforts of the classicists, the inexorable trend toward practicality in higher education continued. In fact, by the early 1830s the academy no longer stood unique in the field of engineering. Norwich established a professorship in that field in 1826; Rensselear awarded its first degrees in civil engineering in 1835, and by mid-century at least fifteen other schools offered courses in the subject, most patterned at least in part after the West Point curriculum.[25] As a matter of fact, the military academy not only provided the model for these courses, West

Pointers established and taught programs in engineering at Yale, Columbia, V.M.I., the naval academy, Lehigh, and the University of Michigan.[26]

Neither its dominance in the utilitarian sphere, nor the fact that its doors were open to boys of all classes spared the military academy from attacks by the Jacksonians in the thirties and forties. The critics alleged that West Point was a bastion of privilege, monopolizing commissions in the regular army, and providing a free education for the unworthy; consequently, the institution should either be abolished or greatly reduced in size.[27] Taken in isolation these attacks would give the impression that the academy was being singled out as a target for the Democrats' abuse, but such was not the case. In actuality the Jacksonians were blasting the entire concept of higher education open to some but not all, and the diatribes against West Point were typical rather than singular—although this was probably cold comfort to those associated with the academy at the time. Not only did civilian colleges come in for their share of criticism, some, lacking Tottens, Poinsetts, and Mahans to defend them, suffered far more severely from these attacks than the military academy. In his history of the American college Frederick Rudolph points out: "The height of the Jacksonian movement was probably a historical low point in legislative generosity to the colleges. The Jacksonians were not hostile to vigorous state governments, but they did object to using the people's money for institutions of privilege."

Rudolph goes on to show that when Lafayette College was chartered in 1826 the Pennsylvania senate took pains to insure that the institution would receive no state funds. New York colleges were also deprived of state aid, and the Missouri legislature petitioned Congress in 1834 for permission to divert funds from the colleges to the common schools. About the same time the Georgia legislature discontinued support of the state university, and in 1845 a Virginia newspaper asked, "Cannot the annual appropriation . . . to the University be more profitably expended for the great cause of education than in instructing . . . one hundred and fifty youths, all of whom have the means of finishing their course through their own resources?"[28]

In the same spirit Davy Crockett, a bitter foe of West Point, complained in a speech before Congress: "This college system went into practice to draw a line of demarcation between the two classes of society—it separated the children of the rich from the children of the poor."[29]

In an effort to adjust to these criticisms the civilian colleges had to inaugurate curricula for part-time students, lower academic and disciplinary standards, and institute manual labor projects so that needy boys could earn their keep.[30] By comparison the military academy escaped relatively unscathed. This was no small accomplishment considering that West Point not only had to face the anti-intellectual attacks along with her civilian sisters, but simultaneously had to cope with traditional American anti-military bias as well.

Thus, in the years between 1833 and 1854 the distinctiveness of West Point was in some respects more apparent than real. The stress on mathematics, science, and engineering was rare early in the period, but before the century was half over other educational institutions had duplicated this feature. Not even the system of military training was peculiar to the academy; it was copied in modified form at Norwich, V.M.I., the Citadel, and Annapolis, all founded before 1850. More importantly, perhaps, the academic atmosphere characteristic of the antebellum academy was closer to that of its civilian counterparts than might be supposed. As Christopher Jenks and David Reisman said in *The Academic Revolution,*

> When West Point opened in 1802 it was the first college in America to emphasize technical subjects, and for a quarter of a century it had no competitors. Annapolis too had a technical bias, albeit of a somewhat different sort. And both institutions, while sharing the interest of their liberal arts rivals in character development, had a distinctive vision of the kind of character they wanted to develop. (Or so one assumes. When we read accounts of nineteenth century college life, however, the clerical emphasis on discipline and manners sometimes seems little different from what we would expect of a West Point Superintendent.)[31]

It is obvious, then, that the so-called Thayer System was in some respects a misnomer. The system was not Thayer's at all in any creative sense, but an adaptation of practices and procedures common to many colleges at the time. Certainly, Thayer and his pre–Civil War disciples deserve credit for successfully implementing this pragmatic approach. It is ironic, however, that with the passage of time what had originally been a practical solution to an immediate educational problem eventually assumed the status of holy writ and stifled the continued growth of the institution it had been designed to improve.

In the aftermath of the Civil War intellectual stagnation and atrophy took over at West Point. Up to then the institution, though faced with an ever-increasing number of competitors, still held primacy in engineering and maintained a place at, or near, the top in mathematics and natural philosophy. Furthermore, a spirit of innovation, one surprisingly bold by the standards of that day, continued to thrive until 1861. This spirit gave birth to the five-year course, a creative attempt to cope with the problem of enriching the quality of education for a student body of widely diverse intellectual caliber and preparatory background.

The Era
of the
Five-Year
Course,
1854−1861

★

More serious than the superficial charges of aristocracy leveled by pothouse politicians in the Jacksonian Era were those made by boards of visitors and boards of officers during the same period. These more knowledgeable critics pointed to several major deficiencies in the curriculum, namely, a weakness in military training and an overemphasis on mathematics, science, and engineering at the expense of the humanities. As early as 1830 reports of boards of visitors commented on these shortcomings,[1] and periodically thereafter, not only these reports but those of army officers as well, noted that the military academy was doing less than it should in English, history, geography, modern languages, and military science. To overcome these defects the critics proposed several alternative solutions. One was to require proficiency in English, geography, and history as prerequisites for admission. Another, borrowed from the British and French, was to establish two separate curricula—one to be composed of more literary subjects and practical military training but less mathematics, science, and engineering for students destined to serve in the infantry, dragoons, and cavalry, while at the same time retaining the traditional program for those deemed worthy of the "scientific corps." A third possibility was to retain the current course but add a year so that the slighted subjects could be covered more adequately.[2]

The chief of engineers and the academic board admitted the validity of these criticisms. They feared, however, that raising the entrance requirements would be unacceptable politically, and they adamantly rejected a two-track curriculum on the grounds that it would destroy the academy. Thus, a five-year program was the only feasible alternative; therefore, in 1846 the academic board recommended adoption of such a course. Joseph

Totten, the chief of engineers, strongly favored the move, but since at that moment the Mexican War was drastically increasing the need for officers, he decided not to press for the reform until a more propitious time. It was also expedient to wait until a class large enough to be split into two groups matriculated so that one could pursue the four-year program while the other followed the new curriculum, thereby avoiding a one-year hiatus in graduating classes.[3] In 1852 Totten thought the ideal moment had arrived, and he urged adoption of the five-year course in his annual report. Secretary of War Conrad curtly vetoed the proposal, arguing that "The object of the institution is not to make finished scholars or accomplished gentlemen, but good officers."[4]

Finally, in 1854 the three prerequisites—a period of stability, a large incoming class, and a sympathetic secretary of war—coincided, and in the summer of that year, Totten, supported by Secretary Davis, ordered Robert E. Lee, the superintendent at West Point, to inaugurate the five-year course.[5] In justifying his decision to lengthen the term rather than increase the entrance requirements, Davis alluded to the anti-democratic aspects of the latter alternative which, as he saw it, "would in some degree deprive the institution of its present popular character by excluding those who from want of early advantages could not pass the preliminary examination. The grade of cadet . . . should be, as it now is, within the reach of youths in every condition of life, and this, together with the fact that by the mode of appointment all sections and all parties are fairly represented, gives to the institution the character which should belong to it as a part of the military establishment of the United States."[6]

In the summer of 1854, 103 boys entered the academy, the largest number to matriculate since 1846,[7] and separating them into classes of roughly equal size did not present a problem. The academic board assigned the forty-seven new students who were eighteen or older to the fourth class and the remainder to the fifth. The former group, along with the three upper classes, was to continue under the four-year program while the fifth class and those to be admitted in subsequent years would pursue the reformed curriculum.[8]

To insure that the intent of the five-year course— that is, enriching the humanities and increasing the effectiveness of military training—was carried out, the implementing directive specified that none of the additional time would be allocated to natural and experimental philosophy, mathematics, French, drawing, chemistry, mineralogy and geology, or to civil engineering. Instead, the increase would be devoted to adding new courses in Spanish, history, geography, and military law and to augmenting the existing programs in English and professional military subjects.[9] (See appendix IV for the five-year course.)

Under the reformed curriculum, as originally implemented, the fifth class studied English grammar and composition, elocution, geography, history, and mathematics, and took practical instruction in fencing, artillery, and infantry. The fourth class continued the study of these subjects and started French.

Third classmen completed French, took one-year courses in Spanish and natural and experimental philosophy, continued their practical work in artillery and infantry, and started the course in drawing. This class also studied the manufacture of ammunition and began equitation. Second classmen completed drawing and took up the study of chemistry, civil engineering, moral and intellectual science (ethics), and logic. In the military area the second class took practical work in infantry and cavalry tactics, and the manufacture of siege ammunition. The first class had both practical and theoretical instruction in infantry, artillery, and cavalry tactics, military engineering, and pyrotechny. In addition, the seniors studied the science of war, international, constitutional, and military law, mineralogy and geology, history, elocution, and composition.[10] Subsequently, as shown in appendix IV, some of these subjects were shifted from one year to another, but the curriculum remained essentially unchanged.

The course in Spanish, inaugurated in September 1856, was originally taught under the auspices of the Department of French, but in February 1857 a separate Department of Spanish was created. Patrice de Janon, a Colombian who had formerly taught fencing at the academy, became the first professor in the new department; he held office until 1882.[11] The purpose of the course was to enable cadets to deal more effectively with the Spanish-speaking natives of the territory acquired from Mexico; therefore, de Janon concentrated more on the spoken idiom and less on grammar and literature than did the instruction in French. A poor disciplinarian in the classroom, the professor could easily be diverted from the subject at hand by questions on dueling etiquette; furthermore, his command of English was so poor, he frequently confused students more than helped them. As a consequence, cadets complained that they received very little from the course.[12]

The Department of Ethics, still directed by the chaplain, presented several new subjects under the enlarged curriculum and also expanded its coverage of English and law. The total increase in one-hour lessons allotted to the department over those in the four-year program was 241.[13]

The fifth class studied English grammar, geography, and universal history (western civilization). Fourth classmen took rhetoric and literature. Both of these courses consisted mostly of the student's reading aloud passages from a text while an instructor corrected his pronunciation. According to the professor of ethics, he did this so the courses in rhetoric and literature would require minimal outside study, thus interfering as little as possible with preparation for more difficult subjects. He also felt that the purpose of these cultural studies was "not to tax the attention but to cultivate the taste," an end better accomplished by classroom drills than study.

Third classmen did not study with the Department of Ethics, but the second class spent a year under its auspices. The curriculum consisted of logic, a continuation of "universal history," theoretical ethics, and the history of philosophy.

The fall term of the first class year in the Department of Ethics consisted of American history, international and constitutional law, military history, and military law, a topic embracing court-martial procedures and the Articles of War.[14]

The five-year course did not provide for an increase in the time allotted to civil engineering, but military engineering and the science of war, the other subjects taught by Professor Mahan's department, were expanded. The revised course in military engineering consisted of ten lessons in field fortifications, twenty-eight in permanent fortifications, eight lessons on the attack and defense of fortified positions, three on sieges, five on frontier defense, twenty-four periods of fortification drawing, and an eighteen-lesson review. The science of war was increased to approximately seventeen lessons followed by an eight-lesson period for review. The total increase of lessons in military engineering and the science of war came to 120.[15]

In September 1859 portions of the science of war—strategy, grand tactics, and army organization—were transferred to the Department of Tactics under the aegis of the commandant of cadets. At the same time these subjects were relocated from the first to the second class year. Thereafter, the seniors recited in civil and military engineering daily for the entire academic year.[16]

Ever the innovator, Mahan used some of the additional time made available to him by the five-year course to institute a series of illustrated lectures in military engineering and the science of war. In order to carry out this project the professor obtained several large maps on which to depict military campaigns, together with drawings of American harbor fortifications and public works.[17] Mahan's rationale for this departure from the daily recitation, a hallmark of the Thayer System, betrays an awareness that the recitation had its limitations. "This plan is one which I have long thought a *desideratum* at the Academy where so much is taught by textbook and blackboard recitations, by which men lose to a degree that habit of attention to oral instruction which is no small accomplishment in the practical pursuits of life, and I would long since have carried it into practice in my own department, could I have found any available opening for it in the crowded course of studies."[18]

Practical military engineering also underwent an expansion with the implementation of the reformed curriculum. In 1854 the course was reorganized to include classroom recitations as well as practical work. Thenceforth, instruction during the academic year consisted of sixteen recitations on the passage of rivers, six on military surveying, and four devoted to a review of the course. Also, a series of drills was conducted each spring. Five of these were spent on military surveying, six on tracing and profiling, and nine on modelling engineering works in sand. In addition, twenty-two drills were held in the summer encampment; these covered the use of siege materiel, mines, saps, and pontoon bridging.[19]

Some of the most radical changes of all took place in the teaching of professional military subjects, both with respect to departmental organization and subject matter. The first of the organizational changes occurred in August 1856 when the commandant of cadets assumed responsibility for instruction in tactics.[20] No longer were the instructors of artillery, cavalry, and infantry independent; now they were subordinates of the commandant. A second structural change took place in June 1857 with the establishment of a Department of Ordnance and Gunnery not under the jurisdiction of the commandant. This new department took over the technical phases of the studies formerly taught by the Department of Artillery, leaving that department responsible only for tactics.[21] Then, the science of war was transferred to the Department of Tactics in 1859. This change, initiated by Secretary of War Floyd in an effort to place all tactical and strategic instruction under the commandant of cadets, remained in effect until the four-year curriculum was resumed at the outbreak of the Civil War. At that time the science of war was returned to Mahan's department.[22]

Important changes were also made in the scope and content of the professional subjects. The number of recitations in artillery tactics increased from thirty-two to forty-five while those pertaining to infantry tactics were expanded from fifteen to thirty-four, and although the number of recitations in cavalry tactics did not increase, a course in veterinary science was added. Likewise, with the advent of the five-year course the number of drills increased: infantry from 540 to 695, artillery from 204 to 252, and fencing from 108 to 216. Moreover, training in rifle marksmanship was expanded, and courses in the use of the bayonet and swimming were instituted.[23]

Instruction in professional military subjects began, as it always had, as soon as the candidates reported to West Point. In their first summer at the academy the fifth classmen learned the rudiments of infantry drill and guard duty. They also took daily instruction in rifle marksmanship for two weeks, then learned how to use the bayonet. Throughout the academic year they attended classes in fencing and also participated in the fall and spring infantry and artillery drills.

118

Fourth classmen continued with artillery and infantry drills in summer camp. In addition, they, along with the second and first classes, fired on the rifle range, shooting five rounds at a six- by three-foot target from the offhand (standing) position at a distance of 150 yards.[24] During the academic year members of the fourth class received lessons in the use of the small sword and the saber. Also, like the other classes, they participated in artillery and infantry drills.[25]

The third class spent the summer on leave. During the academic year third classmen took equitation in addition to attending the spring and fall artillery and infantry drills. Selected members of this class also served as corporals in the cadet battalion. This was their first opportunity to hold rank; all fifth and fourth classmen were privates.[26]

Prior to 1859 equitation was the only military subject pursued by the second class. After the rearrangements of subjects which took place in that year, however, this class carried the heaviest load of all with respect to military studies. Thenceforth, the second class course included cavalry tactics, veterinary science, outpost duty, infantry tactics, strategy, logistics and military administration, heavy and light artillery, and grand tactics. In addition, second classmen rode on alternate days throughout the year, and, of course, attended drills with the rest of the corps. Also, this group furnished all the sergeants for the battalion of cadets.[27]

Before the curricular realignment of 1859 first classmen took the subjects outlined above for the second class, along with practical and theoretical military engineering and the science of war. The seniors also had classes in ordnance and gunnery. The ordnance portion of the course dealt with the manufacture and proof of gunpowder, projectiles, cannon, small arms ammunition, and pyrotechnics. Gunnery, on the other hand, included the study of trajectories, aiming theory, the effects of different types of artillery fire, breaching fortifications, and the organization of field and siege batteries. Also, in the summer encampment the seniors manufactured gunpowder, rockets, and flares in the ordnance laboratory.

After 1859 the first class curriculum in military studies included military engineering, ordnance and gunnery, equitation, and practical military engineering as well as artillery and infantry drills. This class also provided the lieutenants and captains for the battalion.[28]

Possibly the most significant innovation in tactical training occurred when Major William J. Hardee introduced his new system of infantry tactics to the corps of cadets. Hardee, although a cavalryman, had earlier revised the manual on infantry tactics at the direction of Secretary of War Jefferson Davis. Drawing heavily on contemporary French writings, Hardee devised new methods of employment which he tested on the corps of cadets in the summer of 1854. Two years later, after his manual had been published, he became the commandant and instituted the revised system with its emphasis on celerity of movement and looser, more flexible formations.[29]

The increased stress on professional subjects which typified the five-year course provoked second thoughts in some quarters. In 1856 the board of visitors complained that the prominence given to military training was seriously interfering with scientific instruction, and in 1858 Joseph Totten warned that if the authorities continued to yield to demands for additional professional courses West Point would "cease to be a good school of theory without becoming a good school of practice." The views of several officials who appeared before a congressional investigating committee in 1860 expressed similar apprehensions. Professor Bartlett, for instance, claimed that "the tendency of the present system is to break down a scientific academy, and erect upon its ruins a school of practice." Major Alfred Mordecai, a distinguished ordnance officer who had recently served on a committee to evaluate the five-year course, agreed. Mordecai told the congressional commission that he had detected a tendency to overemphasize practical military instruction and cautioned that the academy should not be permitted to degenerate into a school of practice.[30]

Such fears had little basis in fact. The academic board maintained the predominance of mathematics, science, and engineering under the five-year curriculum just as it had earlier. Certainly, the board did not relax its standards. In fact, the failure rate in the era of the five-year course was higher than it had been before, as can be seen from appendix V. Of all the cadets who entered between 1854 and 1860 and who were exposed to the reformed curriculum in part or in its entirety, 31.4 percent failed one or more subjects and were recommended for discharge. Moreover, of the two classes which followed the complete five-year program, 50.8 percent failed. Just as in the pre-1854 era, a majority of the deficiencies continued to occur in the freshman year, and mathematics remained the greatest producer of casualties. Alone, that subject accounted for 35.9 percent of the total losses; in conjunction with one or more others it was responsible for another 35.5 percent. Thus, 71.4 percent of all academic failures were attributable wholly or in part to mathematics. Military subjects, in contrast, accounted for only 1.2 percent of the total number of deficiencies.

The scale for determining order of merit also reflected the continued dominance of mathematics, science, and engineering. Of the total of twenty-five points which determined graduation standing under the five-year curriculum, ten were allotted to those three subjects with the remaining fifteen evenly split between the humanities, drawing, and conduct, on one hand, and military subjects on the other.[31] Despite the increased emphasis on professional military subjects, mathematics, science, and engineering still counted for 40 percent of the total score in computing order of merit, as opposed to the 30 percent contributed by each of the other two categories.[32]

Procedural and substantive changes in the academic structure were not the only novel features of the five-year era; the disciplinary system also underwent modification. In 1855 new rules governing proficiency in conduct were laid down. They specified that any upperclassman who accumulated 100 demerits in a six-month period, and any fifth classman who amassed 150 in the same length of time, was deficient and therefore eligible for discharge. The old limit was 200 a year irrespective of class. The new provision had the aim of halting the practice of relaxing in the second half of the year after having compiled a good conduct record in the first, while at the same time making allowance for the special needs of new boys as they adjusted to the system.[33]

Secretary of War Floyd initiated a more controversial change in the spring of 1860. Convinced that the disciplinary staff tended to punish cadets arbitrarily, Floyd ordered demerits to be given only when students had violated specific articles of the published regulations. He also designated the academic board a court of appeals for cadets who believed they had been given demerits unjustly.[34] This innovation had an immediate adverse effect on discipline, as the board of visitors noted the same June. In January 1861 the academic board reiterated the visitors' complaint, pointing out that the appeal provision had misled cadets into thinking they would automatically have demerits removed whenever they petitioned the academic board.[35] The remonstrances were futile, however; Floyd's directive remained in force until the Civil War.

There were also more positive changes in the disciplinary system. Previously, cadets had received only one summer furlough during their four-year stay at the academy; this followed completion of their second year. Because of the lengthened course the superintendent proposed in 1855 that students whose conduct had been satisfactory be awarded a one-month leave at the end of their third or fourth years in addition to the three-month furlough following their second year. Totten, the chief of engineers, concurred, but Secretary of War Davis, although agreeing in principle, refused to grant a blanket indulgence. He directed instead that individual requests for leaves be forwarded to him for approval. In 1860 Floyd amended this policy so as to give each first classman a one-month summer furlough. To insure that sufficient seniors would always be on hand to help operate the summer camp, the class was divided into two groups, one taking leave in June, the other in July.[36]

Another liberalization took place in 1855 with the granting of short passes to cadets who had shown exemplary conduct for stated periods. In

December of that year John G. Barnard, the superintendent who had also initiated the one-month leave policy, began the practice of giving three-day passes over the Christmas holidays to all students who had gone for six months without accruing more than thirty demerits.[37] In 1858, Richard Delafield, who succeeded Barnard, modified the policy to permit short absences in reward for going three months with no demerits. Any cadet who met this requirement could leave West Point after the end of classes on Saturday morning during the academic year and go where he wanted so long as he returned by 10:45 P.M. that night. In the summer encampment the privilege was extended to permit absence from reveille Saturday morning until 10:45 P.M. the same evening. Surprisingly, considering the stiffness of the requirement, fifteen or twenty cadets qualified for these passes every month. Even George Custer, whose conduct was notorious, managed to win a pass once during his cadetship.[38]

Two other reforms were instituted with an eye toward making life at the academy more pleasant. Both legalized longstanding practices in the corps of cadets. In 1856 Barnard authorized students to play chess in camp, and the following year Delafield permitted smoking in the immediate vicinity of the barracks. Almost immediately, however, the upperclassmen took advantage of the latter reform to devise a new form of hazing, "smoking out"; this consisted of confining a plebe in a closed tent or room and blowing smoke in his face until he fainted or became ill.[39]

Two other features of cadet life during the period eventually became permanent elements of the West Point environment: formal graduation ceremonies and class photographs. The first commencement exercises had been held in 1853, but the following year the superintendent reverted to the old custom of acknowledging the occasion merely by publishing an order which discharged the first class from the corps of cadets. The board of visitors felt that a more impressive ceremony would be appropriate, so in 1857 graduation was celebrated with music, speeches, and the presentation of diplomas.[40] From this point on, except for a temporary interruption in the Civil War years, commencement was celebrated annually. The associated custom of photographing the graduating class also began during the 1854–60 period although the precise date cannot be determined. It is certain that by 1855 the seniors had begun to appoint committees for the purpose of arranging class pictures, but the earliest surviving album of group photographs was made in 1857.[41]

Commencement exercises and class photographs, as well as other features of the 1854–60 era, eventually became traditional, but the five-year curriculum did not enjoy that longevity. Abruptly, in the fall of 1858, before the reform program had completed a cycle, Secretary of War Floyd ordered a return to the four-year course. Floyd's decision to regress was influenced, in part, by the cadets. Bitter at having to spend an extra year at the academy, they followed the advice of the professors and made their unhappiness known to parents and congressmen, thereby generating pressures the secretary felt unable to resist.

The academic board also influenced Floyd's decision. By 1858 the professors had become disenchanted with the experiment and wanted to return to the old curriculum. In their petition for a change they asserted that the five-year course was so exhausting intellectually that it would turn most students against self-study after graduation. The teachers also maintained that the attempt to graft cultural subjects onto the scientific program had failed. For instance, the history being taught consisted of little more than chronology, and the geography was not above the common school level; nor, according to the professors, could the quality of these subjects be raised without lengthening the course even further. More importantly, in the eyes of the hierarchy, the new studies had diverted the time and attention of students from the scientific subjects. As far as a majority of the academic board was concerned, West Point should abandon the field with respect to the humanities, reduce military training to its pre-1854 status, and return to its old preserves: mathematics, science, and engineering.

The lone dissenter was the professor of ethics whose department taught most of the subjects his colleagues wished to diminish or eliminate. He insisted that the experiment had not been continued long enough to give it a fair trial; moreover, the professor discounted the students' protests, declaring that if left to their own devices, cadets would always choose the shortest course of study. These complaints were ignored, however, and the five-year course was dropped on 11 October 1858. The younger group which had entered in 1854 and the class which had matriculated in 1855 were both scheduled to graduate in June 1859.[42]

In April 1859 Floyd, with equal suddenness, reversed himself and ordered resumption of the five-year curriculum. The secretary attempted to justify his change of heart by falling back on the argument of the professor of ethics that the experimental program had not been adequately tested, though he did not explain why the same argument had failed to impress him when the professor had first presented it. A more likely, although unprovable, explanation of Floyd's vacillation is that his decision to return to the five-year course came about as the result of pressure from Jefferson Davis, then chairman of the Senate Military Affairs Committee.[43] There may also have been something to the cadets' claims that the secretary had reinstituted the longer curriculum in order to reduce the number of graduates in 1859, thereby allowing him to appoint more officers from civilian life. Both motives would have been in keeping with Floyd's tendency to bend to the strongest political forces acting on him at any given moment.

123

Whatever the reason, the five-year course was restored, much to the disgust of the corps of cadets and most of the faculty at West Point.[44]

An interesting by-product of this period of experimentation at the military academy was the concept of a permanent, external board of evaluation, empowered to examine the institution periodically and decide on all proposed changes in the curriculum. Sylvanus Thayer had proposed such a device in 1858 when he endorsed the recommendation of the academic board that the four-year program be restored. At that time Thayer was acting as chief of engineers in the temporary absence of Totten. When the board's plea for a return to the status quo ante came to him for comment, the "Father of the Military Academy," conveniently forgetting that he had once advocated a five-year course himself,[45] strongly concurred in the proposal to return to the four-year curriculum, claiming that he had been of that opinion ever since 1817. Thayer then proposed the establishment of a permanent board, to be composed of the superintendent and two other graduates not connected with the academy, which would oversee institutional matters.[46] The secretary of war accepted Thayer's suggestion and appointed a commission consisting of Superintendent Delafield, Major Alfred Mordecai of the ordnance corps, and Captain George W. Cullum of the corps of engineers to examine the curriculum and determine the optimum length and content of the course. The board convened in the early spring of 1860, but before it could complete its business, Secretary Floyd, without explanation, ordered the body to adjourn. Thayer suspected that Floyd, fearing the board was about to recommend a four-year program, had prorogued it to avoid further embarrassment. This was probably the case. The subsequent testimony of the members of the board before the Davis Commission indicates that they would have made such a recommendation.[47]

Floyd's action did not kill the concept of an external regulatory body, nor, for that matter, did it settle the question of the length of the curriculum. Beginning in the winter of 1859 and continuing into the spring of 1860, both houses of Congress debated the issues of who should determine the academic program and what its length should be. A crucial question was whether the secretary of war could arbitrarily change the term of cadetship. One group in the Senate was convinced that Congress had the final say, and to prove its point proposed legislation fixing the term of studies at four years. Jefferson Davis fought to destroy this measure, and though he failed to win unqualified support for the five-year course, Davis did succeed in achieving a compromise: the appointment of an investigatory commission headed by himself to examine the military academy.[48]

The Davis Commission also included Senator Solomon Foote, Representatives Henry W. Davis and John Cochrane, Major Robert Anderson (an artilleryman soon to win fame at Fort Sumter), and Captain Andrew A. Humphreys of the Topographical Engineers, an officer who was also destined for distinction in the Civil War. The group convened at West Point in the summer of 1860 and remained in session there until late November of the same year.[49]

Through personal interviews and questionnaires the Davis committee queried some sixty persons, including the superintendent, the academic staff, cadets, junior officers, the commanding general of the army, other senior military personnel, and several civilians who were familiar with the military academy. Although the questions asked by the commission focused directly on the curriculum, disciplinary system, and organizational structure of the academy, the respondents were free to comment on other matters related to the institution if they so desired.[50]

After analyzing the evidence it had gathered, the Davis committee prepared an exhaustive report which was presented to Congress on 13 December 1860. Foremost among the commission's recommendations was retention of the five-year course. In addition, it advocated establishing a permanent commission, similar in concept to Thayer's, to supervise the operation of the academy and decide on all proposals for change. Unlike Thayer's proposed body, however, that envisioned by the Davis group would have consisted of a senator, a representative, the chief of engineers, an officer of the line, another from one of the scientific corps, and two eminent civilians, one an expert on mathematics and the other an authority on science. In addition, the Davis Commission suggested opening the superintendency to officers of all arms but at the same time retaining general responsibility for the operation of the academy under the chief of engineers. As for the professors, they could retire voluntarily after twenty-five years of service but could be removed at any time by the president on recommendation of the supervisory commission. Finally, the academic board would have retained its functions regarding determination of proficiency and arranging classes according to order of merit, but it would have been required to submit all projected curricular changes to the supervisory commission for approval.

These recommendations were incorporated in a draft bill and submitted to the Senate Committee on Military Affairs in January 1861,[51] but before that body completed its deliberations the shelling of Fort Sumter forced Congress to divert its attention to more important matters. Of the reforms advocated by the Davis Commission only one, opening the superintendency to officers of all arms, was ever implemented, and at the time this was done Jefferson Davis was no longer a senator but a prisoner at Fortress Monroe.

West Point
and the
Civil War

★

On 19 December 1860 Cadet John T. Wofford, having relinquished his appointment, asked permission to leave West Point immediately rather than await the secretary of war's formal approval of his resignation. In justifying this request Wofford wrote "There can be no doubt that my native state, South Carolina, will take her destiny in her own hands for weal or woe . . . And I (being an only son) think it a most sacred duty to protect my mother in time of danger."[1]

Ten days later Charles P. Ball of Alabama, the senior orderly (first) sergeant in the second class, availing himself of a privilege traditionally extended to departing students, called the battalion to "Attention!" in the mess hall after supper and in the ensuing silence sang out, "Good-bye, boys. God bless you all!"[2] The Civil War had come to West Point.

In the months that followed seventy-four Southern cadets either resigned their appointments or suffered dismissal for refusing to take the oath of allegiance to the United States.[3] Neither those who left nor the other Southerners who remained at West Point had a Freeman to record for them, as he did for Lee, the agonies of their dilemma; only their letters and those of their friends can speak for them. Cadet Henry Du Pont of Delaware, for instance, recounted the plight of his comrade John Pelham who wanted desperately to stay at the academy but felt that "it would be his duty to give up his own inclinations and interests if called upon to defend his native state." Edward Anderson of Virginia found himself in the same predicament. Writing his mother in April 1861, Anderson reported, "I have refused to take the oath . . . I actually cried . . . I know well that I resign everything." And the father of Cadet John Marchbank voiced similar regret in his letter to the chief of engineers. "Until lately I had intented [*sic*] him to remain until he graduated and then to enter the service of his country for life. My state, in the present distracted and troubled condition of the country, will not act with your government; therefore, I do not think it right for your department to be at the expense of educating the sons of Tennessee, and for this reason my son has permission to resign his appointment . . . I write this in sorrow."[4]

Most Southern cadets tried to postpone the fateful decision as long as possible, but once their states seceded, they could delay no longer. When that day came, each had to decide whether to stand by the United States or go home. Cadet Thomas Rowland, who had hoped Virginia would remain in the Union, came to realize by mid-April 1861 that he too must make the bitter choice. "We cannot hesitate; we must either make up our minds to fight under the Stars and Stripes . . . or we must resign at once and free ourselves from that solemn oath to serve the United States honestly and faithfully."[5]

Officers also left West Point in the spring of 1861 because of the secession crisis. One was no less a personage than the head of the institution. P. G. T. Beauregard had been appointed to the superintendency in the closing days of John B. Floyd's term as secretary of war. Beauregard had taken command at the military academy on 23 January 1861; however, Joseph Holt, the new secretary of war, suspecting that the superintendent might follow Louisiana into secession, decided to put the academy in safer hands, and ordered Richard Delafield, Beauregard's predecessor, to resume the superintendency he had just given up. The Louisianian protested his summary relief, claiming that he had intended to resign only if secession led to war and adding, as proof of his loyalty, that he had advised several Southern cadets to remain at West Point. His complaint was unavailing, however, and the "Great Creole" was ordered to proceed to New Orleans where he had been reassigned. Ironic coincidence marked this whole affair. Joseph Totten, the chief of engineers, had nominated Beauregard for the superintendency in an attempt to thwart Jefferson Davis's aim of opening that office to all branches of the army. By naming an engineer officer with a reputation for brilliance and well-placed political connections to boot, Totten hoped to make it embarrassing, if not impossible, for Davis to object to Beauregard's designation as superintendent.[6] But as it turned out, the course of events overran both Totten's and Davis's plans.

Another Southern officer who left West Point the same spring was Fitzhugh Lee. At the time the rollicking Virginian was serving as a tactical officer, an assignment which included teaching military science and overseeing discipline in one of the cadet companies. Lee enjoyed great popularity among the officers and ladies of the garrison and with the cadets, too,

Cadet Richard K. Meade, Jr., class of 1857. Meade, a Virginian, served as an engineer officer in the Union garrison at Fort Sumter during the bombardment. Afterwards he became an engineer in the Army of Northern Virginia. Meade is one of the few officers to have participated in combat actions on both sides during the Civil War.

despite the nature of his duties. Indeed, Fitz Lee was one of the few members of the disciplinary staff ever to win the affection of the cadets, a fact probably attributable to his relaxed attitude toward regulations. Because of this universal regard Lee's departure was particularly poignant. The night before he left his brother officers serenaded him; the next morning, with tears in his eyes, he shook hands with every cadet in his company. Then, as Lee rode past the barracks on his way to the riverboat wharf, the students in a spontaneous gesture of esteem formed lines on both sides of the road and doffed their caps as he passed.[7]

But agonizing decisions and tearful farewells should not be permitted to obscure the longstanding tensions and occasional outbursts of violence which sectionalism had fomented at the antebellum military academy.

128

Years before the John Brown incident particularism had surfaced from time to time, and after that momentous event regional disputes and fights became common.

Sectional feeling at West Point could no doubt be traced back to the origin of the institution. In any case, the sentiment certainly existed a quarter-century before the Civil War. In 1833 Cadet Walter Sherwood of New Jersey noted that among his classmates "Each is exceedingly prejudiced in favor of his own section of the country, and several squabbles have been the result of conversation on this subject. The southerners complain bitterly of the hardships while the northerners bare [*sic*] with composure." Three years later Isaac Stevens, a staunch abolitionist from Massachusetts, complained of the contempt with which Southern cadets treated Yankees and their customs. John Tidball observed that although intersectional friendships were common in the corps of the middle and late 1840s, so were regional cliques. And O. O. Howard, a Maine abolitionist, found, on entering West Point in 1850, that the slavery issue was creating several feuding factions, yet sectional differences did not prevent Howard from striking up a friendship with James E. B. Stuart. As for Stuart, he also noticed a tendency for "birds of a feather to roost together," but still felt that cadets from different sections of the country got along better than their civilian contemporaries.[8]

In retrospect, the mid-1850s appear to have formed a vaguely defined but discernible watershed in the evolution of sectionalism at West Point. Up until then regional sentiment generally lay quiescent, bursting forth only rarely into open hostility. Beginning with the fifties, though, sectional feelings grew steadily more intense and overt until they finally erupted into violence on the eve of the Civil War. In that respect the corps of cadets faithfully mirrored the larger society from which it came.

Something of this evolution in attitudes can be sensed when comparing the memoirs of John Tidball, a member of the class of 1848, with those of fellow Ohioan Morris Schaff, who entered West Point exactly ten years later. In his work Tidball commented casually on the presence of sectionalism in the corps, attributing it mainly to different dietary and speech habits, together with the obsessive interest Southern cadets took in politics. Schaff, in contrast, dwelt at far greater length on regional prejudice, finding sectional sensitivities much sharper in the corps than Tidball had. Although he revealed a sincere devotion to his Southern comrades, Schaff still felt compelled to record their arrogance and pugnacity, traits which sparked many fights and a few near-riots. This was not an isolated impression; the writings of Tully McCrea, James H. Wilson, and Eugene Carter, all Schaff's contemporaries, express similar views.[9]

The growing virulence of sectional discord was also reflected in a proposal by Cadet Charles Morgan in 1857 to abolish the moribund Dialectic Society and replace it with two new debating clubs. Morgan believed sectionalism had become so strong that a policy requiring equal representation of Northerners and Southerners in each group was necessary. Otherwise, the two clubs would rapidly degenerate into mere regional gangs.[10] All this was in sharp contrast to the old Dialectic Society which had been free of such problems.

Perhaps the most interesting portent of increasing polarization was the tendency of the companies in the battalion of cadets to become "Northern" or "Southern" in makeup and outlook. This trend, which would have mystified earlier generations of students, had become noticeable by the late 1850s. According to official policy, company assignments were determined solely by height; the taller cadets went to "A" or "D" Companies and the shorter ones to "B" or "C." Clearly, this regulation could not be ignored since the authorities would immediately detect any discrepancies, but somehow, probably with the connivance of the cadet adjutant who handled company assignments, the boys themselves added regional criteria. The lines of demarcation were by no means rigid; Custer, for instance, served happily in a "Southern" company for four years, but the distinctions were real nonetheless. As a matter of fact, the issue of company assignment perplexed an ambitious young Virginian in the summer of 1860. On the one hand, he wanted to join C Company so he could live with fellow Southerners; on the other, his aspirations for rank led him to desire assignment to B Company whose tactical officer selected the corporals for the battalion. Another Virginian of the same era was less ambitious. He was delighted in being assigned to a company "where the treatment of a southern gentleman lessens the annoyance of the West Point Plebe."[11]

Sectionalism persisted at the military academy despite the efforts of the authorities to suppress it. In the early 1840s, for example, the superintendent had forbidden the Dialectic Society to debate the constitutionality of nullification. At about the same time, the professor of ethics, with the concurrence of the academic board, the superintendent, and the chief of engineers, excised chapters touching on the morality of slavery from a text cadets were going to use in his course. Then, in 1858, the superintendent refused students permission to attend a church in nearby Buttermilk Falls because the minister there was preaching abolition. This desire to avoid exacerbating sectional feelings even carried over into the postwar period. In June 1865 the chief of engineers instructed the superintendent to ensure that Confederate war trophies were displayed in a way which would not offend future Southern cadets.[12]

In the opinion of contemporary observers the authorities at West Point were at least partially successful in their efforts to inhibit sectionalism and encourage loyalty to the nation. Several times in the 1830s and 1840s boards of visitors acknowledged that West Point fostered love of country and reduced regional prejudice.[13] Paradoxically, Jefferson Davis saw his alma mater in exactly the same light. During his tenure as secretary of war, Davis, in disapproving a proposal to establish an additional military academy in the South, took occasion to praise the nationalistic spirit of West Pointers. Five years later, while debating a military pay bill in the Senate, he affirmed that alumni of the academy "justify the hope that in bearing the flag of their country, they bear it as citizens whose heart is limited by no section . . . but generalized as broad as the continent."[14]

Apparently, the cadets themselves also felt the unifying influence. Thomas Seymour, a Vermonter of the class of 1846, declared that cadets seldom argued over sectional issues and that the faculty made every effort to stimulate devotion to country. Soon after joining the corps J. E. B. Stuart wrote that, sectional coteries notwithstanding, "there seems to be a sentiment of mutual forbearance . . . as a general thing we know no North, no South." And according to another latter-day cavalryman, James H. Wilson of the class of 1860, the authorities taught that "anyone who had taken the oath of allegiance as an officer had no 'reserved rights,' that as long as two states held together under the Constitution . . . it was the duty of all regular officers to uphold the flag and stand by the government of the United States."[15]

Some observers believed that the nationalism in which West Point took such pride was actually tinged with a pro-Southern coloration. Stuart, for instance, in his "no North, no South" letter also stated that even though the military academy was situated in "the heart of free soil Yankeedom," there was "a strong southern feeling prevalent." With considerably less joy, two Republican senators, Benjamin F. Wade of Ohio and James H. Lane of Kansas, made the identical claim ten years later in their attacks on West Point. Wade bitterly castigated the academy for being "the hotbed in which the rebellion was hatched," while Lane lamented that if the Union should perish in the war, a fitting epitaph would be "Died of West Point pro-slaveryism."[16] Although these charges were rebutted at the time, the notion of a peculiar affinity between the antebellum South and the military academy still survives.[17]

Whatever one wishes to make of the concept of a "Militant South" and the disproportionate number of Southern officers in some branches of the regular army on the eve of the Civil War, the statistical evidence refutes any contention that the South dominated antebellum West Point. Appendix VI plainly demonstrates that there was no imbalance in favor of Southern officers on the staff and faculty in the decade preceding the war. In no department were more than 40.5 percent of the personnel Southern-born, and in only three, including the administrative staff, did the number of Southerners ever exceed one-third of the total. Moreover, of the 155 officers who served at West Point between 1833 and 1861, only twenty-three (14.8 percent) eventually joined the Confederacy, and none of the professors did even though one was a Virginian. Obviously, it is impossible to make a case for undue Southern influence with respect to the staff and faculty.

Nor can it be said that an unusual number of Southerners graduated in the years between 1833 and 1861 (see appendix VII). It is true that in comparison with the total white male population between fifteen and twenty years of age, 4.7 percent more cadets were admitted from the future Confederate states than their proportion of the total population warranted, but this was because more Southern students failed academically or were dismissed for misconduct, necessitating additional appointments to fill the vacancies which resulted from their departures. With respect to graduates, the data reveal that a grand total of seven (0.5 percent) more Southerners graduated than the population of that region merited.

In the panic and confusion of 1861, however, critics of the military academy were in no mood for statistical niceties. In their eyes an inexcusably large number of graduates had deserted the Union, and the performance in the field of those who had remained loyal was not inspiring. Manifestly, something must be fundamentally wrong with the institution. It was in just such a temper that Secretary of War Simon Cameron opened the attacks against West Point. In his annual report for 1861 the secretary first singled out the militia and volunteers for praise, then trained his guns on the military academy. As he saw it, neither sectional ties nor political philosophy could justify the defection of Southern graduates, for in accepting a free education from the government they had become bound "by more than ordinary obligations of honor to remain faithful to their flag." Cameron went on to blame the defections on the disciplinary system at West Point which failed to distinguish between immorality and simple violations of regulations. According to the secretary, this defect had encouraged cadets to substitute "habit for conscience."[18]

Certain Republicans in Congress took up Cameron's cudgel and beat the academy with it at every opportunity. Two of the leaders in these attacks, Wade and Lane, have already been mentioned; Zachariah Chandler of Michigan and Lyman Trumbull of Illinois were also vehement and constant critics. William P. Fessenden of Maine, Charles Sumner of Massachusetts, and John Sherman of Ohio found fault with the academy too, but they refused to join the other senators in advocating its abolition. In fact, they sided with the defenders on that matter. T. Harry Williams has explained that although the major thrust of the case against the military academy was the defection of the Southerners, there were also other reasons for the animosity of the so-called "Radical Republicans." One of these was the conviction that the early Union defeats and McClellan's lack of aggressiveness stemmed from lukewarm patriotism as much as incompetence. Similarly, the Radicals feared that their goal of making emancipation a war aim would be frustrated as long as conservatives like McClellan, Halleck, and Don Carlos Buell held commands. There were other irritants as well, some harking back to the Jacksonian era, such as the alleged West Point monopoly of high military positions, the aristocratic tone of the regular army, and the discrimination which regulars, particularly West Pointers, practiced against militiamen and volunteers.[19]

Arrayed in defense of the academy stood Professor Mahan, Captain Edward Boynton, who published his *History of West Point* in response to the attacks, former superintendent John G. Barnard, and Senator James W. Grimes of Iowa, together with the *Army and Navy Journal* and the *New York Times*. In addition, Senators Fessenden, Sumner, and Sherman eventually joined this group. The defense built its case around several arguments. One was that if some graduates were guilty of snobbery and discrimination, it was in spite of the teachings of the military academy, not because of them. Another was the assertion, backed by statistical evidence, that the corps was, and always had been, democratic in composition; this, of course, was merely an update of the response to the old Jacksonian charge. A third element of the defense was the contention that the percentage of defectors from West Point was considerably lower than that of Southerners in the civil branches of the federal government and that of students and alumni from such Northern educational institutions as Harvard, Yale, Princeton, and Williams. Finally, in an attempt to soften the charges of ineptitude, the defenders maintained that the academy could only provide the educational foundation for generalship—it could not create genius.[20]

The champions of West Point won a significant battle in 1863 when they defeated a Radical effort in Congress to abolish the military academy. By then the improving fortunes of Union forces under Grant, Sherman, George H. Thomas and other graduates, coupled with the less than glittering performance of non-West Pointers such as Benjamin F. Butler, John C. Frémont, Daniel E. Sickles, and Franz Sigel, had robbed the attacks of much of their sting. But even the final victory in 1865 did not completely silence the voices of hostility and suspicion; charges that the academy catered to Southern sensitivities emerged again soon after the war.[21]

The rhetorical honors in these heated debates were probably about even, but statistically the vindicators of the academy had the better case, at least on the sectional issue. Nine hundred and seventy-seven graduates of the classes between 1833 and 1861 were alive at the outbreak of the Civil War.

Of this total, 259 (26.5 percent), including thirty-two graduates from Northern states, joined the Confederacy. Serving in the Union forces were 638 (65.1 percent), including thirty-nine alumni from Confederate states. Eighty (8.4 percent) did not participate on either side. Of the 266 Southern-born alumni who fought, thirty-nine (14.7 percent) served on the Union side, an impressive figure considering the heart-wrenching costs involved. On the other hand, only thirty-two (5.1 percent) of the Northerners fought for the South. [22] Clearly, most graduates on both sides followed their home states, but it is worth noting that among the two groups motivated by something other than geographic loyalty, the percentage of Southerners who chose the Union was three times higher than the percentage of Northerners who went over to the Confederacy. It is equally indicative that while 26.5 percent of these West Point classes defected, 28.8 percent of the regular army officers, not graduates of the academy, who were on active duty when the war began, resigned to join the Confederacy. [23] Thus, the defection rate of non-West Point regulars exceeded that of the classes of 1833 through June 1861 by 2.3 percent and of the staff and faculty for the prewar decade by 10 percent. It would be foolish to argue on the basis of these fragmentary statistics alone that the military academy was necessarily the most important determinant in tipping the scales toward the Union, but by the same token, no claim that in the antebellum era some malign, pro-Southern influence was operating at West Point to seduce cadets away from their loyalty to the United States can be sustained. On the contrary, the views expressed by contemporary observers, the geographic origins of the faculty and student body, and the decisions of graduates at the time of crisis all suggest that the institution was more nationalistic than pro-Southern in its orientation. The extent to which this attitude affected each graduate's choice is, in the final analysis, unanswerable. Sectional loyalties, family ties, political views, friendships, and conscience also played a part. But regardless of the balance in a particular case, it does seem indisputable that West Point strengthened rather than weakened loyalty to the United States.

Dramatic and worrisome though it was, the defection of Southern cadets and alumni was but one of several troubles which plagued West Point during the war years. At the outbreak of hostilities the institution immediately reverted to a four-year curriculum. Soon afterward, the authorities, in an effort to expedite the flow of West Pointers into the depleted Union officer corps, decided to graduate the two senior classes ahead of schedule; consequently, the first class graduated on 6 May 1861 and the second class, a month later, [24] much to the delight of cadets in both groups, most of whom had volunteered for active service as soon as the war began. [25] In addition, the chief of engineers alerted the third class for possible graduation in the summer of 1861 but subsequently decided to retain it at the academy for another year. Thus, in the space of a few months the military academy had lost its Southern cadets, revised the curriculum, graduated two classes, and faced the likelihood of graduating a third. The departure of staff and faculty officers for the field and the transfer of enlisted men from the cavalry, artillery, and engineer detachments to duties elsewhere increased the existing turmoil.[26]

The curriculum to which the military academy returned was essentially the same as that which had been imposed in 1858 when the four-year program had been briefly reinstituted. The fourth class (freshman) course consisted of mathematics, English, United States geography, French, fencing, and bayonet training. The third class completed the study of mathematics and French and began drawing and riding. Second classmen (juniors) took natural and experimental philosophy, chemistry, drawing, infantry and artillery tactics, and continued the course in riding. The first class program consisted of military and civil engineering, the science of war, ethics, law, mineralogy and geology, cavalry tactics, Spanish, equitation, and practical military engineering.[27]

In the summer of 1861 a congressional committee proposed that German be added to the curriculum to better equip graduates to command the large number of Union soldiers who spoke that language, but the academic board vetoed the suggestion on the timeworn grounds that there was no way of introducing a new subject without deleting something more important.[28] The board took a more positive approach to the chief of engineers' request that cadets receive signalling instruction and set aside a period in the summer encampment for that purpose. Third classmen learned visual signals while second classmen studied telegraphy.[29]

Once the transition from the five- to the four-year program was made, the curriculum remained fairly stable throughout the war, but other features of the West Point environment changed drastically. Reacting to the defection of the Southern cadets, Congress twice prescribed more stringent loyalty oaths. A law passed in August 1861 decreed that on receiving his warrant each student must swear, not only to defend the national government and the Constitution, as had hitherto been the case, but in addition, "to maintain and defend the sovereignty of the United States paramount to any and all allegiances, sovereignty, or fealty . . . to any state." Supplementary legislation in July 1863 broadened this requirement to include a demand that each incoming candidate swear he had never borne arms against the United States, given aid to her enemies, held office "under any authority or pretended authority in hostility to the United States," or upheld "any pretended government, authority, power, or constitution within the United States, hostile thereto."[30]

135

Wartime unrest and hysteria created still more problems for the authorities at West Point. When the New York draft riots broke out in 1863, the superintendent had to dispatch a detachment of several officers and fifty-nine men to the city, leaving the cannon and powder magazines at the academy unprotected, this at a time when rumors were rampant that the mob intended to march up the Hudson and seize the materiel. Ultimately, these fears proved baseless, but in the interim the staff at West Point spent some anxious moments. The next summer a tone-deaf super-patriot reported the bandmaster for playing a "disloyal piece of music" at a concert during the encampment. On investigation the allegation turned out to be false, but the incident had been irritating enough to provoke the superintendent into making a rare display of sarcasm in his official report. Noting that the self-appointed loyalty monitor was from New York, the superintendent suggested that he direct his reform efforts to that city, where they were so badly needed, and leave West Point alone. An even more bizarre episode occurred in November 1864. While the chaplain was reading President Lincoln's Thanksgiving Proclamation to the congregation in the cadet chapel, Mrs. D. R. Jones, the widow of a Confederate officer, "committed acts which, if done by a Union woman in Richmond, would have consigned her to Libby Prison." Unfortunately, the record does not reveal the details of the lady's offense, but it was sufficiently grave to necessitate removing her from the post where she had been living with relatives. In this instance the superintendent avoided the risk of public scandal by having Mrs. Jones's brother-in-law discreetly eject her rather than take official action.[31]

The turmoil of war also affected the corps of cadets. Tempted by the lure of volunteer commissions, some students resigned before graduation in spite of the superintendent's efforts to dissuade them. More importantly, the climate of excitement and uncertainty made it more difficult for cadets to concentrate on their studies. This, combined with a chronic shortage of competent instructors, resulted in an increase in the rate of academic failures beyond anything experienced in the antebellum era.[32] Of the 265 cadets admitted between 1861 and 1865, 129 were declared deficient in one or more subjects and recommended by the academic board for discharge (see appendix IX). This failure rate of 48.7 percent exceeded the previous high of 31.4 percent associated with the five-year program. Mathematics continued to be the major source of academic casualties. In the war years this subject alone accounted for 56.6 percent of all failures. In conjunction with one or more others it took an additional toll of 20.9 percent. Thus, 77.5 percent of all deficiencies between 1861 and 1865 stemmed wholly or in part from mathematics.

The high rate of wartime academic failures generated pressures which later would force the imposition of more exacting entrance requirements.

Beginning in 1863 and lasting for the rest of the war, the press, the academic board, congressmen, and boards of visitors campaigned to raise admissions standards. As a result, English, geography, and American history were added to the prerequisites in 1866. Moreover, competitive examinations, which had been used during the war, continued to be employed, but only on a limited basis.[33]

Closely associated with the problem of high deficiency rates was the secretary of war's practice of reinstating cadets who had been discharged. The change of administrations in 1861 did not lessen that hoary abuse. Simon Cameron and Edwin M. Stanton bowed as readily to political pressures in those matters as their Democratic predecessors had. In fact, Stanton went further than any of the antebellum secretaries when he abruptly transferred both the superintendent and the commandant of cadets for court-martialing a student with powerful connections.[34] Congress made a half-hearted effort to abate the evil of arbitrary reappointment in 1861, but the enabling act proved no more effective than earlier attempts. Furthermore, the legislators repealed this law in 1865 when they belatedly realized it had given the academic board more power in matters of reappointment than the politicians had intended.[35]

Another critical difficulty directly related to the Civil War was the problem of obtaining and retaining qualified instructors. In some cases shortages necessitated a return to the unsatisfactory expedient of employing cadets as teachers; in others, courses had to be dropped or curtailed. The War Department assigned paroled and disabled officers to the academy in an effort to alleviate this deficiency. But some of these men fell short of the intellectual requisites, and others were physically unable to carry out their duties properly. Furthermore, the turnover rate was high, with some instructors staying at the academy only one or two years rather than for the longer periods which had been typical before the war. Also, military personnel on duty at West Point sometimes had to leave the post for extended periods in order to assist in mustering and training volunteer units, thereby further disrupting the academic routine. It was not until the summer of 1865 that a sufficient number of officers became available to restore a measure of stability, and even then there was a serious shortage of engineers.[36]

Yet in this same period of wartime chaos reforms which left a permanent impress on West Point were made. George W. Cullum, soon after assuming the superintendency in 1864, decided to reward cadets whose conduct and academic records were exemplary by allowing them to wear tangible proof of their accomplishments. For each of the three upper classes the first five men in the annual deportment standings had stripes of gold lace running diagonally across their sleeves. Seniors wore three of these stripes, second classmen, two, and third classmen, one. At the same time the superintendent sought a way to recognize academic excellence in a more meaningful fashion than the traditional listing in the *Army Register*. Initially, he planned to have the first five men in general order of merit for each upper class wear small metallic stars on their collars, but subsequently Cullum changed his mind and instead substituted medals engraved with the bust of Washington.

These innovations did not noticeably improve the behavior or the scholarship of the corps at the time, and the secretary of war, thinking the reforms too radical, cancelled them almost immediately. The concept of distinctive insignia did not die, however, and in 1899 stripes identical to those Cullum had envisioned were added to the cadet uniform, except that in the later version all cadets of the three upper classes wore them. Then, in 1913 students who had earned distinction in annual order of merit were authorized to wear metallic stars on their collars.[37] Academic stars and service stripes have been part of the cadet uniform ever since.

Two more present-day customs had their origins in the Civil War era at West Point. The class of 1865 began the tradition of presenting a silver goblet to the first son sired by a member after graduation. Likewise, the same class was the first to sing "Army Blue," a tune which had since become de rigeur at cadet social functions.[38]

The military academy also made more substantive contributions to American military science in the wartime years. Soon after hostilities began Professor Mahan made the acquaintance of two members of Lincoln's cabinet, Secretary of the Treasury Salmon P. Chase and Secretary of War Edwin Stanton. The professor used these relationships to advocate important organizational reforms. In 1861 he recommended to both secretaries that the Army of the Potomac adopt the corps structure. Mahan urged, in addition, that the office of chief of staff be established to coordinate the staff bureaus, serve as a communications link between the secretary of war and commanders in the field, and act "as director of our military operations." In fact, the professor had a specific officer in mind for the position— Henry W. Halleck. The ideas of a corps organization and a chief of staff did not originate with Mahan, as he himself admitted; nor was he the only one to press them in 1861.[39] But the professor at least deserves credit for planting these concepts in the minds of the two powerful secretaries.

Mahan was not the only member of the staff and faculty to lend his expertise to the cause. Throughout the war ordnance and artillery officers at West Point carried on the testing program which had begun in the antebellum period. Among the weapons, devices, and explosives subjected to experimentation between 1861 and 1865 were the ten-inch Parrott rifled cannon, the Armstrong and Maxim revolving guns, several calibers of artillery projectiles, the Hawley smooth bore gun with improved shell, and the Beardsley torpedo. In addition, the local authorities tried out pontoon bridging equipment, and conducted tests to determine the effects of rifled cannon against field and permanent fortifications.[40] Each of these experiments had important ramifications for military technology, but the last-named was particularly consequential. Verifying, as it did, what combat experience had already indicated, namely, that the old-style permanent fortifications were no longer effective, this particular test sounded the death knell for long-cherished concepts of strategy and military engineering.

Advising on army organization and assisting in the development of military technology were but ancillary contributions of the academy to the Civil War. Elihu Root once wrote, "The real object of having an army is to provide for war."[41] This being so, it inevitably follows that the most important justification for having a military academy is to provide officers for a nation's wartime armies. Therefore, the transcendent standard for evaluating the quality and extent of West Point's contributions to the Civil War must be the performance of her graduates on the battlefield.

Putting aside such esoteric questions as the influence of strategic principles on campaign planning or the relative merits of regulars and volunteers, and focusing on the more mundane but equally significant issue of leadership at the various levels from company to corps, a simple truth emerges. West Pointers from the classes of 1833 to 1864, taken as a group, acquitted themselves nobly in combat, just as they had earlier in Mexico and against the Indians. In the Civil War 95 graduates of these classes were killed in action and 141 more were wounded. The class of 1854 led the list in total casualties, Union and Confederate, with almost half its members killed or wounded.[42] Of the nineteen alumni from the same classes who won the Medal of Honor, five came from May 1864, making it the most highly decorated class of all.[43] But figures tell only a fraction of the story. Not one graduate on either side ever displayed cowardice in the face of the enemy. Moreover, as the horrendous casualty rates of the Civil War so eloquently attest, these officers not only fought bravely themselves, they inspired their men to do the same. In a similar vein, it was primarily the West Pointers who took huge numbers of raw, unmilitary, young Americans and molded them into the truly formidable soldiers they became. By the same token, it was almost exclusively academy graduates who performed the logistical feats which to this day demand admiration.

Admittedly, alumni on both sides sometimes committed egregious blunders, mistakes which squandered human lives. It is equally true that the vast majority of Civil War West Pointers, while excellent lower-level commanders and staff officers, lacked the intellectual depth and character to earn the appellation, "Great Captain." Yet the fact remains: they established records for courage, dedication, and leadership which still endure.

139

The images their very names evoke—Stuart, Buford, Alonzo H. Cushing, Joseph Wheeler, Pelham, Bayard, Tidball, Sedgwick, McPherson, O'Rorke, Thomas, Winfield Scott Hancock, Gibbon, and A. P. Hill, to name but a few—affirm that fact. If none of them achieved the status of a Lee, a Jackson, a Grant, or a Sherman, they nevertheless validated their alma mater in Root's sense. Or, as Professor Mahan put it, "If the country never has any less competent commanders than McClellan, Buell, and Fitz-John Porter, we need have no fear."[44]

The End
of an Era

★

The restoration of peace in 1865 did
not restore tranquility to West Point. In the immediate postwar era the
academy underwent several unsettling changes to emerge as an institution
which may have seemed a carbon copy of its antebellum predecessor but
which in actuality differed significantly in several respects. Describing what
he considered the most important of the post–Civil War reforms, the removal of the superintendency from the corps of engineers in 1866, William
A. Ganoe wrote, "This change heralded the transition of West Point from a
purely scientific school to one of general education."[1] As a graduate of the
academy, Ganoe should have known better. Not even in his cadet days,
forty years later, could West Point accurately claim to have become a
school of "general education." Clearly, the historian had mistaken an organizational modification for a philosophical reorientation. Ganoe was
not alone in his misconception; others too assumed that changing the superintendency would broaden the perspective of the institution.

The concept of opening the superintendency to officers of all branches
was not new in 1866. As a matter of fact, the idea anticipated the deed by
almost fifty years. In 1820, for instance, Sylvanus Thayer, then superintendent, had proposed just that change as a means of alleviating the shortage of engineer officers. Secretary of War Calhoun had favorably endorsed Thayer's recommendation, but a lethargic Congress had failed to
act, so the proposal died.[2] Then, in the early fifties, Representative
Humphrey Marshall, a graduate of West Point, revived Thayer's suggestion in the House, but on learning that Professor Mahan opposed it, Marshall withdrew his proposal.[3]

Another alumnus, Jefferson Davis, was more persistent in seeking to break the engineer monopoly. In his annual report as secretary of war in 1855 Davis proposed opening the command at West Point to officers of all arms. He did this for two reasons. First, the control structure which permitted a junior officer of engineers to exercise authority over a senior of another branch offended the secretary's sense of military propriety. This had actually happened in March 1855 when John G. Barnard, a captain of engineers, on assuming the superintendency, became the official supervisor of Major William H. T. Walker, the commandant of cadets. Equally important, Davis believed the special tie between the academy and the corps of engineers was inappropriate since West Point was supposed to serve the entire army. At the secretary's suggestion the board of visitors studied the matter in 1856 but recommended against changing the existing relationship. In any case, one aspect of the problem, the issue of relative rank, was temporarily solved the same summer when Richard Delafield, an engineer officer senior to the commandant, became superintendent.[4] A more permanent solution went into effect in 1858 when Congress prescribed that the superintendent and commandant would hold local rank as colonel and lieutenant colonel, respectively, regardless of their actual grades in the army.[5]

Opening the superintendency to all branches remained a lively issue, however, and the desirability of such a change was one of the items examined by the Davis Commission at West Point in the summer and fall of 1860. In every instance the officers of cavalry, infantry, and artillery who testified before the commission preferred opening the superintendency to all arms,[6] whereas the professors and engineers wanted to maintain the status quo.[7] After considering both sets of opinions the Davis Commission recommended a compromise: opening the superintendency to officers of all branches while retaining the chief of engineers as inspector of the academy.[8]

The line officers who had testified before the Davis Commission justified their recommendations with an argument which was difficult to refute: the superintendency should reflect the fact that the academy provided officers for all branches of the army. Altruistic though this view may seem, there can be little doubt that a deep-seated resentment of elitism contributed to it. Not only did the engineers look on themselves as an elect, they actively sought to imbue cadets with the same idea. As John Tidball put it, "We were taught with every breath we drew at West Point, the utmost reverence for this [order of merit] scale; consequently, it becomes [*sic*] a kind of fixture in our minds that the engineers were a species of gods, next to which came the 'topogs' [topographical engineers] . . . only a grade below the first, but still a grade—they were but demi-gods. . . . The line was simply

142

the line, whether of horse, foot, or dragoons. . . . For the latter a good square seat in the saddle was deemed of more importance than brains. These ideas were ground into our heads with such Jesuitical persistency, I do not believe anyone of the old [1840s] regime ever entirely overcame the influence of it."[9]

The testimony of Cadet Adelbert Ames before the Davis Commission in 1860 evinces the success of this kind of indoctrination. Ames, who graduated fifth in the class of May 1861, stated, "The effort to stand high is prompted almost wholly by the prospect it holds out of selecting one's own corps, and being able to enter one of the scientific corps.

"At one time it was reported that all of the graduates were to be put into the line, and afterwards assigned to their respective corps. This occasioned great disgust among the cadets. We in the first section thought it would hardly be worthwhile to study if such was the case. The mere honor of standing high would not be sufficient incentive with many of the class."[10]

This attitude irritated the rest of the army, and it probably was no coincidence that Marshall, Davis, and the officers who recommended the change in 1860 had stood too low in their classes to enter the engineers on graduation. Similarly, it may have been resentment, at least in part, which motivated Grant, Sherman, and Thomas to do nothing which would prevent the separation in 1866 despite pleas for help from Mahan. Grant and Thomas did not record their feelings on the matter, but Sherman made no secret of his contempt for the snobbism associated with the scientific corps, particularly the engineers and ordnance. In his memoirs he criticized the young West Pointers who, on joining those branches, took on the airs of an elite "made of better clay than the common soldier," and in 1873 he told a congressional committee "They [engineer and ordnance officers] are taken from the head of their classes at West Point. They are good scholars, but the difficulty is they are put into these favored corps and begin directly to look down upon the rest of the army. They themselves fail to acquire that practical experience with soldiers which every officer ought to have."[11]

On the other hand, logic as well as spite lay behind the demand for severing the special ties between the corps of engineers and the military academy. Calhoun had seen the need for changing the relationship as early as 1820. Moreover, the Mexican and Civil Wars had demonstrated that the mission of the military academy had expanded greatly beyond its original aim. In addition, a critical shortage of engineer officers, coupled with a glut of high-ranking graduates in other branches during the immediate postwar period, made the change eminently feasible.[12]

The final chapter in the opening of the superintendency to the entire army and removing the academy from the control of the chief of engineers began in June 1865 when the board of visitors assembled at West Point for

143

its annual inspection. This group, under the leadership of Robert C. Schenck, Ohio congressman and former major general of volunteers, conducted a searching investigation of the institution and, unlike most boards of visitors, reported its findings without an eye to pleasing the local authorities. For example, the board criticized the poor performance of the first class on the examinations and the prevalence of hazing, recommending as correctives more stringent entrance requirements, competitive examinations for admission, and a disciplinary system which would make sharper distinctions between minor violations of regulations and offenses involving moral turpitude. The visitors also proposed opening the superintendency to officers of all arms.[13]

Two incidents which occurred during its inspection increased the dissatisfaction of the board of visitors with the control hierarchy at West Point and may have engendered the recommendation concerning the superintendency. First, the members of the board thought that the captured Confederate war trophies on display at West Point were not marked in a manner which drew sufficient attention to the glory of Union arms. Richard Delafield, chief of engineers at the time, had prohibited such ostentation in order to avoid offending future Southern cadets, but the board saw the matter in a different light.[14] Schenck, in particular, was so upset by Delafield's conciliatory directive that he later read it aloud on the floor of the House when proposing an appropriation for exhibiting the trophies in a way he thought more suitable. In his speech the congressman took pains to emphasize that, unlike the chief of engineers, he believed the memory of the war should be perpetuated, not blotted out, and that any Southerner who took offense at the reminders of defeat should be denied admission as a cadet.[15]

Another clash arose over the question of the relative powers of the board of visitors and the superintendent. At the outset the board had decided to deal directly with individual members of the faculty so as to obtain their candid opinions concerning affairs at West Point. George W. Cullum, the superintendent, looked on this as a violation of military protocol and insisted that all statements made by members of the faculty be cleared through him prior to presenting them to the board of visitors. Aware that the superintendent's demand might inhibit frank responses, the visitors protested to the secretary of war. In reply Secretary Stanton stated, "The Department has no authority over the Board of Visitors to direct its course of procedure for acquiring information . . ." Although Stanton's ambiguous statement seemingly reinforced the position of the visitors, Cullum interpreted it as a vindication of his own stand and refused to budge. Nevertheless, the superintendent's insistence on previewing the testimony of the faculty did not deter Captain George Balch, the instructor of ordnance and gunnery, from bluntly telling the visitors what he thought. In his report Balch found fault with the tie between the academy and the corps of engineers, maintaining that it worked against the best interests of the army. "Experience teaches how unwise it is to entrust important national interests to any one set of men who have one [principal] end to serve, whose antecedents and whose professional experiences are identical, and who, from their very habits, no matter what may be the changes in the wants of the army or the country, find it difficult to adjust themselves to the new order of things those changes necessarily create."[16]

Balch went on to suggest that the academy be removed from the supervision of the corps of engineers and placed under a bureau of military education, which would come directly under the control of the secretary of war. At the same time he recommended that the special branch prerequisites for the superintendency be abolished. No halfhearted iconoclast, Balch also condemned the hitherto sacrosanct method of determining order of merit which, as he saw it, was "for the most part entirely arbitrary, and conveyed no exact idea of the fitness of the individual for the duties or pursuits" of a military career. To rectify this defect Balch suggested that every graduate serve a year or so in the line before joining a staff or scientific corps. Finally, the dauntless captain proposed mandatory retirement for superannuated professors, increased stabilization of instructors, and allocation of one-third of the annual cadet appointments to deserving enlisted men. The board of visitors did not act on most of Balch's proposals, but his recommendation on the superintendency did strike a responsive chord, coming as it did in the wake of Cullum's recalcitrance and Delafield's ostensible slighting of the Union war effort. Consequently, in its report the board recommended that officers of all arms be considered eligible for the superintendency.[17]

The chief of engineers commented in detail on some of the recommendations of the board of visitors in his endorsement of their report, but he did not mention the proposal concerning the superintendency. The evidence does not explain Delafield's puzzling silence on that vital matter, but his reticence may have derived from one or more of several sources. In the first place, because of the shortage of engineer officers he may have welcomed relief from the burden of the superintendency. Secondly, Delafield, when superintendent, had wrangled with Professor Mahan on several occasions, and knowing how bitterly Mahan opposed the change, he may have stood mute out of sheer personal rancor. Thirdly, Delafield may have sincerely believed that the proposed modification would best serve the interests of the academy and the army, or more likely, he may have sensed that the pressure for change had become too powerful to resist. Finally, the chief of engineers may have realized that broadening the base of the superintendency would have less impact on the basic orientation of West Point than the reformers supposed. Certainly his own experiences with the academic board would have left him with that impression.

Secretary Stanton showed no reluctance in stating an opinion. He forwarded the report of the board of visitors to Congress with the specific recommendation that "the superintendence of the institution be no longer confined to the Engineer Bureau."[18]

At this point, the early spring of 1866, Professor Mahan once again took up his pen on behalf of the old order. In letters to congressmen and to Generals Grant, Sherman, and Thomas, Mahan argued that the corps of engineers had performed its pedagogical duties well, and that opening the superintendency to other branches would lead to political maneuvering throughout the army. The professor won the support of Senators Fessenden and Edwin D. Morgan and also managed to sway the generals, who originally had supported the change,[19] to a position of neutrality. At the same time Superintendent Cullum, Mahan's partner in this effort, obtained the backing of Senator Henry Wilson. The *New York Times* and the *United States Service Magazine* aided too with editorials opposing the visitors' proposal.[20] The effort failed. Neither Grant, Sherman, Thomas nor any other prominent officer spoke out in defense of retaining the engineer monopoly, and although Senator Fessenden conducted a spirited battle in Congress, he and his allies went down to defeat. On 11 July 1866 the president signed a bill opening the superintendency to all branches of the army. The same measure also removed the inspectorate of the academy from the jurisdiction of the corps of engineers and placed it directly under the secretary of war.[21] This latter proviso, similar to Captain Balch's earlier proposal, had been added to the bill on the recommendation at a joint House-Senate conference which had met to reconcile differences in the drafts prepared by the two houses. John Sherman, the general's brother, was one of the senators at this conference, and Robert Schenck, former president of the board of visitors, attended as a member of the House delegation.[22] Neither politician gave a reason, but the impetus for their joint action to sever all ties between the corps of engineers and the academy probably came from Schenck's experiences at West Point the previous summer and Sherman's knowledge that the separation would not displease his brother.

To carry out the supervisory functions previously performed by the chief of engineers Congress established a separate inspectorate for the military academy directly under the secretary of war. On 10 July 1866 Major General Edmund Schriver, a former line officer, was appointed to that office. A month later Brevet Brigadier General Thomas Pitcher relieved Cullum as superintendent.[23] With the naming of Pitcher to head West Point the "Immortals" came into their own; the new superintendent had graduated next-to-last in the class of 1845.[24]

Contrary to the expectations of the reformers, these changes in the command structure did not presage an era of academic reorientation at West Point. That could have been brought about only by removing the professors who were philosophically wedded to the primacy of mathematics, science, and engineering, or by the secretary of war's imposing a more liberal curriculum. Nothing of the kind took place, the professors remained, and their power to dictate the academic program went untrammeled.[25]

Other features of the academic environment also stayed much the same. A new curriculum went into effect in 1867, but it differed little from that of the early fifties. Fourth classmen took mathematics and French. Third classmen continued those two subjects and studied Spanish, drawing, and equitation. Second classmen learned natural and experimental philosophy, chemistry, drawing, tactics and riding, while first classmen pursued civil and military engineering, the science of war, ethics, law, mineralogy and geology, ordnance and gunnery, tactics, and riding. The only changes from the program of the early fifties were the shift of Spanish from the first to the third class, the transfer of some tactics from the first to the second class, and the addition of penmanship and signalling to the courses in drawing and tactics, respectively. English, history, and geography were altogether omitted from the new program on the grounds that these subjects were required for admission to the academy.[26]

Mathematics, science, and engineering continued to dominate the curriculum inaugurated in 1867 just as they had in the past. For instance, in determining order of merit engineering, mathematics, and natural and experimental philosophy counted 300 points each; chemistry and ethics were valued at 150 apiece; drawing and French counted 100 points each; Spanish, and mineralogy and geology were worth 75 points apiece, and each branch of tactics was weighted at 50. Thus, of a total of 1,775 points, excluding conduct, 1,125 (53.4 percent) were allotted to mathematics, science, and engineering; 425 (23.7 percent) went to the humanities (ethics, law, French, Spanish, and drawing); and 225 (12.7 percent) to professional military subjects. Compared with the curriculum of 1853 the new program represented an increase of 4.5 percent in the influence of mathematics, science, and engineering with corresponding decreases of 2 percent and 2.5 percent in the humanities and military subjects. Moreover, the academic board continued to recommend graduates for the various branches of the army according to their order of merit standings as cadets with only the top men in each class being considered fit for the engineers.[27] Obviously, the removal of the academy from the control of the corps of engineers had not brought a liberalization of the curriculum or a lowering of the prestige of that branch in the eyes of the academic board.

There was a substantive change in the rate of academic failures for the years between 1866 and 1870. As a result of the improved entrance requirements the rate, which had been 48.7 percent during the war, declined to 30.35 percent as shown in appendix X. But even here one constant remained. Mathematics still produced the largest number of casualties, just as it always had (see appendix XI).

Other alterations, subtler but more significant in the long run than opening the superintendency and reducing deficiency rates, also took place in the early postwar years. As several historians have noted, there was a decline in the quality of education at the academy with an accompanying drift toward reaction, inbreeding, and intellectual stagnation.[28] This was in stark contrast to the ferment taking place elsewhere in American higher education during the period following the Civil War. In most colleges the rigid classical curriculum gave way to elective programs, and new instructional techniques replaced, or extensively augmented, the old-style daily recitation which had stressed rote learning.[29] But West Point remained impervious to this spirit. Not only did the 1867 curriculum closely resemble that in use at the academy in 1853, the same held true as late as 1873.[30] Then too, the instructional techniques employed at West Point in 1833 were still in vogue there in the late 1870s. The academy was marking time intellectually, and in doing so the institution forfeited its former eminence in mathematics, science, and engineering to schools like Rensselaer and Massachusetts Institutue of Technology.[31]

Coincident with the onset of intellectual atrophy came an increased inclination toward inbreeding. From the establishment of the academy through the end of the Civil War a sizable fraction of the permanent faculty had always come from outside the institution. For example, in the years between 1833 and 1866 Weir, the professor of drawing, Agnel, the professor of French, and de Janon, the professor of Spanish, had not attended West Point. When these three members of the academic board passed from the scene, however, they were replaced by graduates of the military academy whose knowledge of the fields they were responsible for teaching was limited to what they had learned as cadets.[32]

The advent of reaction and isolation at West Point in the years following the Civil War can be vividly illustrated by contrasting the viewpoints of two professors, each the most notable member of the faculty in his own time. The representative of the old regime until his death in 1871 was Dennis Hart Mahan. The year Mahan died Peter S. Michie, who embodied the postwar generation, assumed the chair of natural and experimental philosophy, a post he held for the next thirty years.

Up until the end Mahan continued his lifelong practice of gathering material wherever he could in order to keep his courses in engineering and the science of war up to date. In 1869, for instance, he visited several schools of engineering as well as public works projects in New York, seeking information for use in the instructional program at West Point. In addition, he labored tirelessly to obtain data on the American Civil War and the Austro-Prussian conflict almost before the guns had cooled in an effort to keep his teachings on warfare current.[33] Nor did Mahan confine his interests to academic matters. In 1867 he proposed a plan for reorganizing the military academy which would have entailed a radical deviation from the past. Fearing that West Point was becoming a "close corporation" ruled by professors and immune to outside influences, Mahan suggested counteracting this trend by interposing a progressive-minded director of studies— that is, a dean—between the superintendent and the academic board, while simultaneously limiting the power of the latter body to ascertaining proficiency on examinations. Prophetically, the professor warned that the governmental structure of West Point "has no vitality within itself and cannot have; as under a certain set of men everything must be kept stationary or retrograde."[34]

Peter Michie, the symbol of the new order at West Point, had graduated second in the class of 1863 and had returned to the academy as an instructor soon after the war. On the retirement of Professor Bartlett in 1871 Michie was appointed to the chair of natural and experimental philosophy. Two years later, he, like Mahan previously, made an extensive tour of educational institutions. Michie visited Yale, Stevens Institute of Technology, Union College, Cornell, The University of Michigan, Massachusetts Institute of Technology, Harvard, Amherst, Dartmouth, Rensselaer, and Columbia, institutions where the postwar educational reforms were beginning to take hold. During his trip the West Point professor attended lectures, observed students working in the laboratory, and talked at great length with his civilian counterparts. On returning to the academy Michie drafted an exhaustive report, one designed as much to defend West Point as to record his observations. The professor described the various techniques of teaching science and engineering he had witnessed and then analyzed each with respect to its applicability at the military academy. Michie found the elective program at Harvard wanting because it provided no safeguards to ensure that students took the necessary courses and also because it tempted professors to curry favor with students in order to keep their classes filled. Likewise, he criticized the practice of having students perform laboratory experiments, as was the case at Massachusetts Institute of Technology, since the exercises merely illustrated principles which should already have been learned from a textbook. The professor also took exception to the heavy reliance on examinations rather than daily recitations which he had noted at a number of schools, inasmuch as this permitted students to postpone studying until examination time. Similarly, he discounted the value of lectures because they spared the student from mental effort. In addition, Michie felt that the close supervision West Point professors exercised over their subordinates made for better teaching than the latitudinarian approach characteristic of the civilian colleges. The professor closed his report with a reaffirmation of faith in the Thayer credo. "It is with pleasure that I have to report that so far as the Military Academy is concerned, the character, scope, and method of its instruction, considering the end in view, is much superior to that of any institution either technical, special [scientific], or general."[35]

Notwithstanding the validity of some of his criticisms, the true significance of Michie's report lies in its isolationist tone. The presumption that the distinctiveness of its mission exempted the academy from educational progress was fatal to continued intellectual improvement.

It is clear that separation from the corps of engineers and the near-simultaneous passing of the most prominent of Thayer's disciples marked the end of an era in the history of West Point. But these changes did not portend a renaissance in which the academy, free from special constraints and prejudices, blossomed into an institution more capable of serving the entire army than its predecessor had been. On the contrary, the "new," postwar West Point chose as its guideposts the curriculum, customs, and parochial biases of a bygone day, while at the same time rejecting the spirit of enlightened conservatism which had also been characteristic of the military academy in the years from 1833 to 1866.

That same span, beginning with the departure of Thayer in 1833 and ending with the abolition of the engineer hegemony in 1866, has been labeled the "Golden Age" of West Point by some writers. The extent to which this title is warranted is largely a matter of judgment and, perhaps, literary taste. But skepticism about the fitness of such accolades cannot obscure the fact that what took place at the academy in those years does merit serious attention. Careful study of antebellum West Point teaches much about how an educational bureaucracy actually works as opposed to the way outsiders think it does. Furthermore, examination of the military academy in the pre–Civil War era permits insights into the influence an educational environment exerts on students and how that influence may produce results the educators had not intended.

150

One especially intriguing feature of antebellum West Point was that the seat of actual power was not where it appeared to be. The academic board stood low in the official hierarchy of control; nonetheless, that body enjoyed a remarkable degree of autonomy in governing the institution and setting its educational tone. It is equally significant that three men— Mahan, Bartlett, and Church—even though vested with no more statutory authority than their colleagues, dominated the board to the extent that they could make their view of the purpose and content of the curriculum prevail. And their view was that the mission of the military academy was to educate "scientific soldiers," or more accurately, engineers who could also serve as line officers. These two factors, the role of the academic board in governing West Point and the outlook of its key members, in great measure determined the other aspects of the educational environment.

The de facto power of the board, together with the orientation of its chief members, readily explains why the Thayer System was so long considered the only appropriate method for instructing cadets; Thayer's disciples, Mahan, Bartlett, and Church, saw to it that the techniques and principles they had inherited from the "Father of the Military Academy" remained intact. In the process, however, what had once been a pragmatic approach to academic problems and national needs took on the status of dogma, as Peter Michie's report so eloquently demonstrates. Similarly, the board perpetuated the primacy of mathematics, science, and engineering in the curriculum. This, as well as the continued reliance on order of merit standings to assign graduates to the branches of the army, insured that the engineers would remain an elite corps even after relinquishing formal control of the academy.

The virtual omnipotence of the academic board was useful for more than perpetuating the Thayer System, frustrating unwanted reforms, and preserving the status of the corps of engineers. The board also exerted its power for the welfare of the academy. For example, it forestalled several attempts to derogate the academic content of the curriculum for the sake of increasing the amount of military training. Moreover, the professors for the most part successfully upheld high academic standards despite political interference. Had the strength of the board been less, these benefits would have been lost to the academy. The major defect in the oligarchical arrangement was that it made progress contingent on the desires and abilities of a small group of men. When authority passed from the hands of enlightened conservatives like Mahan, Bartlett, and Church to professors of less capacity, the academy perforce degenerated into a lifeless simulacrum of the older, more vital institution.

Of only slightly less moment than the power and outlook of the academic

151

board was the influence exerted on the military academy by Joseph Totten, the chief of engineers for much of the antebellum era. Totten labored long and hard to cushion the academy from outside interference and to protect the autonomy of the academic board from assaults by politicians. He also made substantial academic contributions to West Point; the course in practical military engineering and the five-year program both were introduced mainly as a result of his efforts. But despite years of dedication to improving the academy, it was Totten's ironic fate while alive to be downgraded by Thayer and after death to be ignored by the chroniclers of West Point.

Significant though they were, the professors, the chief of engineers, and the other men who helped shape West Point were by no means the only noteworthy figures in the history of the antebellum institution. Most important of all were the cadets themselves. The makeup and interests of the corps, together with the impact of West Point on that body, would be fascinating to study in any case, but the parts alumni of the classes between 1833 and 1866 played in some of the most critical events in the history of the nation lend added consequence to this particular period of the academy's past.

The great majority of the cadets were boys from the middle and lower-middle classes with rural and small-town backgrounds. Thus, the corps represented with a fair degree of accuracy the socioeconomic composition and the demographic distribution of white American society at the time. It is true that the sons of lawyers, editors, and officers of the armed forces enjoyed a slight preference in obtaining appointments, but there is no evidence that students from these groups, once they enrolled as cadets, received favored treatment from the West Point authorities. In fact, the record clearly shows that each student's success or failure depended solely on his ability to cope with the exacting academic and disciplinary demands of the institution. In that regard, at least, the military academy probably came closer to producing the aristocracy of talent espoused by Jefferson and John Adams than any other educational institution in the antebellum United States.

Coming from every congressional district and territory, the cadets naturally brought with them to West Point the sectional biases of their native regions. The academy for its part sought to attenuate the virulence of sectionalism and to foster a spirit of nationalism. The defection of Southern alumni and cadets at the beginning of the Civil War proved that the institution had not been completely successful in its efforts, but even so, the record of West Point was significantly better than those of the other agencies of the federal government and Northern civilian colleges. In a related vein, the charges of Civil War "witch hunters" belied the facts. The antebellum academy was no "hotbed of secession"; nor was it actually pro-Southern in sentiment. The supposed affinity noted by Stuart and other contemporaries stemmed from common preferences for political conservatism, polite manners, and an ordered social structure, together with an understandable desire on the part of the West Point authorities to avoid exacerbating sectional tempers. But as the crisis of 1861 conclusively demonstrated, the identity of interests between the academy and the South was apparent, not real.

Another long-lived myth is the claim that Professor Mahan's emphasis on Jomini became a dominating influence on Civil War strategy. T. Harry Williams, one of the leading exponents of the thesis, saw fit to repeat it in his last book on American military history.[36] This view not only exaggerates the impact of one small segment of the curriculum, while ignoring the effects of other characteristics of the West Point environment, it also overlooks such factors as differences in intellect and the influence of military experiences after graduation. In addition, the fixation on Jomini excludes the possibility that other military figures, such as Winfield Scott, may have played instrumental roles in molding Civil War strategic thought, such as it was. If, in fact, there is a single culprit which should bear the blame for unimaginative and inept generalship, it may be the total West Point environment which stressed strict adherence to texts and regulations, and promoted a mechanistic approach to human problems. Recent work in educational psychology supports the claim that academic environments have a definite effect on students' personalities.[37] It seems logical to suggest, therefore, that the strategic and tactical failures so typical of the Civil War stemmed less from following abstract principles per se, than from a lack of the mental flexibility necessary to modify those principles to fit the situation at hand. Mahan may indeed have preached "cobbon sense"; the question is whether the West Point environment fostered or discouraged it.

Less controvertible is the assertion that the academy helped nurture a military aristocracy. The "Plebe System," the Darwinian process of elimination, the social customs of the staff and faculty, and the pronounced Episcopal flavor of the chapel services certainly encouraged caste-consciousness. In that regard the Jacksonian and Radical Republican critics were on target with their charges. In both the Mexican and Civil Wars the West Pointers' condescension created animosity among volunteer officers. What the critics failed or refused to see was that the officer corps of a regular army is by its very nature aristocratic, nor is this necessarily an evil as long as the feeling of superiority is affirmed by superior performance on the battlefield. Some insensitive graduates needlessly provoked antagonism by advertising their contempt for citizen-soldiers, but such stupid behavior does not gainsay the fact that, as a general rule, the West Pointers were better officers. Had the case been otherwise, the military academy would have had no reason to exist.

On the walls of Cullum Hall and a few of the other older buildings at the military academy hang the portraits of antebellum West Pointers. Famous or obscure, successes or failures, Union or Confederate, the men in those portraits all have the same look: stiff dignity and grim, humorless dedication. The portraits are but half-truths. They betray no hint that the stone bastions at which the warrior-subjects eternally frown once echoed with the shouts, the laughter, and the sobs of their vibrant, grey-clad youth.

Appendix One

★

OCCUPATIONAL AND FINANCIAL STATUS OF PARENTS OF CADETS, 1842–1854

Compiled from "Circumstances of Parents of Cadets, 1842–1879"
(R–Rural; T–Town; C–City.)

Occupation	Indigent			Reduced			Moderate			Affluent		
	R	T	C	R	T	C	R	T	C	R	T	C
Planter				1	2		29	7	3	2		2
Farmer	3	2		33	4		165	39	4	4	2	1
Physician				2	1	4	21	43	8		2	
Merchant				2	7	3	18	48	43	1	2	4
Army Officer		1					14	15	24			2
Lawyer		1		3	6	2	31	51	24	1	5	2
Editor		1		1		1		6	7			2
Clergy		1		1	1		1	8	9			
Naval Officer							2	5	4			
Mechanic		1		1		1	5	12	2			
Hotel Proprietor				1					1			
Sea Captain				1	1		1	2	1			
Judge					1		1	3	2		1	1
Bank Officer								5	2			
School Teacher	1				2		1	1	1			
Congressman							2	6				
Engineer						1		3	3			
Printer				2	1			3				
Professor								1	2			
Laborer		1		1			2					
Manufacturer							5	5	1			1
Sheriff		1		1				2	1			
Clerk								3	3			
Grocer								2	1			
Bank President								2	1			
Bank Cashier								2	1			

APPENDIX ONE

Occupation	Indigent R	T	C	Reduced R	T	C	Moderate R	T	C	Affluent R	T	C
Railroad Agent					1			2				
Hotel Keeper					1		1	7	2	1		
Clerk of Court								3				
Saddler					1		2					
Blacksmith					1		1	1				
Hatter								3				
Carpenter	2						2	1				
Shoemaker					2		1	1				
Mason				2					1			
Marine Officer						3						
Stage Proprietor								1	1			
Machinist							1	2				
Jeweler									2			
Ironmaster							3					
Sutler							2					
Miller								2				
Cashier							1	1	1			
Land Agent							1	2				
Customs Officer									2			
Postmaster					1			1	1			
Gentleman							1	2	1			2
Seaman		1			1							
Surveyor				1			1	1				
Cabinet Maker				1			1					
Government Officer							1	2				
Innkeeper							2	1				
Broker							1	2				
Revenue Collector								2				
Carriage Maker							1	1				
Inspector of Customs						1			1			
Tavern Keeper								2				
TOTAL (952)	6	9		49	38	17	316	312	167	9	12	17

The above is a summary of all reports of two or more entries in the same occupational category. Single entries (i.e., only one listing in a category) have not been itemized but are summarized below:

	Indigent R	T	C	Reduced R	T	C	Moderate R	T	C	Affluent R	T	C
		3	2	1	6		13	20	33	1	2	2
GRAND TOTAL (1035)	6	12	2	50	44	17	329	332	200	10	14	19

156

RECAPITULATION

Occupation	Total Number	Percentage of Grand Total
Planter	46	4.4
Farmer	257	24.8
Physician	81	7.8
Merchant	128	12.4
Army Officer	56	5.4
Lawyer	126	12.2
Editor	18	1.7
Clergy	20	1.9
Naval Officer	11	1.0
Mechanic	22	2.1
Hotel Proprietor	2	.2
Sea Captain	6	.6
Judge	9	.9
Bank Officer	7	.8
School Teacher	6	.6
Congressman	8	.8
Engineer	7	.8
Printer	6	.6
Professor	3	.3
Laborer	4	.4
Manufacturer	12	1.2
Sheriff	5	.5
Clerk	6	.6
Grocer	3	.3
Bank President	3	.3
Bank Cashier	3	.3
Railroad Agent	3	.3
Hotel Keeper	12	1.2
Clerk of Court	3	.3
Saddler	3	.3
Blacksmith	3	.3
Hatter	3	.3
Carpenter	5	.5
Shoemaker	4	.4
Mason	3	.3
Marine Officer	3	.3
Stage Proprietor	2	.2
Machinist	3	.3
Jeweler	2	.2
Ironmaster	3	.3
Sutler	2	.2
Miller	2	.2

Occupation	Total Number	Percentage of Grand Total
Cashier	3	.3
Land Agent	3	.3
Customs Officer	2	.2
Postmaster	3	.3
Gentleman	6	.6
Seaman	2	.2
Surveyor	3	.3
Cabinet Maker	2	.2
Government Officer	3	.3
Innkeeper	3	.3
Broker	3	.3
Revenue Collector	2	.2
Carriage Maker	2	.2
Inspector of Customs	2	.2
Tavern Keeper	2	.2
TOTAL	952	92.6
Others (One only)	83	7.4
GRAND TOTAL	1,035	100

MAJOR (1 PERCENT OR MORE) OCCUPATION CATEGORIES OF CADET PARENTS COMPARED TO THE PERCENTAGES OF THESE CATEGORIES 1N THE GENERAL POPULATION (BASED ON THE CENSUS OF 1850)

Occupation	Percentage of Corps of Cadets	Total in Population	Percent of Total [3]	Differential
Farmer	24.8	2,363,958	44.0	−19.2
Merchant	12.4	100,752	18.8	− 6.4
Lawyer	12.2	23,939	4.5	+ 7.7
Physician	7.8	40,564	7.8	0
Army Officer	5.4	948[1]	.02	+ 5.3
Planter	4.4	27,055	5.0	− .6
Mechanic	2.1	16,004	2.9	− .8
Clergy	1.9	26,842	4.9	− 3.0
Editor	1.7	1,372	.2	+ 1.5
Manufacturer	1.2	2,046	.4	+ .8
Naval Officer	1.0	567[2]	.01	+ .9

[1] Not included in Census of 1850. Figure taken from Heitman, 2:626.

[2] Not included in Census of 1850. Figure taken from *Register of Commissioned and Warrant Officers of the Navy of the United States . . . for the year 1850* (Washington. D.C.: G.A. Alexander, 1850).

[3] Total Working Population according to Census of 1850 was 5,371,876.

FINANCIAL STATUS OF PARENTS

Category	Number in the Category	Percentage of Total
Indigent	20	1.9
Reduced	111	10.7
Moderate	861	83.2
Affluent	43	4.2
TOTAL	1,035	100

COMPOSITION BY RURAL, TOWN, AND CITY

Category	Number in Category	Percent of Total
Rural	395	38.2
Town	402	38.8
City	238	23.0
TOTAL	1,035	100

The same pattern for fathers' occupations held through 1867. This was verified in a separate study conducted by Peter Karsten at West Point in 1977. Peter Karsten, ed., *The Military in America from Colonial Times to the Present* (New York: Free Press, 1980), 87.

159

Appendix Two

★

SUBJECTS BY SEMESTER, 1833–1854

Department of Mathematics

Class	Fall Term	Spring Term
Fourth	Algebra	Plane & Solid Geometry, Plane & Spherical Trigonometry, Mensuration, Analytical Geometry, Review
Third	Analytical Geometry, Descriptive Geometry, Review	Shades, Shadows, Perspectives, Differential and Integral Calculus, Surveying, Review

Daily recitations, one and one-half hours in length, throughout the academic year for third and fourth classes.

Department of French

Class	Fall Term	Spring Term
Fourth	1833–1846 Daily recitations, one hour	1833–1846 Daily recitations, one hour 1846–1854 Alternate days, one hour recitations (spring only)
Third	1833–1839 Daily recitations, one hour 1839–1845 Alternate days, one hour recitations 1845–1854 Daily recitations, one hour	1833–1839 Daily recitations, one hour 1839–1845 Alternate days, one hour recitations 1845–1854 Daily recitations, one hour

No detailed schedules for French instruction are available, but the text-listings indicate that both French literature and grammar were studied.

Department of Ethics

Class	Fall Term	Spring Term
First	1833–1842 Rhetoric, Moral Science 1842–1854 International Law, Constitutional Law	Moral Science, Political Science Moral Philosophy, Logic

One hour recitations on alternate days throughout the year.

Class	Fall Term	Spring Term
Third	1839–1845 English grammar, Composition, Rhetoric*	Rhetoric*, Geography

*Rhetoric transferred from first to third class in 1839.

One hour recitations on alternate days throughout the year.

Class	Fall Term	Spring Term
Fourth	1854–1864 Same as third class course from 1839–1845.	

Department of Chemistry, Mineralogy, and Geology

Class	Fall Term	Spring Term
Second	1833–1854 Chemistry	Chemistry

One hour recitations, alternate days throughout the year.

Class	Fall Term	Spring Term
First	1833–1839 1840–1854	Geology Mineralogy and Geology

One hour recitations, alternate days, spring term only.

Chapter 6 discusses course content. It is impossible to break this out by term.

Department of Natural and Experimental Philosophy

Class	Fall Term	Spring Term
Second	1833–1854 Mechanics	Accoustics, Optics, Astronomy

Daily recitations throughout the academic year, each recitation one and one-half hours in length.

Department of Drawing

Class	Fall Term	Spring Term
Third	1833–1839	
	Human Figure	Human Figure
	1839–1854	
	Topography	Topography, Human Figure
Second	1833–1839	
	Landscape	Topography
	1839–1854	
	Landscape	Landscape

Recitations: Third class—two hours on alternate days throughout the year.
Second class—two hours daily throughout the year.

Department of Civil and Military Engineering and the Art [Science] of War

Class	Fall Term	Spring Term
First	1833–1854	
	Civil Engineering, Drawing	Military Engineering, Science of War, Drawing, Review

Daily recitations throughout the year. Drawing recitation, three hours in length; others, one and one-half hours.

Department of Practical Military Engineering

Class	Fall Term	Spring Term	Summer Camp
First	1851–1854		
	Drills after class, 4:00 P.M. to sunset.	Drills after class, 4:00 P.M. to sunset.	Drills

Department of Tactics

Class		Fall Term	Spring Term	Summer Camp
First	1833–1854			
	Recitations	Infantry	Infantry	Infantry
	Recitations	Artillery	Artillery	
	1853–			
	Recitations	Cavalry	Cavalry	
	Graded Exercise	Fencing	Fencing	

APPENDIX TWO

Class		Fall Term	Spring Term	Summer Camp
	1839–			
Practical Work		Equitation	Equitation	Equitation
Drills		Infantry & Artillery	Infantry & Artillery	Infantry & Artillery
Second	1846–			
Practical Work		Equitation	Equitation	
	1833–			
Drills		Infantry & Artillery	Infantry & Artillery	Infantry & Artillery
Third	1851–			
Practical Work		Equitation	Equitation	
	1833–			
Drills		Artillery & Infantry	Artillery & Infantry	Artillery & Infantry
Fourth	1852–			
Graded Exercise		Fencing	Fencing	
	1833–			
Drills		Infantry	Infantry	Infantry

Recitations in infantry, artillery, and cavalry tactics were one-hour long, held on alternate days from September to November, from March to June, and in summer camp.

Equitation periods were one hour in length, on alternate weekdays throughout the year.

Fencing periods were one half-hour in length, on alternate days throughout the year.

Drills were held between 4:00 P.M. and sundown in the spring and fall and were two hours in length in summer camp.

Total number of recitations (first class only):
   Artillery, 32
   Infantry, 15
   Cavalry, 15
Cumulative total of drills: (entire four year course)
   Artillery (first, second, third classes), 104
   Infantry (first, second, third, fourth classes), 540
Cumulative total of equitation periods: (entire four years)
   (first, second, and third classes), 268
Cumulative total of fencing periods: (entire four years)
   (first and fourth classes), 108

Sources: USMA Regulations, 1832, 1839, and 1853.
   Official Registers, 1833–1854, inclusive.
   Staff Records (Academic Board Proceedings), 1833–1854.
   Centennial of the United States Military Academy at West Point, New York, 1802–1902, vol. 1.
   Report of the Jefferson Davis Commission, 1860.

Appendix Three

DEFICIENCIES BY CLASS AND SUBJECT, 1833–1854

Class and Subject	No. of Cadets	% of Total Deficiencies
First (Senior)		
Conduct	3	0.6
Engineering	7	1.3
Second (Junior)		
Chemistry & Conduct	1	0.2
Natural Philosophy & Drawing	1	0.2
Conduct	2	0.4
Natural Philosophy, Chemistry, & Drawing	2	0.4
Natural Philosophy & Chemistry	6	1.1
Chemistry	15	2.8
Natural Philosophy	24	4.5
Third (Sophomore)		
Drawing	1	0.2
English Grammar & Geography	1	0.2
Mathematics, English Grammar, & Geography	1	0.2
Mathematics & Conduct	1	0.2
Mathematics, French, & Drawing	1	0.2
Conduct	2	0.4
French	2	0.4
French & English Grammar	2	0.4
Mathematics & Drawing	2	0.4
English Grammar	5	0.9
Mathematics, French, & English Grammar	6	1.1
Mathematics & English Grammar	10	1.9
Mathematics & French	16	3.0
Mathematics	49	9.2
Fourth (Freshman)		
Mathematics & Conduct	1	0.2
Mathematics, English Grammar, & Conduct	1	0.2

Class and Subject	No. of Cadets	% of Total Deficiencies
English Grammar & Conduct	2	0.4
English Grammar & French	2	0.4
Mathematics, French, & Conduct	2	0.4
Mathematics, French, & English Grammar	3	0.6
Conduct	7	1.5
English Grammar	10	1.9
French	21	4.0
Mathematics & English Grammar	64	12.1
Mathematics & French	77	14.5
Mathematics	180	33.9

RECAPITULATION:	Cadets Deficient	% of Total Deficiencies
First Class	10	1.9
Second Class	51	9.6
Third Class	99	18.6
Fourth Class	370	69.9

Of the 2,112 cadets who entered between 1833 and 1854, 25% failed academically:

First Class	0.5%
Second Class	2.4%
Third Class	4.7%
Fourth Class	17.4%

FAILURES DUE TO MATHEMATICS
(Percentage of Total Failures)

Class	Math Only (%)	Math plus one or more other subjects (%)
Fourth	33.9	28.0
Third	9.2	7.0

The Department of Mathematics alone accounted for 43.1% of all academic failures, and accounted in part for an additional 35% of failures. Thus, that department, wholly or partially, accounted for 78.1% of all academic failures.

Of 2,112 entering cadets, 8.5% failed fourth class math and no other subject; another 7.0% failed fourth class math and one or more other subjects.

Of the same number of entering cadets, 2.3% failed third class math and no other subject; another 1.8% failed third class math and one or more other subjects.

In summary, 10.8% of all entering cadets failed mathematics and no other subject. An additional 8.8% failed mathematics and one or more other subjects. Or, 19.6% of all entering cadets failed, solely or in part, because of mathematics.

Source: SR, 1833–1854 inclusive.

Appendix Four
★

THE FIVE-YEAR PROGRAM IN 1860

Year	Class	Studies	Time	
First	Fifth	Mathematics	8 to 11	Daily
		English studies	12 to 1, 2 to 4	Daily, except Saturday
		Fencing	12 to 1, 3 to 4	Every other day except Saturday
Second	Fourth	Mathematics	8 to 11	Daily
		French	2 to 4	Daily
		English studies	11 to 1	Every other day
		Fencing	11 to 1	Every other day
Third	Third	Philosophy, natural & experimental	8 to 11	Daily
		French & Spanish alternating till January		
		Spanish	11 to 1	Alternating with each other—Sept., Oct., Nov., & Dec.; daily—Jan., Feb., Mar., Apr., & May; recitation in Spanish after Jan.; may be from 11 to 4 P.M.
		Drawing (alternating)	2 to 4	Five times in two weeks.
		Riding		Riding may be from 2 to 5 P.M.
Fourth	Second	Moral science, history of philosophy, logic & conduct	8 to 11	Every other week day

Class	Subject	Hours	Schedule
	Cavalry tactics, equitation, & outposts; infantry tactics & strategy; artillery & grand tactics, & organization of armies	8 to 11	Every other weekday, alternating with moral science & conduct
	Chemistry	11 to 1	Every other weekday
	Riding	11 to 1	Every other weekday, alternating with Chemistry
	Drawing	2 to 4	Every weekday except Saturday
Fifth	Civil & military engineering	8 to 11	Every weekday
First	Law, history, & conduct	2 to 4	Every other weekday except Saturday, five recitations in two weeks
	Mineralogy & geology	11 to 1, 2 to 4	Every other weekday except Saturday, from 1st Sept. to end of 1st week in Dec., from 2 to 4, alternating with law, & conduct, and last three weeks of May to review, from 1 to 1, every other weekday
	Ordnance & gunnery	11 to 1 or 2 to 4	Every other weekday, from 1st Oct. to end of 1st week in Dec., from 11 to 1, alternating with riding; then from 2 to 4 every other weekday, except Saturday, until Apr. 1, alternating with law, history, & conduct
	Riding	11 to 1 and 2 to 4	Every other weekday except from st Oct. to end of second week in Nov., and last three weeks in May
	Practical engineering	11 to 1 and 2 to 4	Every other weekday, Apr. and May, from 11 to 1, alternating with riding, until end of 1st week in May, and then with mineralogy and geology; also from 2 to 4; alternating with law, history, & conduct; five recitations in two weeks

U.S. Congress, Senate Misc., Doc. no. 3, *Report of the Commission Appointed Under the eighth section of the act of Congress of June 21, 1860, to examine into the organization, system of discipline, and course of instruction of the United States Military Academy at West Point, 36th Cong. 2d sess.,* 1860, p. 31.

Appendix
Five

★

ACADEMIC FAILURES DURING THE FIVE-YEAR COURSE
January 1855–January 1861

	Fifth class					
	Mathematics	*English*	*Mathematics & English*	*Mathematics, English, & Conduct*	*Mathematics & Conduct*	*Conduct*
1855	5	2	9			
1856	4		7	2	1	
1857	3	1	5			
1858	4	2	5	1		
1859	4					
1860	8	1	4			
1861	3	1	5	2	2	1
TOTAL	31	7	35	5	3	1

Fourth class

	Mathematics	English	Mathematics & English	Mathematics, French, & English	French & English	Mathematics & French	Conduct	French	Mathematics & Conduct
1855*									
1856		3						4	
1857	3				2	3			
1858	4			1				1	
1859	7	1	6						
1860	4					2	4	5	
1861	3								1
TOTAL	21	4	6	1	2	5	4	10	1

Third class

	Mathematics	Mathematics & Conduct	Drawing	Mathematics & French	Conduct
1855*					
1856*					
1857					
1858			2		
1859	4			1	
1860					
1861					5
TOTAL	4		2	1	5

169

	Conduct	Infantry Tactics	Ethics	Ethics & Infantry Tactics
Second class				
1855*				
1856*				
1857*				
1858	1			
1859				
1860		1		
1861	2		2	1
TOTAL	3	1	2	1

	First Class Conduct
1855*	
1856*	
1857*	
1858*	
1859	
1860	
1861	1
TOTAL	1

RECAPITULATION

Failures by Class	No. of Failures	% of Total Failures
FIFTH CLASS	82	52.6
FOURTH CLASS	54	34.6
THIRD CLASS	12	7.7
SECOND CLASS	7	4.5
FIRST CLASS	1	0.6
TOTAL	156	

*Was not affected by the Five-Year Curriculum.

FAILURES BY SUBJECT

Class	Subject	No. of Failures	% of Total Failures
Fifth	Mathematics & English	35	22.4
Fifth	Mathematics	31	19.9
Fourth	Mathematics	21	13.5
Fourth	French	10	6.4
Fifth	English	7	4.5
Fourth	Mathematics & Engiish	6	3.8
Fifth	Mathematics, English, & Conduct	5	3.2
Fourth	Mathematics & French	5	3.2
Third	Conduct	5	3.2
Fourth	Conduct	4	2.6
Fourth	English	4	2.6
Third	Mathematics	4	2.6
Fifth	Mathematics & Conduct	3	1.9
Second	Conduct	3	1.9
Fourth	French & English	2	1.3
Third	Drawing	2	1.3
Second	Ethics	2	1.3
Fifth	Conduct	1	0.6
Fourth	Mathematics, French, & English	1	0.6
Fourth	Mathematics and Conduct	1	0.6
Third	Mathematics & French	1	0.6
Second	Infantry Tactics	1	0.6
Second	Ethics & Infantry Tactics	1	0.6
First	Conduct	1	0.6
TOTAL		156	

IMPACT OF MATHEMATICS ON FAILURES

	No. of Failures	% of Total Failures
Mathematics Alone	56	36.0
Mathematics plus one or more other subjects.	57	36.5
TOTAL	113	72.5

Between 1854 and 1860, 497 cadets were admitted and pursued the Five-Year Curriculum, wholly or in part. Of this number 156 (31.4%) failed one or more subjects and were recommended for discharge by the Academic Board.

Two classes completed the Five-Year Program. Of the 55 admitted with the class of 1859, 22 (40.0%) graduated. Of the 80 admitted with the class of 1860, 41 (51.3%) graduated. Thus, of the 135 cadets admitted in these two classes, 63 (46.7%) graduated.

Sources: SR, 1854–1861.
      Boynton, 320–31.
      Register of Graduates and Former Cadets of the United States Military Academy (1948; reprint, West Point, N.Y.: West Point Alumni Foundation, 1963), 247–49.

Appendix
Six

STAFF AND FACULTY, 1850–1861:
STATE OF RESIDENCE, REGIONAL GROUPINGS,
CONFEDERATE SERVICE

STAFF AND FACULTY, 1850–1861:
STATE OF RESIDENCE
When two states are given, first indicates state of birth,
second indicates state of residence when staff
or faculty member joined West Point.

State	Number	Percentage of Total No.
New York	25	16.1
Pennsylvania	17	11.0
Virginia	13	8.4
Ohio	11	7.1
Massachusetts	10	6.5
Connecticut	6	3.9
Georgia	5	3.2
Kentucky	5	3.2
New Hampshire	4	2.6
New Jersey	4	2.6
North Carolina	4	2.6
South Carolina	4	2.6
Vermont	4	2.6
Maryland	3	1.9
District of Columbia	2	1.3
Florida	2	1.3
Illinois	2	1.3
Maine	2	1.3
Tennessee	2	1.3
New York/Pennsylvania	2	1.3
New York/Michigan	2	1.3

State	Number	Percentage of Total No.
France/New York	2	1.3
Kentucky/Ohio	2	1.3
Indiana	1	0.7
Michigan	1	0.7
Pennsylvania/Missouri	1	0.7
Kentucky/Indiana	1	0.7
Massachusetts/Rhode Island	1	0.7
New Hampshire/New York	1	0.7
Vermont/Ohio	1	0.7
District of Columbia/Pennsylvania	1	0.7
South Carolina/Georgia	1	0.7
North Carolina/Tennessee	1	0.7
Pennsylvania/North Carolina	1	0.7
New York/Illinois	1	0.7
Alabama/New York	1	0.7
Connecticut/District of Columbia	1	0.7
Maine/North Carolina	1	0.7
South Carolina/Ohio	1	0.7
Virginia/Alabama	1	0.7
Ohio/Indiana	1	0.7
Cartagena, Colombia, South America	1	0.7
France	1	0.7
Unknown	2	1.3
TOTAL	155	

STAFF AND FACULTY GROUPED REGIONALLY

Confederate		Border		New England		Middle Atlantic		Midwest	
Va.	13	Ky.	5	Mass.	10	N.Y.	25	Ohio	11
Ga.	5	Md.	3	Conn.	6	Pa.	17	Ill.	2
S.C.	4	D.C.	2	N.H.	4	N.J.	4	Ind.	1
N.C.	4	Pa./Mo.	1	Vt.	4	N.Y./Pa.	2	Mich.	1
Fla.	2	Ky./Ind.	1	Maine	2	N.Y./N.H.	1	N.Y./Mich.	2
Tenn.	2	D.C./Pa.	1	Mass./R.I.	1	Fr./N.Y.	2	Vt./Ohio	1
S.C./Ga.	1	Ky./Ohio	2					N.Y./Ill.	1
N.C./Tenn.	1	Conn./D.C.	1					Ohio/Ind.	1
Pa./N.C.	1								
Ala./N.Y.	1								

Confederate		Border	New England	Middle Atlantic	Midwest
Maine/N.C.	1				
S.C./Ohio	1				
Va./Ala.	1				
TOTAL	37	16	27	51	20

REGIONAL PERCENTAGE OF TOTAL:

Confederate 23.9
Border 10.3
New England 17.4
Mid-Atlantic 32.9
Midwest 12.9
Other 2.6

REGIONAL GROUPING, STAFF AND FACULTY, BY DEPARTMENT
1850–1861

Department	Confederate	Border	Other	% Confederate	% Border
Superintendent	1*		4	20.0	
Engineering	4		7	36.4	
Natural & Expl. Philosophy		3	10		23.1
Mathematics	5	1	15	24.0	4.8
Chemistry, Mineralogy, & Geology			7		
Ethics	3	3	13	15.8	15.8
Drawing			6		
Practical Military Engineering	3		7	30.0	
Tactics	15	5	17	40.5	13.5
French			6		
Fencing			2		
Ordnance			1		
Spanish	1	1	1	33.3	33.3
Staff (Adjutant, Quartermaster, & Surgeon)	5	3	6	35.7	21.4
TOTAL	37	16	102		

*Does not include P. G. T. Beauregard, Superintendent, 23–28 January 1861, but not listed in *Annual Register.*

Departments in Order of Concentration of
Personnel from Confederate States

Tactics 40.5%
Engineering 36.4%
Staff 35.7%
Spanish 33.3%
Practical Military Engineering 30.0%
Mathematics 24.0%
Superintendent 20.0%
Ethics and Chaplain 15.8%

STAFF AND FACULTY ASSIGNED TO U.S. MILITARY ACADEMY, 1833–1861, WHO SERVED IN THE CONFEDERATE ARMIES

Department	No. Serving in Confederate Army
Tactics	13
Mathematics	2
Practical Military Engineering	2
Engineering and Science of War	1
Ethics	1
Chemistry, Mineralogy, Geology	1*
Spanish	1
Staff (Adjutant, Quartermaster, Surgeon, etc.)	1
Superintendent	1
TOTAL	23

Of a total of 155 officers assigned to the academy during this period, 23 (14.9%) later joined the Confederacy.

*Caleb Huse, class of 1851, a native of Massachusetts, assistant professor of chemistry, mineralogy, and geology, 1852–1859. Served as major, CSA, assigned as a purchasing agent in Europe. After the Civil War Huse returned to Highland Falls, New York, just outside West Point, and operated a preparatory school for the military academy. *Dictionary of American Biography,* s.v. "Huse, Caleb."

Appendix
Seven

CADETS AT WEST POINT, 1830–1860:
CENSUS STATISTICS, FAILURES BY STATE,
FAILURES BY REGION

GRADUATES FROM CONFEDERATE STATES, 1830–1860

Class	Total	Alabama	Arkansas	Florida	Georgia	Louisiana	Mississippi	No. Carolina	So. Carolina	Tennessee	Texas	Virginia
1830	42				1	1		2	1	2		2
1831	33	1			1			2	1	1		2
1832	45	2					1	1	1	3		4
1833	43				1			1	2	2		5
1834	36	1		1	1				1	1		5
1835	56				3			3	2	1		4
1836	49	1						2	2	1		5
1837	50	2			2			2		1		6
1838	45				2	2	2	1	2	2		3
1839	31							1	1	1		1
1840	42			1		1		3		3		4
Subtotal	472	7		2	11	4	3	18	13	18		41 (117)
1841	52		1					3	3	1		7
1842	56	1			1	1	1	2	3	1		7
1843	39									1		3
1844	25		1					2		1		1
1845	41			1	2	1		2		1		2
1846	59				4			1	1	3		5
1847	38								2			2
1848	38		1		2			2	3	2		1

Class	Total	Alabama	Arkansas	Florida	Georgia	Louisiana	Mississippi	No. Carolina	So. Carolina	Tennessee	Texas	Virginia
1849	43			1	2					2		5
1850	44	2				2	2	2	1	2		2
Subtotal	435	3	3	2	11	4	3	14	13	14		35 (102)
1851	42	1				1		3		3		2
1852	43	2					1	2		1		
1853	52	1		1	3				2	2	1	5
1854	46	2			2	1	2	2	3	1	1	4
1855	34				1	1		2				
1856	48	1			4		1	1		2		2
1857	39	2			2				2	1	1	3
1858	27	1						2	1	1		
1859	22	1								1		1
1860	41	1	1					2	2			
Subtotal	394	12	1	1	12	3	4	14	10	12	3	17 (89)

RECAPITULATION

Years	Total Confederate State Graduates	Total Graduates	Percentage of Confederates
1830–1840	117	472	24.8
1841–1850	102	435	23.4
1851–1860	89	394	22.6
TOTAL	308	1,301	23.7

Source: Boynton, 322–23; *Register of Cadets*, 1963, 215–48.

Cadets admitted from Confederate States, 1830–1860	701
Total cadets admitted, 1830–1860	2,513
Confederate percentage of total admissions	27.9

Source: Boynton, 320–21.

CENSUS STATISTICS, CONFEDERATE STATES 1830–1860

State	White Males Between Fifteen and Twenty				
	1830ₐ	1840	1850	1860	
Alabama	21,638	16,222	30,145	29,889	
Arkansas	2,898	3,863	11,930	17,810	
Florida	1,804	1,305	3,077	4,099	
Georgia	33,770	20,987	37,075	33,354	
Louisiana	9,459	7,218	14,103	16,295	
Mississippi	8,214	8,662	21,105	19,620	
No. Carolina	55,979	24,819	37,577	33,976	
So. Carolina	30,458	13,719	18,842	15,994	
Tennessee	65,291	34,218	54,444	46,727	
Texas			10,346	21,651	
Virginia	80,234	38,263	59,955	56,601	
					AGG.
Subtotals	309,745	169,276	298,599	296,016	1,073,636
Entire U.S.	1,242,698	756,106	1,225,575	1,402,432	4,626,811
% of Confederates in Total	24.9	22.4	24.4	21.1	23.2

Sources: *Sixth Census of the United States . . . As Corrected by the Department of State in 1840,* (Washington, D.C.: Thomas Allen, 1841), 474.

Historical Statistics of the United States, Colonial Times to 1957, (Washington, D.C.: Government Printing Office, 1961), 10.

U.S. Congress, House, *Abstract of the Returns of the Fifth Census,* 22d Cong., 1st sess., May 1832, 48.

The Seventh Census of the United States: 1850, (Washington, D.C.: Robert Armstrong, Public Printer, 1851), 13.

Population of the United States in 1860 . . . (Washington, D.C.: Government Printing Office, 1864), 593.

ᵃThis figure includes ages between ten and twenty. The Census of 1830 did not break the group down further.

CADET STATISTICS WITH RESPECT TO STATE
OF BIRTH OR RESIDENCE 1833–1860

State	Admitted	Academic Number	Failure %	Dismissed No.	Dismissed %	Graduated No.	Graduated %
New Hampshire	29	3	10.3	0	.0	23	79.3
Indiana	73	9	12.3	0	.0	36	49.3
Massachusetts	94	17	18.1	3	3.2	61	64.9
At Large	275	52	18.9	4	1.5	120	43.6
Maine	58	11	19.0	1	1.7	34	58.6
New York	293	61	20.8	9	3.1	172	58.7
Vermont	31	7	22.6	0	.0	24	77.4
Ohio	159	39	24.5	5	3.1	80	50.3
Arkansas	12	3	25.0	0	.0	4	33.3
Utah	4	1	25.0	0	.0	1	25.0
Connecticut	43	11	25.6	2	4.7	22	51.2
Kentucky	96	25	26.0	1	1.0	49	51.0
Pennsylvania	223	63	28.3	8	3.6	120	53.8
No. Carolina	87	25	28.7	4	4.6	37	42.5
Illinois	60	18	30.0	2	3.3	25	41.7
Delaware	13	4	30.8	0	.0	9	69.2
Wisconsin	13	4	30.8	1	7.7	5	38.5
Louisiana	43	14	32.6	0	.0	10	23.3
Dist. of Columbia	33	11	33.3	1	3.0	21	63.6
Rhode Island	18	6	33.3	0	.0	11	61.1
Texas	9	3	33.3	0	.0	3	33.3
New Mexico	3	1	33.3	0	.0	0	.0
Maryland	65	22	33.8	1	1.5	33	50.8
Georgia	79	27	34.2	1	1.3	32	40.5
Virginia	157	54	34.4	5	3.2	85	54.1
Michigan	23	9	39.1	0	.0	11	47.8
Alabama	62	25	40.3	3	4.8	22	35.5
Missouri	32	13	40.6	1	3.1	13	40.6
Mississippi	36	15	41.7	2	5.6	10	27.8
Tennessee	107	45	42.1	4	3.7	38	35.5
New Jersey	49	21	42.8	2	4.1	25	51.0
Florida	11	5	45.5	0	.0	5	45.5
So. Carolina	71	33	46.5	4	5.6	33	46.5
Kansas	2	1	50.0	0	.0	0	.0
Oregon	2	1	50.0	0	.0	0	.0
Iowa	19	12	63.2	0	.0	5	26.3
California	6	4	66.6	1	1.7	0	.0
Minnesota	3	2	66.6	0	.0	1	33.3
TOTALS	2,393	677	28.3	65	2.7	1,180	49.3

CADET STATISTICS WITH RESPECT TO REGION 1833–1860

State	Admitted	Academic Failures	Dismissed	Graduated
Confederate				
Virginia	157	54	5	85
Florida	11	5	0	5
Tennessee	107	45	4	8
No. Carolina	87	25	4	37
Louisiana	43	14	0	10
So. Carolina	71	33	4	33
Alabama	62	25	3	22
Mississippi	36	15	2	10
Georgia	79	27	1	32
Texas	9	3	0	3
Arkansas	12	3	0	4
TOTALS	674	249 (36.9%)	23 (3.4%)	249 (36.9%)

Remaining 153 voluntarily resigned for unknown reasons.

State	Admitted	Academic Failures	Dismissed	Graduated
Border				
Kentucky	96	25	1	49
Maryland	65	22	1	33
Dist. of Columbia	33	11	1	21
Missouri	32	13	1	13
TOTALS	226	71 (31.4%)	4 (1.8%)	116 (51.3%)
Middle Atlantic				
New York	293	61	9	172
Pennsylvania	223	63	8	120
Delaware	13	4	0	9
New Jersey	49	21	2	25
TOTALS	578	149 (25.8%)	19 (3.3%)	326 (56.4%)
New England				
Massachusetts	94	17	3	61
Rhode Island	18	6	0	11
Maine	58	11	1	34
New Hampshire	29	3	0	23
Connecticut	43	11	2	22
Vermont	31	7	0	24
TOTALS	273	55 (20.1%)	6 (2.2%)	175 (64.1%)

State	Admitted	Academic Failures	Dismissed	Graduated
Midwest				
Indiana	73	9	0	36
Ohio	159	39	5	80
Michigan	23	9	0	11
Illinois	60	18	2	25
Iowa	19	12	0	5
Wisconsin	13	4	1	5
Minnesota	3	2	0	1
Kansas	2	1	0	0
TOTALS	352	94 (26.7%)	8 (2.3%)	163 (46.3%)
Far West and Southwest				
California	6	4	1	0
Oregon	2	1	0	0
New Mexico	3	1	0	0
Utah	4	1	0	1
TOTALS	15	7 (46.7%)	1 (6.7%)	1 (6.7%)

RECAPITULATION

Regions Arranged in Order of Percentage of Academic Failures

Far West and Southwest 46.7%
Confederate 36.9%
Border 31.4%
Midwest 26.7%
Middle Atlantic 25.8%
New England 20.1%

Regions Arranged in Order of Percentage of Graduates

New England 64.1%
Middle Atlantic 56.4%
Border 51.3%
Midwest 46.3%
Confederate 36.9%
Far West and Southwest 6.7%

Appendix Eight

PARTICIPATION IN THE CIVIL WAR, GRADUATES, CLASSES OF 1833–1861

Class	Number Living in 1861	Confederate	Union	Northerners in Confederate Army*	Southerners in Union Army*
1833	23	6	11	1	1
1834	21	6	11	3	1
1835	32	6	18		
1836	27	4	13	1	
1837	32	10	18	2	1
1838	26	10	11		
1839	20	3	15		
1840	28	10	15	2	2
1841	37	11	23	3	2
1842	37	13	21	1	2
1843	27	4	18	3	
1844	15	3	7	1	
1845	25	7	15		1
1846	43	10	28		1
1847	33	4	27	1	
1848	28	10	16	2	1
1849	31	13	24	1	4
1850	40	18	19	1	
1851	37	8	29	1	5
1852	40	12	24	2	2
1853	48	12	35		4
1854	39	14	24	2	3
1855	31	6	25	3	1
1856	46	10	36	1	2
1857	37	15	22		2

Class	Number Living in 1861	Confederate	Union	Northerners in Confederate Army*	Southerners in Union Army*
1858	26	11	14		1
1859	22	5	17	1	1
1860	41	9	32		1
1861 (May)	45	6	39		1
1861 (June)	34	3	31		
TOTALS	977	259	638	(32)*	(39)*

26.5% of the graduates from these classes served in the Confederate Army, 65.1% in the Union Army.

*Figures included in appropriate columns to the left.

Sources: *Register of Cadets*, 1948, 386–88; 1963, 218–51.

Elsworth Eliot, *West Point In The Confederacy* (New York: G. A. Baker & Co., 1941), 20–23, 31–32.

Appendix Nine

ACADEMIC FAILURES BY CLASS AND SUBJECT
1861–1865

First Class	
Class	*Conduct*
1861	1
1862	
1863	
1864	
1865	
Subtotal	1

Second Class						
Class	*Conduct*	*Drawing*	*Natural Philosophy*	*Natural Philosophy & Chemistry*	*Chemistry*	*Conduct & Natural Philosophy*
1861						
1862						
1863		1	1			
1864	1			2	1	
1865			4			1
Subtotal	1	1	5	2	1	1

Third Class

Class	Conduct	Mathematics	French	French & Conduct	Mathematics & Conduct	Drawing	Mathematics & French
1861	2						
1862		2			1		
1863		3	1				2
1864	1	8					
1865		10				1	
Subtotal	3	23	1		1	1	2

Fourth Class

Class	Mathematics	Mathematics & Conduct	Mathematics, English, & Conduct	English	Conduct	Mathematics & English	Mathematics & French
1861	2	1					
1862	13	2	1	1	6	3	
1863	11				1	1	4
1864	8	4			3	5	1
1865	12					2	
Subtotal	46	7	1	1	10	11	5

Fifth Class

Class	Mathematics	Conduct	
1861	4	1	(fifth class discontinued after 1861)

APPENDIX NINE

RECAPITULATION

Total Failures		Total Admissions		Rate of Failure Failures/Admissions
First Class	1	1861–1865	265	48.7%
Second Class	11			
Third Class	31			
Fourth Class	81			
Fifth Class	5			
	129			

SUBJECT IN ORDER OF MAGNITUDE

Fourth Class	Mathematics	46
Third Class	Mathematics	23
Fourth Class	Mathematics & English	11
Fourth Class	Conduct	10
Fourth Class	Mathematics & Conduct	7
Second Class	Natural Philosophy	5
Fourth Class	Mathematics & French	5
Fifth Class	Mathematics	4
Third Class	Conduct	3
Second Class	Natural Philosophy & Chemistry	2
Third Class	Mathematics & French	2
First Class	Conduct	1
Second Class	Conduct	1
Second Class	Drawing	1
Second Class	Chemistry	1
Second Class	Natural Philosophy & Conduct	1
Third Class	Mathematics & Conduct	1
Third Class	French	1
Third Class	Drawing	1
Fourth Class	Mathematics, English, & Conduct	1
Fourth Class	English	1
Fifth Class	Conduct	1

Appendix Ten

ADMISSIONS AND GRADUATIONS

CLASSES ENTERING BETWEEN
1866 and 1870

Year Entered	Number Entering	Number of These Who Graduated	Percentage of Graduates
1866	70	52	74.3
1867	55	37	67.3
1868	76	55	72.4
1869	70	44	62.9
1870	65	46	70.8
TOTALS	336	234	69.6

PERCENTAGE OF ACADEMIC FAILURES (102/336), 30.25%

Sources: SR 8 and 9.

"Cadets Admitted Book," 1846–1912, USMA Archives.

Appendix Eleven

ACADEMIC FAILURES

CLASSES ENTERING BETWEEN
1866 and 1870

Fourth Class

Class	Mathematics	Mathematics & English	English	Mathematics & French	Mathematics, French, & English	Conduct	French
1866	7	6	2	2	1		
1867	8	3		1		1	
1868	4			4		2	
1869	5						
1870	8			4			2
1871	4			2			
TOTALS	36	9	2	13	1	3	2 (66)

Third Class

Class	Mathematics	Conduct	French, Spanish, & Conduct	Mathematics & French
1866				
1867	10			
1868	3	1		
1869	1			
1870	4	1	1	2
1871	4			
TOTALS	22	2	1	2 (27)

Class	Natural Philosophy	Second Class Natural Philosophy & Chemistry	Artillery & Infantry	Chemistry	
1868	1	3		2	
1869		1			
1870					
1871	3		1		
1872	2	2	1		
1873	2				
1874					
TOTALS	8	6	2	2	(18)

Class	First Class Mineralogy & Geology	Engineering	
1870			
1871			
1872	1		
1873		1	
1874			
TOTALS	1	1	(2)

RECAPITULATION

Fourth Class	66
Third Class	27
Second Class	18
First Class	2
Total	113

FAILURES IN ORDER OF MAGNITUDE

	Subject	Percentage of Total Failures
Fourth Class	Mathematics	31.9
Third Class	Mathematics	19.5
Fourth Class	Mathematics & French	11.5
Fourth Class	Mathematics & English	8.0
Second Class	Natural Philosophy	7.1
Second Class	Natural Philosophy & Chemistry	5.3
Fourth Class	Conduct	2.7
Fourth Class	English	1.8
Fourth Class	French	1.8
Third Class	Conduct	1.8
Third Class	Mathematics & French	1.8
Second Class	Artillery & Infantry Tactics	1.8
Second Class	Chemistry	1.8
Fourth Class	Mathematics, French, & English	.9
Third Class	French, Spanish, & Conduct	.9
First Class	Mineralogy & Geology	.9
First Class	Engineering	.9

Sources: SR 8 and 9.

Appendix
Twelve

CONTEMPORARY FOREIGN MILITARY SCHOOLS, 1833–1866

This appendix examines the undergraduate military educational institutions of Great Britain, France, and Eastern Europe from the standpoints of mission, structure of the governing body of the school, makeup of the student body, means of gaining admission, entrance requirements, curriculum, and assignment of graduates to the services. In comparing these characteristics with the corresponding features of West Point it becomes readily apparent that the British and continental concepts of military education varied drastically from those characteristic of the United States. Briefly stated, the fundamental differences were the British and French demands for higher standards of attainment prior to admission, early professional specialization, and shorter periods of attendance on the one hand and the East European system of commencing military education with eleven-year-old boys on the other.

L'ÉCOLE POLYTECHNIQUE (FRANCE)

A. *Missions.*
 (1) To provide officers for the artillery, ordnance, staff corps, and engineers of the army.
 (2) To provide naval architects, marine artillerists, and officers for the Hydrographic Corps.
 (3) To provide civil servants, mining, telegraphic, and civil engineers.
B. *Organizational Structure.*
 The school was under the jurisdiction of the Ministry of War. A commandant was the head. Under him came in order of rank, the director of studies, the professors, teachers, and examiners.
 Operations were supervised and controlled by four boards—administration, discipline, instruction, and improvement. The first three of these were composed of members of the school staff. The board of improvement, which supervised the curriculum and made changes where required, consisted of the commandant, his as-

sistant, the director of studies, two delegates from the Department of Public Works, one delegate from the Ministry of the Navy, one delegate from the Ministry of Interior, three delegates from the Ministry of War, two delegates from the Academy of Sciences, together with three professors and two examiners from the school.

c. *The Student Body.*

Three hundred and fifty cadets, arranged in a battalion of four companies.

d. *Means of Admission.*

Competitive examinations open to all citizens.

e. *Entrance Requirements.*

(1) The candidate had to be between sixteen and twenty years of age. (Soldiers could be admitted up to age twenty-five). He had to hold a bachelor of science degree from a lycée.

(2) Entrance Examinations.

Arithmetic, geometry, algebra, plane and spherical trigonometry, analytical geometry, solid geometry, descriptive geometry, mechanics, natural philosophy, chemistry, French, German, Latin (optional), and drawing.

f. *The Curriculum.*

(1) Course lasted two years. Each year was divided into three terms. Each of the first two terms was four months in length and consisted of instruction by lecture. The third term, two months in length, was devoted to individual study and the final examinations.

(2) First Year.

(a) First Term. Calculus, descriptive geometry, physics, chemistry, French literature, German, and drawing (figure and landscape).

(b) Second Term. Mechanics, geodesy, physics, chemistry, French literature, German, and drawing (figure and landscape).

(3) Second Year.

(a) First Term. Calculus, mechanics, physics, chemistry, French literature, German, and drawing (figure and landscape).

(b) Second Term. Stereotomy, the art of war and fortification, topography, architecture and construction, physics, chemistry, French literature, German, and drawing (figure and landscape).

(4) Military Instruction. There were three periods of infantry drill each week in the spring and summer. Also, fencing and gymnastics were offered on a voluntary basis. There were no provisions for instruction in riding, swimming, or firing weapons.

g. *Assignment of Graduates.*

Each subject in the curriculum was assigned a numerical value and weight for use in determining order of merit. Graduates selected their service based on order of merit standing. The usual preferences in order of priority were: civil and mining engineering, ordnance, naval architecture, military engineering, army artillery, army staff corps, the hydrographical corps, the Tobacco Department, the Telegraph Department (Ministry of the Interior), the navy, and marine artillery. After selecting a branch the graduate was sent to an appropriate school of application.

THE SCHOOL FOR INFANTRY AND CAVALRY AT ST. CYR (FRANCE)

A. *Mission.*

To provide officers for the infantry and cavalry.

B. *Organizational Structure.*

The school was under the jurisdiction of the War Department. A commandant was the head of the school. Under him came a director of studies, the professors, teachers, and examiners. There were two supervisory councils—a council of instruction and a council of administration—each composed of representatives of the commandant's office, the instructional staff, and the administrative staff.

C. *The Student Body.*

The corps of cadets consisted of between five hundred and six hundred boys, organized into a battalion of eight companies.

D. *Means of Admission.*

Competitive examinations open to all citizens.

E. *Entrance Requirements.*

(1) The candidates had to be between sixteen and twenty years of age. (Soldiers could be admitted up to age twenty-five). Each candidate had to hold a bachelor of science degree from a lycée.

(2) Entrance Examinations.

Arithmetic, algebra, geometry, plane trigonometry, solid geometry, French grammar, German, drawing, physics, chemistry, French history, and French geography.

F. *The Curriculum.*

(1) The course lasted two years.

(2) First Year. Descriptive geometry, physics, military literature, history, military geography, German, landscape and military drawing.

(3) Second Year. Topography, fortification, artillery, military law, military administration, military art and history, German, and military drawing.

(4) Military Instruction. Cadets drilled two hours daily. Cavalry cadets rode three hours daily; infantry cadets rode one hour a week. All cadets received instruction in infantry, cavalry, and artillery.

G. *Assignment of Graduates.*

(1) Graduates were arranged by general order of merit similar to L'École. The top twenty-five to twenty-seven men in each class were allowed to compete for appointments to the staff college after graduation from St. Cyr.

(2) Graduates were permitted to select their regiments according to their order of merit standing.

ROYAL MILITARY ACADEMY AT WOOLWICH (GREAT BRITAIN)

A. *Mission.*

To provide officers for the artillery and engineers.

B. *Organizational Structure.*

The academy was under the jurisdiction of the secretary of war. A council on military education, consisting of high-ranking officers and members of the staff of the academy exercised general supervision over the operation. A governor was at the head of the academy. The professors and instructors came under him.

C. *The Student Body.*

Approximately two hundred cadets were divided into five classes, or terms. A cadet spent six months in each term.

D. *Means of Admission.*

Competitive examinations open to all citizens.

E. *Entrance Requirements.*

(1) The candidate had to be between sixteen and nineteen years old.

(2) The entrance examinations included mathematics (arithmetic, algebra, Euclid, plane and spherical trigonometry, and calculus), statics, dynamics, hydrostatics, English composition, English history, geography, the classics, French, German, chemistry, mineralogy, geology, and drawing. All candidates had to take the mathematics examination and up to four of the other subjects.

F. *The Curriculum.*

(1) The course lasted two and one-half years. A cadet could fail one term and remain, but three years was the limit.

(2) Program of Instruction. (Each class lasted six months).

Fifth class (lowest): mathematics, practical geometry, topography, drawing, French, German, gymnastics, infantry drills.

Fourth class: same program as fifth class with the addition of fortifications.

Third class: surveying, higher mathematics, practical geometry, topographical drawing, French, German.

Second class: artillery, surveying, riding, chemistry, French, German, military history, mechanics, natural philosophy.

First class (senior): military history, chemistry, artillery practice, riding, surveying, drawing, mechanics, natural philosophy.

G. *Assignment of Graduates.*

Cadets chose the artillery or engineers, according to class standing.

THE ROYAL MILITARY COLLEGE AT SANDHURST (GREAT BRITAIN)

A. *Mission.*

To provide officers for the infantry and cavalry.

B. *Organizational Structure.*

Like Woolwich, the college was under the jurisdiction of the Secretary of War, and supervised by the council on military education. A governor was in charge of Sandhurst; the instructors and professors were under him.

c. *The Student Body.*

Approximately 180 cadets were organized into three terms. Each term lasted six months. At the end of the first term a cadet could, by passing a special examination, advance directly to the third term. A cadet who failed one term could be held over, but for no longer than two years.

D. *Means of Admission.*

Competitive examinations open to all citizens. Also, the sovereign could make appointments. Candidates with university training were exempt from the entrance examinations.

E. *Entrance Requirements.*

(1) All candidates had to be between sixteen and nineteen years old.

(2) Entrance examinations: The classics, mathematics (algebra, trigonometry, arithmetic, Euclid), English grammar, modern languages, history and geography, natural science, experimental science, geometric drawing, free-hand drawing.

F. *The Curriculum.*

(1) The length of the course varied from time to time; generally speaking, it was between eighteen months and two years in length.

(2) First Term. Mathematics (algebra, trigonometry), practical mechanics, hydrostatics, field fortifications, military history and geography, drawing, military surveying, French, German, chemistry, geology.

(3) Second Term. Same as first.

(4) Third Term. Same as first and second terms except that permanent fortifications was studied in place of field fortifications.

(5) Military Training. Gymnastics was taught in the first term; gun drills and riding in the second term, and riding in the third term. Infantry drill was taught for eighty minutes daily throughout the course.

G. *Assignment of Graduates.*

Cadets who completed the course of instruction in three terms or less were given commissions in the infantry or cavalry without being required to purchase them. Those who took four terms to complete the course were given first priority in purchasing commissions.

THE UNDERGRADUATE LEVEL SYSTEM OF MILITARY EDUCATION IN PRUSSIA

Prussian military education was centered about four junior cadet schools, located in the provinces, and one upper cadet school at Berlin. All were under the command of a single officer.

Boys entered the junior schools at the age of ten or eleven and remained until they were fifteen or sixteen. Although the junior school cadets wore uniforms, lived in dormitories, and were subject to military discipline, the academic program of the junior schools was not military, but similar to what was offered at civilian preparatory schools.

Boys who had graduated from one of the junior cadet schools could enter the senior cadet school at Berlin without examination. Boys from civilian preparatory schools could also enter the senior school at Berlin but only after passing a qualifying examination.

The Berlin Upper Cadet School program consisted of a three-year curriculum.

First Year. Latin, German, plane and solid geometry, quadratics, geography, ancient and medieval history, natural philosophy, military drawing, religion, conversational French.

Second Year. Latin, advanced algebra, trigonometry, physical geography, modern history, natural philosophy (heat, electricity, magnetism, sound, light), conversational French, history of German literature, German composition, military drawing.

Third Year. Arms, munitions, artillery, fortification, tactics, military literature, practical exercises, military drawing and surveying, French and German, mental philosophy, chemistry, calculus.

After completing the second year cadets could be admitted to the army as aspirant officers. They joined their regiments and attended division schools while engaged in their military duties. When they felt qualified, they could take the examinations for commissions.

About one-third of each class, the top students, were held over at the Upper Cadet School for the third year program. On graduation they were commissioned immediately without further examination.

The Bavarian, Austrian, and Russian systems were similar to the Prussian.

Sources: Henry Barnard, *Military Schools and Courses of Institutions in the Science and Art of War*, rev. ed. (New York: E. Steiger, 1872).

Rene Desmazes, *Saint-Cyr, son histoire ses gloires-ses leçons* (Paris: La Saint-Cyrienne, 1948).

L'École Polytechnique, livre du centenaire, 1794–1894, 3 vols. (Paris: Gauthier Villars et fils, 1895).

Frederick G. Guggisberg, *"The Shop": The Story of the Royal Military Academy* (London: Cassell and Co., 1900).

Paul Jazet, *Histoire de L'École Spéciale Militaire de Saint-Cyr*, (Paris: Delagrave, 1893).

Abbreviations
Used in
Notes

AGO	Office of the Adjutant General, U.S. Army
ALB	Adjutant's Letter Book, USMA
ALR	Adjutant's Letters Received, USMA
DAB	*Dictionary of American Biography*
ELS	Engineer Letters Sent
LR	Letters Received
LS	Letters Sent
MA	"Military Academy" when used with correspondence of chief of engineers; "Military Affairs" when used with correspondence of Secretary of War
OCE	Office of the Chief of Engineers, U.S. Army
OR	*The War of the Rebellion: A Compilation of the Official Records of the Union and Confederate Armies*
OSW	Office of the Secretary of War
SLB	Superintendent's Letter Book, USMA
SR	Staff Records
USMA Regulations	*Regulations Established for the Government of the Military Academy at West Point*

Notes

CHAPTER ONE

1. U.S. War Department, *Report of the Secretary of War*, 1844, no. 6, Report of the Chief Engineers, 205.

2. Edgar Denton III, "The Formative Years of the United States Military Academy, 1775–1833" (Ph.D. dissertation, Syracuse University, 1964), 1–54, 79, 81–83, 89–91, 98–105, 121–280, passim; Theodore J. Crackel, "The Founding of West Point: Jefferson and the Politics of Security," *Armed Forces and Society* 7 (Summer 1981): 529–37.

3. Crackel, "Founding of West Point," 529–43.

4. Francis B. Heitman, *Historical Register and Dictionary of the United States Army, From Its Origins, September 29, 1789, to March 2, 1903*, 2 vols. (Washington, D.C.: Government Printing Office, 1903), 1:582; Leonard D. White, *The Jacksonians, A Study in Administrative History: 1829–1861* (New York: Free Press, 1954), 189; William A. Ganoe, *The History of the United States Army* (Ashton, Md.: Eric Lundberg, 1964), 191; Francis P. Prucha, *Army Life on the Western Frontier, Selections from Official Reports Made Between 1826 and 1845 by (Colonel) George Croghan* (Norman, Okla.: Univ. of Oklahoma Press, 1958), xiii.

5. Ganoe, 162, 196; Russell F. Weigley, *History of the United States Army* (New York: Macmillan, 1967), 163–65.

6. William H. Goetzmann, *Exploration and Empire: The Explorer and the Scientist in the Winning of the West* (New York: W. W. Norton & Co., 1978), 316.

7. Weigley, *History of the Army*, 163; Robert M. Utley, *Frontiersmen in Blue: The United States Army and the Indian, 1848–1865* (New York: Macmillan, 1967), 2–5, 108, 349; *The Centennial of the United States Military Academy*, 2 vols. (Washington, D.C.: Government Printing Office, 1904), 1:835 ff.; Goetzmann, *Exploration and Empire*, 184, 271, 285, 286–91, 306–22, 325–28; Robert V. Hine, *The American West, An Interpretive History*, 2d ed. (Boston: Little, Brown and Co., 1984), 63, 159; William H. Goetzmann, *Army Explorations in the American West, 1803–1863* (Lincoln: Univ. of Nebraska Press, 1979), 9–14, 267.

8. Walter Millis, *Arms and Men: A Study of American Military History* (New York: G. P. Putnam's Sons, 1956), 97–98; John K. Mahon, *History of the Second Seminole War 1835–1842* (Gainesville: Univ. of Florida Press, 1967), 321–27; Weigley, 160–63.

9. Utley, 18, 39, 40–41, 309; Ganoe, 175, 202, 218 ff.; Weigley, 168–69; Francis P. Prucha, *Broadax and Bayonet: The Role of the United States Army in the Development of the Northwest, 1815–1860* (Madison: State Historical Society of Wisconsin, 1953), 36–45.

10. Heitman, 2:596, 626; White, 189; *Official Army Registers, 1833–1860*; Marvin A. Kreidberg and Martin G. Henry, *History of Mobilization in the United States Army, 1775–1945* (Washington, D.C.: Government Printing Office, 1955), 61–95; *The War of the Rebellion: A Compilation of the Official Records of the Union and Confederate Armies*, 4 ser., 68 vols., (Washington, D.C.: Government Printing Office, 1880–1902), ser. 1, 1:524; ser. 3, 1:22, 301, 775 (hereafter cited as O.R.); Fred A. Shannon, *The Organization and Adminis-*

tration of the Union Army, 1861–1865, 2 vols. (1928; reprint, Gloucester, Mass.: Peter Smith, 1965), 1:27.

11. *Registers,* 1833–60; Heitman, 2:584–97; White, 190–94.

12. Russell F. Weigley, *Quartermaster General of the Union Army, a Biography of M. C. Meigs* (New York: Columbia Univ. Press, 1959), 31–112; Montgomery Meigs, diary, 1838–43, John M. Toner MSS, 16793, Library of Congress; Cadet James B. McPherson to Catherine Stem, 13 Feb. 1853, no. 106, Stem Papers, Rutherford B. Hayes Presidential Center, Fremont, Oh.; James L. Morrison, Jr., "Getting Through West Point: The Cadet Memoirs of John C. Tidball, Class of 1848," *Civil War History* 26 (Dec. 1980): 323.

13. Chief of Engineers to Superintendent, USMA, 13 July 1848. Office, Chief of Engineers, Letters Sent, 40 Record Group 94, National Archives (hereafter cited as OCELS); Heitman, 2:582–95; *Centennial* 2:106.

14. Weigley, *History of the Army,* 166–67; Ganoe, 170.

15. Statistics gathered from *Register of Graduates and Former Cadets of the United States Military Academy, 1802–1963* (West Point, N.Y.: West Point Alumni Foundation, 1963), 218–56; *The Centennial of the United States Military Academy at West Point, 1802–1902,* 2 vols. (Washington, D.C.: Government Printing Office, 1904), 1:486–87; Gustavus W. Smith, "John Newton," *Annual Reunion U.S. Military Academy, 10 June 1895* (West Point, N.Y.: Association of Graduates, 1895), 107–10; Goetzmann, *Exploration and Empire,* 363; William H. Baumer, Jr., *Not All Warriors: Portraits of 19th Century West Pointers Who Gained Fame in other than Military Fields* (New York: Smith and Durrell, 1941), xi; Heitman, 2:580–88.

16. William E. Birkhimer, *Historical Sketch of the Organization, Administration, Material, and Tactics of the Artillery, United States Army* (Washington, D.C.: James Chapman, 1864), 169–73; Weigley, *History of the Army,* 142; Ganoe, 159; Heitman, 2:584–97.

17. Birkhimer, 57–75; Weigley, *History of the Army,* 139–40; Journal of John W. Turner, Third Regiment of Artillery, 26 Mar.–28 July 1856, photocopy in possession of author, given to him by its owner, Mr. J. W. Turner, York, Pa., now deceased.

18. Heitman, 2:584–97.

19. Ibid.

20. Ganoe, 22; Heitman, 2:580–83; Utley, 22.

21. Utley, 22–27; U.S. Army, Office of the Adjutant General, Order no. 69, 14 Aug. 1833, USMA Post Orders, 6, USMA Archives; Ganoe, 173; Heitman, 2:584, 586, 596; Weigley, *History of the Army,* 159, 190.

22. Heitman, 2:583–97; *Army Registers,* 1848–60.

23. Utley, 58–77; James L. Morrison, Jr., ed., *The Memoirs of Henry Heth* (Westport, Conn.: Greenwood Press, 1974), 81, 94, 121–37.

24. Ganoe, 192; Weigley, *History of the Army,* 189.

25. Oliver S. Spaulding, *The United States Army in War and Peace* (New York: G. P. Putnam's Sons, 1937), 147–53, 240; Weigley, *History of the Army,* 189; Utley, 50; Ganoe, 192.

26. Philip St. George Cooke, *Scenes and Adventures in the Army, or Romance of Military Life* (Philadelphia: Lindsay & Blakiston, 1857), 205–21; White, 188–91; Russell F. Weigley, *The American Way of War, A History of United States Military Strategy and Policy* (New York: Macmillan, 1973), 69–71; Russell F. Weigley, *Towards an American Army, Military Thought From Washington to Marshall* (New York: Columbia Univ. Press, 1962), 36, 176, 189–90; Utley, 17; William B. Skelton, "Officers and Politicians: The Origin of Army Politics in the United States Before the Civil War," *Armed Forces and Society* 6 (Fall 1979): 27, 40; Robert M. Utley, "The Army and the Frontier, 1848–1890," taped lecture, *Voices of History* (Michael Glazier, Inc., M-9); T. Harry Williams, *The History of American Wars from*

Colonial Times to World War I (New York: Alfred A. Knopf, 1981), 195; John K. Mahon, *History of the Militia and the National Guard* (New York: Macmillan, 1983), 78–84.

27. *Army Registers, 1841–61*; White, 191–94; Charles W. Elliott, *Winfield Scott, the Soldier and the Man* (New York: Macmillan, 1937), 385–87, 574 ff.; Winfield Scott, *Memoirs* (New York: Sheldon & Co., 1864) 258–59, 589–93; Hudson Strode, *Jefferson Davis*, 3 vols. (New York: Harcourt, Brace, 1955), 1:287–90; Weigley, *History of the Army*, 135, 178–79, 193–94.

28. J. D. Hittle, *The Military Staff, Its History and Development*, 2d ed. (Harrisburg, Pa.: Military Service Publishing Co., 1952), 175–85; Weigley, *History of the Army*, 315.

29. Hittle, 166; White, 191–93, citing U.S. Senate Exec. Doc. 11, 35th Cong., 1st sess., *Report of the Secretary of War, 1857*, 9; Weigley, *History of the Army*, 135, 178–79, 315.

30. Heitman, 1:573, 582, 326, 228–29, 150, 966.

31. The statistics on the graduates in the regular army and their distribution in the corps and regiments are derived from a detailed analysis of the *Official Army Registers, 1833–60*.

32. John L. Smith entered the corps of engineers from civilian life in 1813 and served until he died in 1858. Smith was made a brevet colonel for services in the Mexican War. Heitman, 1:900; Thomas H. Hamersley, *Complete Regular Army Register of the United States for One Hundred Years, (1799–1879)* (Washington, D.C.: T. H. Hamersley, 1880), 768.

33. Secretary of War to Hon. John McKeon, H.R., 20 Jan. 1837, Office of the Secretary of War, Letters Sent, Military Affairs, 17:95, RG 107, NA (hereafter cited as OSWLSMA); Secretary of War to George W. Claxton, 16 June 1840, ibid., 22:269; Chief of Engineers to Secretary of War, 9 Mar. 1848, OCELS, Abstract of Letter Book, 2:21, RG 94, NA.

34. *Congressional Globe*, 23d Cong., 1st sess., 1834, 1:452; ibid., 24th Cong., 2nd sess., 1837, 4:247; "Miscellany," *Army and Navy Chronicle* 9 (Sept. 1839): 182–83; *Congressional Globe*, 35th Cong., 1st sess., 1858, 36:1962–63; Weigley, *History of the Army*, 154–55.

35. Ganoe, 206; *Army Registers, 1836–38, 1846–48, 1855–56*; Weigley, *History of the Army*, 182–83; Utley, 34.

36. Secretary of War to Vice-President R. M. Johnson, 24 Oct. 1847, OSWLSMA, 17:79; Secretary of War to candidates, 1 Aug. 1838, ibid., 12:305; U.S. Army, Office of the Adjutant General, General Orders no. 14, 23 June 1859; "Proceedings of Examining Board," 5 Sept. 1839, USMA Archives; White, 200.

37. Mahan to Secretary of War, 1 Aug. 1840, Poinsett Papers, 15:11, Historical Society of Pennsylvania MSS (USMA microfilm).

38. "Miscellany," *Army and Navy Chronicle* 9 (Sept. 1839): 182–83.

39. "Appointments in the Army," *Army and Navy Chronicle* 8 (Jan. 1839): 50.

40. *USMA Regulations, 1832*, 22; 1857, 38; Superintendent to Chief of Engineers, 17 Sept. 1839, Superintendent's Letter Book, 1:262, USMA Archives (hereafter cited as SLB).

41. Secretary of War to Taylor, 15 Mar. 1838, OSWLSMA, 18:457; U.S. Congress, House, Ex. Doc., no. 88, 24th Cong., 2nd sess., 1–3; White, 201; Weigley, *History of the Army*, 154.

42. Samuel P. Huntington, *The Soldier and the State: The Theory and Policy of Civil-Military Relations* (Cambridge: Harvard Univ. Press, Belknap Press, 1959), 206; Utley, 35; White, 194–96.

43. Ulysses S. Grant, *Personal Memoirs*, 2 vols. (New York: Charles L. Webster, 1885), 1:44; White, 187–88.

44. White, 187–88; Weigley, *History of the Army*, 156; Huntington, 224–27; Utley, 158.

45. Weigley, *History of the Army*, 168; John Hope Franklin, *The Militant South* (Cambridge: Harvard Univ. Press, Belknap Press, 1956), 138–70.

46. "United States Military Academy," *Army and Navy Chronicle* 2 (Sept. 1839): 182;

201

U.S. Army, Office of the Adjutant General, General Order no. 3, 1860; Weigley, *History of the Army,* 153; Ganoe, 164; Spaulding, 154; Birkhimer, 122–41.

47. Adjutant General's Order no. 6, 14 Feb. 1835, USMA Post Orders, 6:238, USMA Archives; AGUSA to Chief of Engineers, 17 Oct. 1844, USMA Adjutant's Letters Received, Box 2, USMA Archives (hereafter cited as ALR); John Bratt, diary, 22 Oct. 1857, USMA Archives; Chief of Ordnance to Superintendent, USMA, 6 Oct. 1857, ALR, 17-C; USMA Endorsements and Memos, 1:111; Chief of Engineers to Superintendent, 8 June 1852, OCELS, 18:384; Secretary of War to Chief of Engineers, 1 Nov. 1853, OSWLSMA, 35:30; Silas Casey, President of Board, to Superintendent, 8 Sept. 1854, ALR, C-11; Casey, President of Board, to Adjutant General, USA, 23 Sept. 1854, ALR, Box 1, 164; George Bayard to Sister Esther, 7 Oct. 1854, USMA MSS; Bratt diary, 29 July 1855, USMA Archives; USMA Endorsements and Memos, 1:71, USMA Archives; Adjutant, USMA to Board of Officers on Rifle-Musket Manual, 31 Mar. 1858, USMA Adjutant's Letter Book, no. 3, 2; Superintendent to Adjutant General, USA, 1 Apr. 1858, ibid., 3; Chief of Engineers to Superintendent, 25 June 1858, ALR, Box 5, 80 1/2; Order no. 41, 25 Oct. 1859, USMA Post Orders, no. 5, 301; Chief of Engineers to Superintendent, 25 May 1860, OCELS, 23:142; H. A. Du Pont to Father, 8 Oct. 1859, and to Mother, 28 Mar. 1857, H. A. Du Pont Papers, Hagley Museum and Library, Wilmington, Del.; Morrison, *Heth's Memoirs,* xxxi, 140–42.

48. Hamersley, 190–93; *Army Registers,* 1833–60 Weigley, *History of the Army,* 169.

49. Frederick Rudolph, *The American College and University* (New York: Alfred A. Knopf, 1962), 193–200; Daniel H. Calhoun, *The American Civil Engineer: Origins and Conflict* (Cambridge: MIT Press, 1960), 167–73.

50. Ganoe, 121, 153, 180, 200, ff.; Secretary of War to Hon. Joseph Duncan, H.R., 1 May 1834, OSWLSMA, 14:27; White, 199–200, Weigley, *History of the Army,* 110–11, 229–30; Morrison, *Heth's Memoirs,* xxviii, 123.

51. Utley, 42; Weigley, *History of the Army,* 240; Robert M. Utley, "The Army on the Frontier, 1848–90," taped lecture, *Voices of History* (Michael Glazier, Inc., M-9).

52. Grier to Superintendent, 20 Jan. 1841, ALR.

53. Morrison, *Heth's Memoirs,* 118, Turner journal, 26 Mar.–20 July 1856; John H. Calef, "A Distinguished Horse Artilleryman," *The Journal of the Military Service Institution of the United States* 43 (June–Aug. 1908): 113; Hyland C. Kirk, *Heavy Guns and Light, A History of the Fourth New York Heavy Artillery* (New York: C. R. Dillingham, 1890), 439; U.S. Congress, Senate, 33d Cong., 2nd sess., Exec. Doc. no. 78, *Reports of Explorations and Surveys,* vol. 13, pt. 3, 6–36, and vol. 11 ("Maps"), 84; Dabney H. Maury, *Recollections of a Virginian in the Mexican, Indian, and Civil Wars,* 3d ed. (New York: Charles Scribner's Sons, 1894), 95–130; Philip H. Sheridan, *Personal Memoirs,* 2 vols. (New York: Charles L. Webster, 1888), 1:15–104; Burke Davis, *Jeb Stuart: The Last Cavalier* (New York: Rinehart and Co., 1957), 29–49; John W. Thomason, Jr., *Jeb Stuart* (New York: Charles Scribner's Sons, 1948), 21–22, Zenas R. Bliss Papers, MSS, U.S. Army Military History Insitute, Carlisle Barracks, Pa; Eugene A. Carr Papers, ibid.; David S. Stanley Memoirs, West-Stanley-Wright Papers, ibid.

CHAPTER TWO

1. Denton, 269–77.

2. *Register of Graduates,* 1963, 202; Weigley, *History of the Army,* 145–47, 155; Maurice Matloff, ed., *American Military History* (Washington, D.C.: Office, Chief of Military History 1969), 155. *Centennial* 1:230 erroneously credits Thayer with several reforms initiated by his predecessors.

3. Denton, 60, 73, 81–86, 122, 127–35.

4. Ibid., 182, 227, 231.

5. Inspector general to Calhoun, n.d., 1819, USMA Archives; Reports of Boards of Visitors, June 1833, June 1838, and June 1842, USMA Archives; U.S. Congress, Senate, *Report of the Commission on the U.S. Military Academy,* Misc. Doc. no. 3, 35th Cong., 2nd sess., 1860, 12–19.

6. Thayer to Cullum, 23 Jan. 1865, Sylvanus Thayer Papers, USMA MSS.

7. Thayer to Delafield, 1 Oct. 1838, Richard Delafield Papers, USMA MSS.

8. Thayer to Cullum, 18 Dec. 1855, Thayer Papers.

9. Secretary of War to Chief of Engineers, 31 Aug. 1835, OSWLSMA, 14:167; Secretary of War to Superintendent, 1 Sept. 1835, ibid., 173; USMA Post Orders, 6, no. 96, 4 Sept. 1835, USMA Archives.

10. USMA Post Orders, 6:352, USMA Archives.

11. James D. Richardson, ed., *A Compilation Of The Messages and Papers of the Presidents,* 10 vols. (Washington, D.C.: Bureau of National Literature and Art, 1904) 2:456.

12. Ibid., 3:169–70.

13. John Spencer Bassett, *Correspondence of Andrew Jackson,* 7 vols. (Washington, D.C.: Carnegie Institute, 1928), 3:190–91.

14. Richardson, 2:390.

15. *Register of Graduates,* 1963, 213.

16. Order no. 20, 4 Feb. 1848, USMA Post Orders, 3, USMA Archives.

17. Chief of Engineers to Superintendent, 15 Sept. 1848, with indorsement by President, ALR, 227.

18. Superintendent to Col. George Wright, 17 Nov. 1849, SLB, 2:40; Secretary of War to Wright, 28 Nov. 1849, OSWLSMA, 29:387; Superintendent to Wright, 20 Dec. 1849, SLB, 2:50.

19. Milo M. Quaife, ed., *The Diary of James K. Polk During His Presidency,* 4 vols. (Chicago: A. C. McClurg Co., 1910), 1:31–32.

20. Roy F. Nichols, *Franklin Pierce: Young Hickory of the Granite Hills* (Philadelphia: Univ. of Pennsylvania Press, 1931), 77–88, 90–91, 174; David W. Bartlett, *The Life of Gen. Frank Pierce of New Hampshire* (Buffalo: George H. Derby & Co., 1852), 61–80; *Congressional Globe,* 24th Cong., 1st sess., Appendix, 513–15; Robert Seager, *And Tyler Too: A Biography of John and Julia Tyler* (New York: McGraw-Hill, 1963), 443.

21. U.S. Congress, *American State Papers,* Class 5, Military Affairs, 7 vols. (Washington, D.C.: Gales & Seaton, 1861), 5:18–19, 629, 170; Secretary of War to Superintendent, 15 Apr. 1835, OCELS, 4:461.

22. Secretary of War to Cadet E. M. Clarke, 16 Apr. 1835, OCELS, 4:462; Secretary of War to Chief of Engineers, ibid., 296; Secretary of War to unidentified addressee, 22 Oct. 1835, OSWLSMA, 14:305.

23. Minutes of the Academic Board, USMA Staff Records, 2, Oct. 1836, 49–51, USMA Archives (hereafter cited as SR); Secretary of War to Superintendent, 9 Oct. 1836, OSWLSMA, 16:422; Chief of Engineers to Superintendent, 24 Jan. 1837, OCELS, 6:88; Secretary of War to President, 11 Mar. 1837, OSWLSMA, 17:200.

24. Chief of Engineers to Superintendent, 20 Apr. 1837, OCELS, 6:215; *Centennial* 1:97–99; Boynton, 226.

25. Poinsett's nominee for the chaplaincy was his fellow South Carolinian Jasper Adams. Although a scholar, Adams was also a meddler and a gossip who embarrassed West Point authorities. Mahan to Poinsett, 17 May 1837, Poinsett Papers, 8:86; Mahan to Poinsett, 14 Feb. 1838, ibid., 10:45; Mahan to Poinsett, 4 June 1839, ibid., 12:153; Poinsett to Gouvernor Kemble, 13 Nov. 1847, Thayer Papers.

26. Memorandum to the Commanding General, 1 Mar. 1838, OSWLSMA, 18:397; W. W. Bliss to Henry Du Pont, 2 Jan. 1837, Du Pont Papers.

27. Secretary of War to Mahan, 17 Aug. 1841, OSWLSMA (Confidential and Unofficial), 118; Chief of Engineers to Superintendent, 20 Sept. 1841, OCELS, 9:365; Adjutant to Mahan, 27 Sept. 1841, USMA Adjutant's Letter Book, 1, USMA Archives (hereafter cited as ALB).

28. Chief of Engineers to Secretary of War, 27 Jan. 1842, OCELS, Abstract of Letters Sent, 1; Report of Committee of Academic Board, Feb. 1842, ALR; Secretary of War to Chief of Engineers, 18 July 1842, OCELS, 10:204; *Centennial* 1:302.

29. Secretary of War to Chief of Engineers, 5 Feb. 1844, and 28 Feb. 1845, OSWLSMA, 25:279, 483; Superintendent to Chief of Engineers, 15 May 1848, SLB, vol. 1, pt. 2, 174; Superintendent to Chief Clerk, War Department, 28 June 1848, ibid., 196; Superintendent to Capt. F. A. Smith, Office of the Chief of Engineers, "Unofficial," 17 July 1851, SLB, 2:184.

30. Secretary of War to Academic Board, 23 Aug. 1852, SR, 5:214-19.

31. Proceedings of Academic Board, Sept. 1852, SR, 5:223-29. One took the examination and failed. The other never reported.

32. Douglas S. Freeman, *R. E. Lee: A Biography*, 4 vols. (New York: Charles Scribner's Sons, 1937), 1:321; U.S. Congress, Senate, Doc. 98, *Report of the Secretary of War*, 32nd Cong., 1st sess., 1852, 1-3.

33. "I give it as my fixed opinion, that but for our graduated cadets, the war between the United States and Mexico might have lasted some four or five years, with, in its first half, more defeats than victories falling to our share." Winfield Scott, quoted in U.S. Congress, Senate, Misc. Doc. no. 3, *Report of Commission*, 36th Cong. 2d sess., 1860, 176.

34. Grant, 1:41; Charles W. Elliott, *Winfield Scott, The Soldier and The Man* (New York: Macmillan, 1937), 237, 256, 564, 663; Morrison, 24-25, 36-37; Joseph H. Martin, "Journal of a Cadet, 1838-41," 31, USMA Archives (microfilm); Catherine S. Crary, ed., *Dear Belle: Letters from a Cadet and Officer to his Sweetheart, 1858-1865* (Middletown, Conn.: Wesleyan Univ. Press, 1965), 14, 103; James H. Wilson, *Under the Old Flag*, 2 vols. (New York: D. Appleton Co., 1912), 1:59, 62; Morrison, "Getting Through West Point," 311.

35. Thayer to Cullum, n.d., Dec. 1865, and notes by Cullum on conversation between himself and Prof. Bartlett, 26 Sept., 1877, Thayer Papers; "Charles Gratiot," no. 16, George W. Cullum MSS, USMA MSS.

36. U.S. Congress, *Annual Report of the Secretary of War*, 23d Cong., 1st sess., 1833, 112, 113; ibid., 23d Cong., 2nd sess., 1834, 112, 113; ibid., 24th Cong., 1st sess., 1835, 114, 115; ibid., 24th Cong., 2nd sess., 1836, 207.

37. Francis P. Prucha, *The Sword of the Republic: The United States Army on the Frontier, 1783-1846* (New York: Macmillan, 1969), 350; K. Jack Bauer, *The Mexican War, 1846-1848* (New York: Macmillan, 1974), 146, 252-53; *Register of Graduates*, 1963, 201; *Dictionary of American Biography* (hereafter cited as *DAB*), s.v. "Totten, Joseph G"; Cullum, 1:96.

38. Totten to Mahan, 26 Jan. 1839, OCELS, Totten Letters, 4:7; Chief of Engineers to Superintendent, 7 Mar. 1839, OCELS, 7:397.

39. Annual Report of the Superintendent of the United States Military Academy, 1896 (Washington, D.C.: Government Printing Office, 1896), 172; Ganoe, 206; Chief of Engineers to Superintendent, 30 June 1841, OCELS, 9:278; U.S. War Department, *Annual Report of the Secretary of War*, 1846, no. 3, 135-37.

40. Totten to Superintendent, 18 Nov. 1842, OCELS, 10:300-305; 11 Dec. 1844, 12:351; 4 May 1840, 8:317-21; 6 Sept. 1850, 18:221-26; 2 Jan. 1851, ALR, 324.

41. Totten to Superintendent, 15 Feb. 1842, OCELS, 10:8-11.

42. Totten to Superintendent, 24 Apr. 1844, OCELS, 12:264; 3 Nov. 1842, 10:281; Totten to Adjutant General, 31 May 1841, OCELS, 9:326; 31 May 1841, 9:248–51; Totten to Secretary of War, 2 July 1839, OCELS, 7:544.

43. Superintendent to Totten, 4 Nov. 1848, SLB, vol. 1, pt. 2, 239; Totten to Superintendent, 2 Nov. 1848, ALR; Totten to Secretary of State, 8 Nov. 1848, ALR; Totten to President Polk, 3 Aug. 1848, OCELS, Extract of Letter Book, 40–49; Totten to President Fillmore, 31 Mar. 1851, OCELS, 17:510–13.

44. Swift to Thayer, 27 Apr. 1864, Thayer Papers, 10.

CHAPTER THREE

1. Ambrose, 62.

2. *Register of Graduates,* 1963, 16; Chief of Engineers to Superintendent, 1 Aug. 1837, OCELS, 6:292; Gouverneur Kemble to Thayer, 30 July 1838, Thayer Papers; Thayer to Kemble, 9 Aug. 1838, ibid.; Poinsett to Kemble, 13 Nov. 1837, ibid.; Mahan to Poinsett, 17 May 1837, Poinsett Papers, 8:36; Robert E. Lee to Jerome Bonaparte, 11 Apr. 1853, R. E. Lee Papers, MS. 23737 L15, 3, Virginia State Library, Richmond; Lee to Mahan, 16 Aug. 1852, Lee Papers, MS. 10734.

3. *Register of Graduates,* 1963, 205; Heitman, 1:43.

4. Academic board minutes, Oct. 1839, SR 2:161–62, USMA Archives.

5. *Register of Graduates,* 1963, 16.

6. *DAB,* s.v. "Delafield, Richard"; Heitman, 1:365; *Register of Graduates,* 1963, 16; Beauregard to chief of engineers, 23 Jan. 1861, SLB, 4, USMA Archives; Special Order no. 6, 23 Jan. 1861, USMA Post Orders, 5; Chief of Engineers to Delafield, 28 Jan. 1861, Engineer Letters Sent, 33:288, RG 94, NA (cited hereafter as ELS).

7. J[oseph] Stewart, "The Class of 1842," *Army and Navy Journal* 39 (14 June 1902): 1028; Crary, 24.

8. John C. Tidball [Class of 1848], "Getting Through West Point by One Who Did," 71, 103–4, 166–67, 183, USMA MSS (hereafter cited as Tidball Papers); Stewart, 1028.

9. E. P. Alexander, "The Class of 1857," *Army and Navy Journal* 39 (14 June 1902): 1031.

10. Tully McCrea to Belle, 6 Feb. 1859, in Crary, 49; Tidball Papers, 98.

11. Tully McCrea to Belle, 26 Jan. 1861, in Crary, 38; Tidball Papers, 71, 103–04.

12. *Regulations Established for the Government of the Military Academy at West Point* (New York: Wiley and Putnam, 1839), 18 (five books on regulations were published between 1832 and 1866; see bibliography for publishing facts. These are hereafter cited as *USMA Regulations* with year). Order no. 7, 18 Jan. 1839, USMA Post Orders, 7; Superintendent to Chaplain Adams, 21 Feb. 1840, SLB, 1:346; J. W. Bailey to Superintendent, 19 June 1843, ALR, 104.

13. *USMA Regulations,* 1839, 33; Lt. Minor Knowlton to Adjutant, 21 Oct. 1839, ALR, 98; Weir to Adjutant, 6 Jan. 1840, ibid., 4; Adjutant to Bailey, 31 Jan 1842, ALB, 1; Superintendent's Indorsement to Adjutant's note, 16 Apr. 1842, ibid.

14. Circular, 24 Nov. 1849, USMA Post Orders, 3; Adjutant to Lt. S. B. Buckner, 27 Nov. 1849, ALB, 2; Adjutant to Bvt. Capt. George B. McClellan, 28 Nov. 1849, ibid.; Adjutant to Dr. Southgate, Capt. McClellan, Lt. Deshon, 26 Nov. 1849, ibid.; Adjutant to Bvt. Capt. G. B. McClellan and Lt. S. B. Buckner, 29 Nov. 1849, SLB, 2; Chief of Engineers to Superintendent, 17 Dec. 1849, OCELS, 16, 456; Secretary of War to Chief of Engineers, 19 Dec. 1849, ibid., 461; Chief of Engineers to Superintendent, 27 Dec. 1849, ALR.

15. Mahan to Poinsett, 20 Sept. 1838, Poinsett Papers, 2:10.
16. Denton, 182–85; *USMA Regulations,* 1832, 5; 1853, 2–3; 1866, 4; SR, 1833–66; Chief of Engineers to Secretary of War, 1 Apr. 1841, OCELS, Abstracts, 1:17.
17. Ibid.
18. SR, 2, June 1835, 8.
19. SR, 2, June 1836, 50–51.
20. SR, 2, Feb. 1839, 139–40; Chief of Engineers to Superintendent, 7 Mar. 1839, ALR, 60.
21. SR, 2, Oct. 1843, 187; SR, 4, Feb. 1852, 134–37, 144–46; Davis Report, 11; T. Harry Williams, "The Attack Upon West Point During the Civil War," *Mississippi Valley Historical Review* 25 (Mar. 1939): 493–96; *Centennial* 1:245.
22. *USMA Regulations,* 1839, 17, Table A.
23. SR, 2, Mar. 1839, 141; SR, 2, Oct. 1841, 320–30; SR, 5, Sept. 1852, 231–40; SR, 6, Aug. 1858, 348–50, 353–64; SR, 6, Oct. 1858, 385–86.
24. *Register of Graduates,* 1963, 210, 212, 214, 217, 221.
25. *USMA Regulations,* 1832, 20; 1839, 23; 1853, 21–22; *Centennial* 1:292, 325, 368.
26. Ibid., 379, 422.
27. Mahan to Superintendent, 6 Apr. 1840, ALR, 74; Mahan to Superintendent, 6 July 1843, OCE Mahan Papers, D-2402; Secretary of War to Chief of Engineers, 20 July 1843, OSWLSMA, 25:171; Mahan to Major Kurtz, OCE, 26 May 1864, OCELRMA, 3134; *DAB,* s.v., "Mahan, Dennis Hart"; Mahan to Chase, 27 Oct. 1861, Salmon P. Chase Papers, Library of Congress; Mahan to President Lincoln, 20 Jan. 1862, USMA Mahan Papers, M55 (photocopy); Mahan to Sherman, 28 Aug. 1863, W. T. Sherman Papers, 13:1699–1701, General Correspondence, Library of Congress.
28. Mahan to Chief of Engineers, 30 June 1836, OCELR, 1727, E 1836; George Cadwallader to Mahan, 1 July 1848, Cadwallader Collection, Pa. Historical Society MSS (USMA photocopy); Weigley, *Toward An American Army,* 43–53; *Centennial* 2:310; Thomas E. Greiss, "Dennis Hart Mahan: West Point Professor and Advocate of Military Professionalism, 1830–1871," (Ph.D. dissertation, Duke University, 1968), 301–5.
29. Mahan to Poinsett, 1 Aug. 1840, Poinsett Papers 4:11; Mahan to Superintendent, 2 July 1841, ALR, 109; Chief of Engineers to Mahan, 13 Aug. 1847, OCE, Totten Letters, 6:431; Mahan to Cadet James B. McPherson, 28 July 1852, McPherson Papers, Library of Congress; Mahan to Fred Harris, 5 Apr. 1834, D. B. Harris Papers, William R. Perkins Library, Duke University; SR, 5, June 1853, 277–88; Weigley, *Toward An American Army,* 45–46; Sherman to Cullum, 15 Feb. 1868, MS. 1282, Cullum MSS; Crary, 33–35; Chief of Engineers to Superintendent, 21 May 1834, OCELS, 4:186–87; Mahan to Superintendent, 2 July 1841, ALR, Box 109; Morris Schaff, *The Spirit of Old West Point* (New York: Houghton, Mifflin Co., 1908), 68; Morrison, "West Point Memoirs," 322; Mahan to Bache, 22 Mar. 1846, Mahan Papers; Greiss, 173; Samuel B. McIntire, "Echoes of the Past," *Army and Navy Journal* 39 (14 June 1902): 1026; Denton, 231–32; *Centennial* 1:278; William S. McFeely, *Grant, A Biography* (New York: W. W. Norton Co., 1981), 15.
30. Edward S. Holden, "Biographical Memoir of William H. C. Bartlett, 1804–1893," *National Academy of Sciences Biographical Memoirs* (Washington, D.C.: National Academy of Sciences, 1911), 175, 192–93; *DAB,* s.v., "Bartlett, William Holmes Chambers"; SR, 5, Sept. 1852 141; Oct. 1841, 320–30.
31. Holden, 175, 192–93; *Centennial* 1:265; 2:180.
32. "Observatories in the United States," *Harper's New Monthly Magazine* (Mar. 1874), 539–41; Holden, 176–77.
33. Crary, 27, 35–36; *Annual Reunion of the Graduates of the United States Military*

Academy (Saginaw, Mich.: Seaman and Peters, 1893), 110; Tidball Papers, 65, 105; Holden quoted in *DAB*, s.v., "Bartlett, William Holmes Chambers."

34. *Register of Graduates*, 1963, 214; *Centennial* 1:248; 2:216; Heitman 1:301.

35. Florian Cajori, *The Teaching and History of Mathematics in the United States* (Washington, D.C.: Government Printing Office, 1890), 121; *Centennial* 2:216.

36. Schaff, 68; Hardy quoted by Cajori, 124.

37. Stanley MSS, 81, 90, West-Stanley-Wright Papers; Tidball Papers, 85; Ambrose, 74–75, 93, 132; *Centennial* 1:243.

38. *DAB*, s.v., "Bailey, Jacob Whitman"; Heitman, 1:181; *Register of Graduates*, 1963, 217; *Centennial* 1:353; Bailey to Mother, 4 Feb. 1832, Jacob W. Bailey Papers, MS. 1546, USMA MSS.

39. Order no. 3, 26 Feb. 1857, USMA Post Orders, 5; Announcement, 16 Sept. 1853, no number, Bailey Papers; Stanley Coulter, "Jacob Whitman Bailey," *Botanical Gazette* (May 1888), 118–24; Goetzmann, *Explorations and Empire,* 321.

40. Baumer, 228–29; Zenas R. Bliss, Reminiscences, Bliss Papers, 2:1, E181B 69 1936; Stanley MSS, 90, West-Stanley-Wright Papers; John M. Schofield, *Forty-Six Years in the Army* (New York: Century Co., 1897), 9.

41. *Register of Graduates*, 1963, 221; Heitman, 1:591–92; *Centennial* 1:353; David S. Stanley MSS, 106–9, West-Stanley-Wright Papers.

42. Samuel B. McIntire, "Echoes of the Past," *Army and Navy Journal* 39 (14 June 1902): 1026; S. G. Merce, "Class of 1848," ibid., 1028; H. A. Du Pont to Mother, 17 Oct. 1858, H. A. Du Pont Papers; Tidball Papers, 73.

43. *Centennial* 1:291–92; Heitman, 1:1015.

44. Denton, 34–40, 54, 79–80; *USMA Regulations,* 1832, 20; 1839, 23; 1853, 21; 1857, 36.

45. *DAB*, s.v., "Weir, Robert Walter."

46. Ambrose, 94, 155–56; Baumer, 328; Thomas J. Fleming, *West Point: The Men and Times of the United States Military Academy* (New York: William Morrow & Co., 1969), 135; SR, Feb. 1852, 143; E. R. and J. Pennell, *The Life of James McNeill Whistler,* 2 vols. (Philadelphia: J. B. Lippincott & Co., 1911) 1:3–32; Tidball Papers, 81–83.

47. Heitman 1:213, 154; Forman, 52; *Centennial* 1:312 23; H. L. Welch, "Early West Point Teachers and Influences," *American Legion D'Honeur Magazine* (Spring 1855), 37–38.

48. *Centennial* 1:322; 2:185; Ambrose, 92; Crary, 31–32; Tidball Papers, 297–304; Superintendent to Chief of Engineers, 6 May 1848, SLB, 1:172; Superintendent to Agnel, 3 Dec. 1839, SLB, 1:303.

49. *Centennial* 1:368; *Register of Graduates,* 1963, 212; Joseph H. Martin, Journal, 1838–41, 34, Pa. Historical Society MSS (USMA microfilm); J[oseph] Stewart, "The Class of 1842," *Army and Navy Journal* 39 (14 June 1902): 1028; Crary, 92; Secretary of War to Superintendent, 13 Apr. 1835, OCELS, 4:457; Secretary of War to Chief of Engineers, 24 Apr. 1835, OSWLSMA, 14:127; AGO Order no. 50, 21 Aug. 1835, USMA Post Orders 6; AGO Order no. 63, 15 Sept. 1835, ibid.; Denton, 220; Ambrose, 151, 165; Schaff, 104; Bratt diary, 25 Aug. 1856; *New York Times,* 13 Sept. 1856, 3; Secretary of War to Sprole, 26 Aug. 1856, OSWLS, 38:239.

50. Peter S. Michie, *The Life and Letters of Emory Upton* (New York: D. Appleton Co., 1885), 39.

51. *Army and Navy Chronicle* 6 (1 Mar. 1833): 138; *Register of Graduates,* 1963, Cullum numbers: 966, 1350, 1273, 1585, 1344, 1353, 1325, 1634, 1084, 1112, 1308, 1755, 1176, 1216, 1259, 1433, 1238, 1115, 1266, 1085, 1262.

52. SR, vols. 2–6; *USMA Regulations,* 1832, 20; 1839, 23; 1853, 21–22; "Report of the

Board of Visitors," *The North American Review* 34 (Jan. 1832): 260; Reports of Board of Visitors, 1838, 1843, 1844, USMA Archives; U.S. Congress, Senate, Ex. Doc. no. 1, *Report of the Chief Engineer,* 32nd Cong., 2nd sess., 1852, 171–83; SR, Aug. 1852, 171–83; Boynton, 320–21; SR, Aug. 1858, 348–50, 353–64, 385, 86; Chief of Engineers to Superintendent, 23 Aug. 1858, ELS, 22:234, RG 94, NA; Special Orders no. 143, 11 Oct. 1858, USMA Post Orders 6; Secretary of War to Chief of Engineers, 31 Mar. 1859, OSWLSMA, 41:184, RG 107, NA.

CHAPTER FOUR

1. U.S. Congress, Senate, Doc. 247, 23d Cong., 1st sess., 1834, 1; U.S. Congress, House, Report no. 303, 24th Cong., 2nd sess., 1837, 15–30; U.S. War Department, *Annual Report of the Secretary of War,* 1861, 27–28; T. Harry Williams, "The Attack on West Point During the Civil War," *Mississippi Valley Historical Review* 24 (June 1939): 492–501; White, 208–12.

2. White, 208–12; Peter S. Michie, "Reminiscences of Cadet and Army Service," *Personal Recollections of the War of the Rebellion* (New York: G. P. Putnam's Sons, 1897), 192–97; Arthur Tremaine, (untitled article), *The Military and Naval Magazine of the United States* 4 (Oct. 1834): 81–90; Report of the Board of Visitors, U.S. Military Academy, 1835, 1838, 1839, 1845, M85, USMA Archives.

3. U.S. Congress, Senate, Doc. no. 1, 28th Cong., 2nd sess., 1844, *Annual Report of the Secretary of War* 194–95; "Circumstances of Parents of Cadets, 1842–1879" ledger, USMA Archives; U.S. Congress, House, Ex. Doc. no. 2, 27th Cong., 3d sess., 1842, *Report of the Board of Visitors* 271–75; U.S. Congress, House, Report no. 476, 28th Cong., 2nd sess., 1844, *Report of Mr. Fish* 15–16; Boynton, 324.

4. George C. Strong, *Cadet Life at West Point* (Boston: T. O. H. P. Burnham, 1862), 128–31. The categories were not further defined. The authorities took the cadets' word at face value.

5. U.S. Congress, *An Act making appropriations for the support of the military academy . . . for the fiscal year beginning the first day of July, one thousand eight hundred and forty three,* chap. 52, sec. 2; Leonard D. White, *The Jeffersonians: A Study in Administrative History, 1801–1829* (New York: Macmillan, 1951), 256; Denton, 251.

6. *USMA Regulations,* 1832, 7; Superintendent to President Fillmore, 20 Jan. 1851, SLB, 2; Superintendent to Chief of Engineers, 25 June 1850, SLB, 2; Battalion Orders no. 39, 27 May 1833, USMA Post Orders, 6; Special Order no. 61, 24 May 1844, ibid.; Superintendent to Capt. H. Canfield, 24 June 1852, SLB, 2.

7. This figure is based on the records of 1,928 candidates contained in USMA Staff Records for the period.

8. This figure is based on the 518 cadets recommended by the academic board for discharge because of failures at the examinations in January and June each year, USMA Staff Records.

9. "Proceedings of the Academic Board," SR, 3 Oct. 1843: 89–190; "Report of Committee of Academic Board," Feb. 1842, ALR, Box E; "Report of the Board of Visitors for 1840," *The North American Review* 53 (Jan. 1841): 26–28; U.S. Congress, Senate Doc. no. 1, *Report of the Chief of Engineers,* 29th Cong., 1st sess., 1845, 269–77.

10. *USMA Regulations,* 1866, 6; U.S. Congress, *Joint Resolution relative to appointments to the Military Academy of the United States,* no. 49, June 1866, sec. 3; Secretary of War to John P. Richardson, H.R., 6 Feb. 1837, OSWLSMA 14; Secretary of War to Fitz-John Porter, 6 Dec. 1838, ibid.; *Niles Weekly Register* 63 (4 Feb. 1843): 357; *New York Times,* 21 Jan. 1863, 4; U.S. Congress, House, 38th Cong., 1st sess., *Report of the Board of Visitors,* June 1863, 85–88; Superintendent to Chief of Engineers, 24 Aug. 1863, SLB, 4; Adjutant to

Chief of Engineers, 3 Oct. 1863, ALB, 3; SR, 7, Dec. 1863, 330; *Army and Navy Journal,* 20 Feb. 1864, 402; *Congressional Globe,* 38th Cong , 1st sess., 12 Mar. 1864, 1053–54, 1084–88, 1220; ibid., 26 Mar. 1864, 1226; SR, 7, June 1864, 361; *New York Times,* 9 June 1864, 4; Thayer to Superintendent, 30 Jan. 1866, USMA Thayer Papers, vol. 10; *Congressional Globe,* Appendix, 39th Cong., 1st sess., June 1866, 429; U.S. Congress, 39th Cong., 2nd sess., Exec. Doc. no. 1, *Report, Office of the Inspector of the Military Academy,* June 1866, 37–40; Stanley Memoirs, 76, West-Stanley-Wright Papers; Tidball Memoirs, 56, Tidball Papers.

11. Battalion Order no. 39, 27 May 1833, USMA Post Orders, 6; Special Order no. 71, 17 June 1843, ibid., 3; Special Orders no. 61, 24 May 1844, ibid.

12. Morrison, "Getting Through West Point," 306.

13. *USMA Regulations,* 1832, 31; 1839, 35; 1853, 35; Schofield, 3.

14. "Animal" or "Thing" was the unofficial term used by old cadets to designate candidates who had not yet been issued uniforms. "Plebe" was the unofficial designation of a cadet in the fourth class. The date of origin of this term is unknown but it was in common use before 1833. Strong 55; Schaff, 29; Morrison, 14.

15. Morrison, "Getting Through West Point," 307.

16. Ibid., 308.

17. Strong, 65.

18. Morrison, "Getting Through West Point," 312 13; Strong, 100; SR, 1833–54.

19. Morrison, "Getting Through West Point," 312–15; Strong, 104–5, 112–14; Schaff, 38–40.

20. Morrison, "Getting Through West Point," 313–15; Morrison, xvii, 23–24; Benjamin Perley Poore, *The Life and Public Services of Ambrose E. Burnside* (Providence: J. A. & R. A. Reid, 1882), 36–39.

21. Morrison, 14; Commandant to Superintendent, 15 July 1844, ALR, Box C, no. 128.

22. Superintendent to Chief of Engineers, 25 June 1846, 24 July 1846, SLB, 1:2; Chief of Engineers to Secretary of War, 21 July 1846, ALR, 46.

23. Morrison, 27–30; Strong, 80–81.

24. Poore, 39; Tidball Papers, 124–27.

25. Strong, 73–75.

26. Strong, 139; Battalion Order no. 48, 8 July 1838, USMA Post Orders, 7; Bayard to Mother, 25 June 1853, George D. Bayard Papers, USMA MSS; Schaff, 46–49; Crary, 57.

27. "Casualties, U.S. Corps of Cadets," 57, 52; Special Order no. 104, 17 July 1852, USMA Post Orders, 3; Superintendent to Chief of Engineers, 25 June 1846, SLB, 1:2; Order no. 57, 31 May 1849, ibid.; Order no. 29, 31 May 1850, ibid.; Schofield, 10–11.

28. Tidball Memoirs, 35, Tidball Papers; Stanley Memoirs, 77, West-Stanley-Wright Papers; Sheridan, 1:9; James H. Wilson, *Under The Old Flag,* 2 vols. (New York: D. Appleton Co., 1912), 1:8.

29. Strong, 63.

30. Superintendent to Hon. J. C. Calhoun, 12 Apr. 1839, SLB, 1; Superintendent to Chief of Engineers, 30 Apr. 1839, ibid.; Morrison, "Getting Through West Point," 320.

31. Order no. 10, Hq. Corps of Cadets, 25 June 1843, ALR, Box 17; Bayard to Mother, 25 June 1853, Bayard Papers; Special Order no. 42, 25 Aug. 1845, ALR, Box 16; Superintendent to C. W. Lawrence, 4 July 1848, SLB, 1, pt. 2; Superintendent to Chief of Engineers, 9 Apr. 1852, SLB, 2; Morrison, "Getting Through West Point," 321.

32. W. T. Sherman to P. B. Ewing, 12 Apr. 1837, Philomen Ewing Papers, Ohio Historical Society (USMA photocopy); Order no. 60, 8 July 1844, USMA Post Orders, 6; Battalion Order no. 82, 30 July 1838, ibid., 7; Superintendent to John Noverre, 3 May 1839, SLB, 1; Special Order no. 31, 17 July 1843, ALR, Box 17.

33. W. D. Wallace to Superintendent, 3 Apr. 1843, ALR, Box D, no. 37; Tidball Mem-

oirs, 112–16, Tidball Papers; Bayard to Father, 21 Aug. 1853, Bayard Papers; Strong, 132–42.

34. Order no. 80, 4 July 1833, USMA Post Orders, 6; Bayard to Sister, 19 July 1855, Bayard Papers; Bayard to Mother, 1 July 1855, ibid.; Forman, 104–5; *Centennial* 2:96, 97.

35. Mahan to Poinsett, 20 Sept. 1838, Poinsett Papers, 2:10.

36. Superintendent to Chief of Engineers, 24 Feb. 1848, SLB, 1:2, 162; Order no. 10, 29 Mar. 1841, USMA Post Orders, 1; R. W. Weir to Superintendent, 28 Aug. 1851, ALR (all categories).

37. Sherman to Ewing, 29 Apr. 1838, Ewing Papers.

38. Battalion Order no. 98, 21 Aug. 1838, ALR, Box 14; Special Order no. 41, 23 Aug. 1845, ALR, Box 16; Battalion Order no. 70, 23 Aug. 1839, Box 17; Sherman to Ewing, 15 Dec. 1838, Ewing Papers; Superintendent to Major General Patterson, 10 Dec. 1846, SLB, 1:2; Morrison, 21–22.

39. U.S. War Department, *Annual Report of the Secretary of War*, 1836, Report of the Chief Engineer, 299; ibid., 1838, 243; ibid., 1845, 269, 277; Superintendent to Chief of Engineers, 12 Jan. 1839, SLB, 1; Report of Board of Officers, 5 Feb. 1839, ibid.

40. U.S. Congress, Exec. Doc., *Report of the Chief Engineer*, 31st Cong., 2nd sess., June 1850, 274; Order no. 134, 22 Nov. 1849, USMA Post Orders, 3.

41. *Centennial* 2:103, 112; Boynton, 261; Maury, 23; Morrison, "Getting Through West Point," 307; Order no. 44, 23 Dec. 1857, USMA Post Orders, 5; Boynton, 249.

42. Secretary of War to Chief of Engineers, 24 Nov. 1838, OSWLSMA, 29:485; Battalion Order no. 25, 30 Mar. 1839, ALR, Box 17.

43. Mahan to McPherson, 28 July 1852, McPherson Papers; Commandant to Superintendent, 6 Aug. 1840, ALR, Box 14, no. 155; Morrison, "Getting Through West Point," 308.

44. Cadet captains wore four chevrons on each arm. Lieutenants wore three. The adjutant's three chevrons were subtended by an arc, the quartermaster's by a straight bar. Chevrons were of gold lace; they were worn with the points up. *USMA Regulations*, 1839, 64–65; 1853, 42–43.

45. Sergeants wore two gold-lace chevrons, points up, on each upper sleeve. The sergeant major's chevrons were subtended by an arc, the quartermaster sergeant's by a straight bar. First sergeants wore a lozenge, and the color sergeant a star, just below the chevrons. Corporals wore two gold-lace chevrons, points up, on each lower sleeve. Color corporals (guards) wore a star just below the chevrons. Ibid.

46. *USMA Regulations*, 1839, 40; 1853, 40; Commandant to General Wiley, Board of Visitors, 10 June 1849, ALR, Box 15.

47. "High Privates," although holding no official rank, were temporarily detailed to leadership positions, such as Officer of the Day, and acting officers at drills. Sherman to Ewing, 1 Dec. 1839, Ewing Papers; Morrison, "Getting Through West Point," 315–16; Tidball Memoirs, 97, Tidball Papers; Battalion Order no. 6, 21 Apr. 1845, ALR, Box 16; Battalion Order no. 37, 8 Apr. 1837, ALR, Box 17; Battalion Order no. 39, 15 May 1839, ibid.; Stanley Memoirs, 87–91, West-Stanley-Wright Papers; J. M. Wright, "Class of 1860," *Army and Navy Journal* 39 (14 June 1902): 1029; E. P. Alexander, "The Class of 1861," ibid.; 1031.

48. *USMA Regulations*, 1832, 14 and Table A; 1853, 14 and Table A.

49. Ibid., 1832, 20–21; 1839, 24; 1853, 22–23; Superintendent to Dwight Jarvis, 24 Feb. 1853, SLB, 3; Morrison, "Getting Through West Point," 318–19.

50. Commandant to Superintendent, 1 June 1841, ALR, Box C, no. 80; Chief of Engineers to Cadet H. L. Crittenden, 14 Jan. 1841, OCELS, 9:31; Secretary of War to Superintendent, 24 Dec. 1852, OSWLSMA, 34:41; *USMA Regulations*, 1832, 26–27; 1839, 31; 1853, 31.

51. Commandant to Adjutant, 1 Sept. 1842, ALR, Box 14, no. 176; Adjutant to Com-

mandant, 16 Sept. 1842, ALR, Box 1; Record of Garrison Court-Martial, 12 Apr. 1842, USMA Post Orders, 2:326.

52. Tidball Memoirs, 68, Tidball Papers.

53. Secretary of War to Superintendent, 24 Dec. 1852, OSWLSMA, 34:41; Superintendent to Chief of Engineers, 8 July 1854, SLB, 3; Order no. 20, 4 Feb. 1848, USMA Post Orders, 3. See also chapter 2.

CHAPTER FIVE

1. Roswell Park, *A Sketch of the History and Topography of West Point* (Philadelphia: Henry Perkins, 1840), 117–19; *Centennial* 2:70, 86; Order no. 107, 22 Sept. 1837, USMA Post Orders, 6.

2. "Dialectic Society Journal, 1840–1844," USMA MSS, 6, 11, 20, 23, 27, passim; Hazard Stevens, *The Life of Isaac Ingalls Stevens*, 2 vols. (New York: Houghton, Mifflin Co., 1901), 1:38.

3. "Dialectic Society Journal," 6; Burke Davis, *Jeb Stuart, The Last Cavalier* (New York: Rinehart & Co., 1957), 24.

4. SR, 3:290; Chief of Engineers to Superintendent, 27 July 1842, OCELS, 1:220; Commandant to Adjutant, 16 Feb. 1840, ALR, Box 14; Order no. 107, 22 Sept. 1837, USMA Post Orders, 6.

5. Special Order no. 120, 2 Sept. 1847, USMA Post Orders, 3; S. Moody to Superintendent, 9 Oct. 1847, ALR, Box 7; Battalion Order no. 60, 8 July 1833, USMA Post Orders, 6; Battalion Order no. 2, 20 Jan. 1835, ibid.; Bratt diary, 13 May 1837; Superintendent to Spencer Beaver, 9 Jan. 1839, SLB, 1; Lt. Knowlton to Superintendent, 16 May 1841, ALR, Box C, no. 84; Bayard to Mother, 14 Mar. 1854, Bayard Papers; Tully McCrea to Belle McCrea 6 Feb. 1859, cited in Crary, 46–49.

6. Order no. 5, 2 Feb. 1846, USMA Post Orders, 3; Special Order no. 14, 3 Feb. 1846, ibid.; Capt. E. D. Keyes to adjutant, 3 Feb. 1846, ALR, Box 7.

7. Order no. 22, 12 Feb. 1833, USMA Post Orders, 6; Order no. 1, 4 Jan. 1839, ibid., 7; *Catalogue of the Library of the U.S. Military Academy . . . 1852* (New York: John F. Trow, 1853), iv; Morrison, "Getting Through West Point," 319; Wilson, 1:9.

8. U.S. Military Academy Library Circulation Records, entries for 14 Oct. 1837, 28 Jan. 1838, 5 Nov. 1842, 25 Feb. 1843, 26 Jan. 1846, 9 Dec. 1846, 10 Mar.–26 Oct. 1850, USMA Archives; Grant, 1:39; McFeely, 16; Stanley Memoirs, 91, West-Stanley-Wright Papers.

9. Superintendent to Lt. Col. Henry Whiting, 23 Jan. 1839, SLB, 1; *USMA Regulations*, 1832, 35; 1853, 39–40.

10. Bratt diary, 23 Dec. 1854; McPherson to Catherine Stem, 13 Feb. 1853, Stem Papers, 106.

11. Superintendent to Mrs. W. F. Tirron, 28 Dec. 1852, SLB, 2; Battalion Order no. 13, 10 Mar. 1835, USMA Post Orders, 6; Battalion Order no. 29, 15 Apr. 1835, ibid.; Bratt diary, 11 Apr. 1836, 26 Sept. 1836; Sherman to Ewing, 30 Sept. 1837, Ewing Papers.

12. Post Order no. 191, 11 Dec. 1838, USMA Post Orders, 7; Post Order no. 189, 24 Dec. 1835, ibid.; Commandant to Superintendent, 26 Dec. 1838, ALR, Box 14; Superintendent to Chief of Engineers, 25 Dec. 1839, SLB, 1; Special Orders no. 154, 19 Dec. 1843, USMA Post Orders, 3.

13. Order no. 133, 13 Dec. 1834, USMA Post Orders, 6; Hon. James G. Clinton to Superintendent, 10 Oct. 1843, ALR, Box D, 101; Order no. 104, 15 Nov. 1843, USMA Post Orders, 3; Special Order no. 102, 29 July 1843, ibid.; Order no. 29, 27 Feb. 1837, ibid., 6; Bratt diary, 5 Feb. 1837, 16 Apr. 1837; Bailey to Brother, 11 Mar. 1843, Bailey Papers.

14. U.S. Congress, Ex. Doc. no. 1, *Report of the Chief of Engineers,* 30th Cong., 2nd sess., 1848, 300; Morrison, "Getting Through West Point," 308; Forman, 97; Strong, 70; Thomas K. Jackson, "Class of 1848," *Army and Navy Journal* 39 (14 June 1902): 1028; Crary, 19–22.

15. Bayard to Mother, 4 Oct. 1854, Bayard Papers; Chief of Engineers to Secretary of War, 16 Mar. 1835, ELS, 4:435; Bailey MS. 1495, Bailey Papers; Tidball Memoirs, 118, Tidball Papers; Special Orders no. 146, 1 Oct. 1849, USMA Post Orders, 3.

16. *USMA Regulations,* 1832, 27; 1839, 113; 1853, 31; Sherman to Ewing, 5 Nov. 1837, Ewing Papers; Lloyd Lewis, *Captain Sam Grant* (Boston: Little, Brown & Co., 1950), 75; Strong, 301–13; Morrison, 19–20, 33; Poore, 41–42; Superintendent to Chief of Engineers, 28 Dec. 1853, SLB, 3; Superintendent to Chief of Engineers, 24 July 1854, ibid.; Freeman, 1:332–34.

17. Secretary of War to Cadet W. W. Wessells, 4 Apr. 1833, ELS, 3:344; Order no. 3, Mar. 1845, ALR, Box 16; Superintendent to Hon. A. C. Neven, 8 Feb. 1847, SLB, 1:2; Superintendent to Chief of Engineers, 11 Mar. 1848, ibid.; Superintendent to Col. G. Loomis, 25 May 1851, ALB, 2; Morrison, 21, 33; D. A. Kinsley, *Favor the Bold,* 2 vols. (New York: Promontory Press, 1957), 1:10–11; Morrison, "Getting Through West Point," 114.

18. Acting Chief of Engineers to Superintendent, 11 Oct. 1838, ELS, 7:354; Unnumbered Draft Order, 14 Oct. 1838, USMA Post Orders, 7; "Pledge of Cadets," 13 May 1840, ALR, Box 14, no. 5; Superintendent to Chief of Engineers, 20 June 1842, ALB, 1; Chief of Engineers to Superintendent, 27 June 1842, ELS, 10:164–66; Commandant to Superintendent, 28 Jan. 1845, ALR, Box 16; "Pledge, Members of the Third Class," 25 Apr. 1846, ALR, Box 15; Order no. 143, 29 Dec. 1849, USMA Post Orders, 3; Edward Anderson to Mother, 28 Feb. 1861, "Letters of a West Pointer, 1860–1861," *American Historical Review* 18 (Apr. 1928): 608; Superintendent to Chief of Engineers, 7 Mar. 1861, SLB, 4.

19. Memorandum from the Secretary of War, 27 June 1836, USMA Post Orders, 6; *USMA Regulations,* 1832, 29; 1839, 33; 1853, 32; Strong, 300–309, 250–56; Poore, 41–42; Morrison, xix, 31–32; Morrison, "Getting Through West Point," 314; Wilson, 1:15; Schofield, 7.

20. *USMA Regulations,* 1832, 28; 1839, 32; 1853, 34; Battalion Order no. 59, 25 Apr. 1857, USMA Post Orders, 5; Special Order no. 59, 25 Apr. 1857, USMA Post Orders, 5.

21. Superintendent to Chief of Engineers, 30 Sept. 1857, SLB, 2, and 2 Sept. 1849, SLB, 1.

22. Superintendent to Chief of Engineers, 30 Sept. 1851, SLB, 2; 15 July 1847, SLB, 1, pt. 2; Report, Commandant to Adjutant, 8 Dec. 1852, ALR, Box 16.

23. Report, Commandant to Superintendent, 8 June 1844, ALR, Box C, no. 84; 28 Oct. 1844, no. 199.

24. Bayard to Sister, 6 Mar. 1853, Bayard Papers; "Register of Delinquencies, U.S.M.A.," entry for 6 Mar. 1853, 137, USMA Archives; H. B. McClellan, *The Life and Campaigns of Major-General J.E.B. Stuart* (New York: Houghton, Mifflin Co., 1885), 7–8; Davis, 20; Cadet W. C. Paine to Superintendent, 18 Aug. 1856, ALR, Box 11; Schaff, 260; "Register of Delinquencies, U.S.M.A.," 1856–57, USMA Archives; Superintendent to Chief of Engineers, 1 July 1861, SLB, 4; Special Order no. 114, 17 July 1861, USMA Post Orders, 6; Crary, 64; Ambrose, 160–61; Michie, xi.

25. Order no. 23, 1 Mar. 1835, USMA Post Orders, 6; Sherman to Ewing, 11 July 1837, Ewing Papers; Order no. 1, 14 Jan. 1843, OCE, Record of Orders and Letters, 473, RG 94, NA; Totten to Delafield (Private), 19 Jan. 1843, Delafield Papers; Superintendent to Chief of Engineers, 29 Nov. 1841, ALB, 1; Tidball Memoirs, 7, 30, Tidball Papers; Morrison, xviii, 26–27; Du Pont to Mother, 2 Jan. 1858, H. A. Du Pont Letters; Tully McCrea to Belle McCrea, 1 Dec. 1860, quoted in Crary, 58; Edward Anderson to Mother, 16 Oct. 1860, "Letters of a West Pointer," 606; Schaff, 196; *Centennial* 2:112. "Hash" in cadet usage did not

signify any particular dish, but rather a haphazard collection of whatever edible materials were available, mixed together and cooked over grate fires. Stanley Memoirs, 85–86, West-Stanley-Wright Papers.

26. Secretary of War to Hon. G. B. Samuels, H. R., 20 July 1840, OSWLSMA, 23:359; and 8 Aug. 1840, ELS, 8:436; Adjutant to Commandant, 21 July 1840, ALB, 1.

27. Superintendent to Thomas Phenix, 12 Feb. 1846, SLB, 1:2; Superintendent to Chief of Engineers, 2 June 1847, SLB, 1:2, and 13 July 1849, SLB, 2; Cadet B. C. H. Phenix to Superintendent, 7 June 1847, ALR, Box 16; "Alphabeta Cards," Cadets S. Koockogey, J. W. C. Smith, B. C. H. Phenix, and R. H. Adams, USMA Archives.

28. Order no. 23, 23 Apr. 1845, USMA Post Orders, 6; Commandant to Superintendent, 26 Nov. 1841, ALR, Box C, nos. 200, 202, 208, 210; Report, Lieutenant Andrews to Commandant, 5 Jan. 1840, ALR, 3; Chief of Engineers to Superintendent, 21 Nov. 1855, enclosing extracts from Proceedings of Court of Inquiry, Orlando M. Poe Papers, USMA MSS.

29. Superintendent to Chief of Engineers, 3 Dec. 1839, SLB, 1; 7 Apr. 1854, SLB, 3; 30 Jan. 1849, SLB, 1:2; 1 May 1850, SLB, 2; Cadet Henry Martin to Superintendent, 9 Apr. 1854, USMA Post Orders, 4.

30. Order no. 16, 13 Mar. 1839, USMA Post Orders, 7; Cadet C. Best to Commandant, 14 Aug. 1841, ALR, Box 14, no. 29; Order no. 90, 9 Sept. 1842, USMA Post Orders, 3; Superintendent to Chief of Engineers, 29 Oct. 1862, 21 Jan. 1863, and 25 Dec. 1865, SLB, 4; Tully McCrea to Belle McCrea, 1 Nov. 1852, quoted in Crary, 41; Chief of Engineers to Superintendent, 7 Nov. 1862, 10 Jan. 1863, ALR, Box 9, nos. 31 and 9; Adjutant to President, Board of Inquiry, 17 Nov. 1862, ALB, 3; "Statements Pertaining to Cadet French," 18 June–2 July 1863, ALR, Box F; Chief of Engineers to Secretary of War, 29 Dec. 1865, OCE, Abstract of Letter Book, 3:110, RG 94, NA; Adjutant to Commandant, 6 Jan. 1866, ALB, 3; Special Order no. 10, 24 Jan. 1863, USMA Post Orders, 6.

31. Edward Anderson to Mother, 29 June 1860, "Letters of a West Pointer," 603; Superintendent to Chief of Engineers, 13 Feb. 1862, and 8 July 1863, SLB, 4; Statement, Cadet Kane to Lieutenant James, 28 Aug. 1864, ALR, J, Box H; Order no. 13, Engineer Department, 1 July 1864, OCE, Records of Letters and Orders, 620, RG 94, NA; F. A. Conklin to Superintendent, 10 July 1865, ALR, Box C; Superintendent to Secretary of War, 18 Sept. 1863, SLB, 4; Chief of Engineers to Superintendent, 23 Nov. 1863, ELS, 24:415, RG 94, NA; Special Order no. 9, 15 Jan. 1864, SLB, 4; Special Order no. 67, 3 June 1864, USMA Post Orders, 6; Special Order no. 179, ibid.

32. Strong, 186–89; Report, Assistant Professor of Drawing to Professor, 5 Apr. 1852, ALR, Box I; Proceedings of Court of Inquiry, 6 Apr. 1849, ALR, Box G; Report, Teacher of French to Superintendent, 6 Nov. 1838, ALR, Box C, no. 91; Adjutant to Commandant, 22 June 1845, ALB, 1; Report, Assistant Professor of Ethics to Professor, 3 Dec. 1852, ALR, Box I; Tully McCrea to Belle McCrea, 19 Jan. 1861, quoted in Crary, 43–46; SR, 7, Jan. 1861, 128–29, and May 1861, 171.

33. Superintendent to Mrs. T. Garesche, 31 Dec. 1850, SLB, 1; Superintendent to Mr. James Webb, 8 Aug. 1851, SLB, 2; Superintendent to Mr. I. R. Torbert, 6 Oct. 1852, SLB, 2; Superintendent to B. O'Connor, 17 Dec. 1852, SLB, 2; "Register of Delinquencies," entry for Henry M. Judah, 16 Aug. 1840, 56; Cadet Horace Randal to Superintendent, 24 Oct. 1852, ALR, Box 13, Superintendent to Chief of Staff, U.S. Army, 17 Feb. 1955, enclosing extracts from Bernard Postal and Lionel Kopman, *A Jewish Tourist's Guide to the U.S.* (Philadelphia: 1954), 366–88, and "Jews at West Point," Maurice J. Bloom, *Liberal Judaism* 11 (Sept. and Oct. 1943); York (Pa.) *Dispatch,* 26 Sept. 1983, 10.

34. Bratt diary, entries for 25 Feb. 1855, 28 Aug. 1855, 6 Feb. 1856; Thomas Rowland to Mother, 10 July 1859, 10 June 1860, 1 Jan. 1860, "Letters of A Virginia Cadet at West Point, 1859–1861," *South Atlantic Quarterly* 14 (July 1915): 211, 197, 337; Bayard to Mother, 4 July

1855, Bayard Papers; Du Pont to Mother, 22 Jan. 1860, 13 Nov. 1859, H. A. Du Pont Letters; U.S. Congress, Senate, Executive Documents, *Report of the Chief Engineer,* 34th Cong., 1st sess., 1855, 227; Superintendent to Secretary of War, 20 Mar. 1856, SLB, 3; Special Order no. 218, 28 Dec. 1855, ibid.; Special Order no. 219, 29 Dec. 1855, ibid.; Battalion Order no. 33, 5 Apr. 1838, USMA Post Orders, 7; Schofield, 8; Michie, 20; McClellan, 7; Superintendent to Mr. John Gray, 8 Feb. 1840, SLB, 1.

35. Lewis, 71; Schofield, 9; O. O. Howard to Brother, 8 Sept. 1850, USMA MSS.

36. Sherman to Ellen Ewing, 8 Dec. 1839, Sherman Family Papers, Notre Dame Univ. Microfilms (USMA Archives); Ambrose, 152; Tidball Papers, 108.

37. Superintendent to President, Mass. Temperance Society, 2 Jan. 1839, SLB, 1; Superintendent to John Gray, 8 Feb. 1840, ibid.; *Quarterly Christian Spectator* 6 (Sept. 1834): 348.

CHAPTER SIX

1. *USMA Regulations,* 1832, Table B, and 17–18; 1839, Table B, and 20–21; 1853, Table B, and 18; *Centennial* 1:231.

2. SR, "Reports of the progress, aptitude, and habits of certain cadets . . .", 1833–54; John Pemberton to Mother, 21 May 1834, Pemberton Family Papers, Pa. Historical Society, USMA microfilm.

3. *USMA Regulations,* 1832, 20; 1839, 23; 1853, 21–22.

4. The formula for computing the grade differential between two cadets adjacent to each other on the list was $\frac{L-A}{n-1}$ where the L= the largest number of points awarded, A= the smallest number of points awarded, and n= the total number of proficient cadets. For example, in a class of thirty-five cadets in freshman mathematics, the first man would receive 200 points; the last man proficient would receive 66.67. The second man in the class would get 3.9 points less than the first, the third man would get 3.9 points less than the second, and so on $\frac{(200-66.67)}{(35-1)}$. The formula is on an unnumbered sheet in the front of "Staff Records," 6, 1854–59.

5. SR, 1833–54; *Official Army Registers,* 1833–54.

6. Secretary of Academic Board to Chief of Engineers, 3 July 1849, ALR, Box H; Superintendent to Chief of Engineers, 12 July 1849, SLB, 2; Order no. 20, Hq. Eng. Dept., 18 July 1849, OCE, Orders and Letters, RG 94, NASR, 4:373.

7. *USMA Regulations,* 1832, 16–17, 1839, 18–19; 1853, 15–17; Bayard to Sister, 4 Sept. 1852, Bayard Papers; "The Military Life of Benjamin Bastion, Late of the Army," *Military and Naval Magazine of the United States* 4 (Jan. 1835): 362.

8. Isaac Stevens to Father, 8 Sept. 1835, quoted in Stevens, 1:29; Bayard to Sister, 4 Sept. 1852, Bayard Papers; Bayard to Mother, 2 Nov. 1853, ibid.; Morrison, "Getting Through West Point," 322; William Harris to Father, 27 Mar. 1859, David B. Harris Papers, Duke University, USMA photocopy; H. A. Du Pont to Mother, 28 June 1857 and 17 Oct. 1857, H. A. Du Pont Papers; Wilson 1:22. Edward Anderson to Mother, 28 Feb. 1861, "Letters of a West Pointer," 607.

9. *USMA Regulations,* 1832, 15–16; 1839, 18–19; 1853, 15–16; SR, 1:523–26; Secretary of War to Second Auditor of Treasury, 24 Aug. 1835, OSWLSMA, 14:162, RG 105, NA; Order no. 139, Post Orders, 6; Professor of Chemistry to Adjutant, 18 Aug. 1847, ALR, Box 7; Sherman to Ewing, 15 Sept. 1838, Ewing Papers.

10. *Catalogue of the Library of the U.S. Military Academy, May 1830* (New York: J. Des Nouss, 1830), i–vi.

11. Chief of Engineers to Superintendent, 15 Mar. 1844, ALR, no. 65, Box 2; *Catalogue of the Library . . . 1852* i–vi; Librarian to Superintendent, 3 Sept. 1853, ALR, Box 1.

12. *Catalogue of the Library* . . . *1852*, iv–v; Librarian to Superintendent, 3 Sept. 1853, ALR, Box 1.

13. Superintendent to Hon. Hamilton Fish, 30 Sept. 1851, SLB, 2; Superintendent to Chief of Engineers, 24 Jan. 1852, ibid.; Superintendent to Secretary of the Senate, 5 Aug. 1851, ibid.; Superintendent to Secretary, Board of Regents, 28 Apr. 1852, ibid.; W. L. Macker to Superintendent, 16 Sept. 1843, ALR, Box D, no. 92; Superintendent to Ministers of Public Works, War, Interior, Marine, and Public Instruction of France, 11 Nov. 1849, SLB, 2.

14. *Library Catalogue*, 1852, v, 14; Librarian to Superintendent, 15 Mar. 1844, ALR, Box 2, no. 65; Order no. 1, 4 Jan. 1839, Post Orders 7, USMA Archives.

15. "Circulation Records and Entry of Books Issued to Cadets . . ." 1833–1852, USMA Archives; *Library Catalogue*, 1852, v.

16. *USMA Regulations*, 1832, Table A, 20; "Superintendent's Curriculum Study: Report of the Working Committee on the Historical Aspects of the Curriculum . . . ," July 1958, appendix 12, 12, USMA Archives.

17. *USMA Regulations*, 1853, Table A, 21; "Superintendent's Curriculum Study," 25.

18. Isaac Stevens to Sister, 8 Sept. 1835, quoted in Stevens, 1:29; Isaac Stevens to Father, 11 Mar. 1836, ibid., 44; Reports of the Board of Visitors, 1837 and 1839, USMA Archives; Assistant Professor of Mathematics to Superintendent, 13 Feb. 1841, ALR, G, Box C; SR, 4: 136–45; Bayard to Sister, 4 Sept. 1852; to Mother, 2 Nov. 1853, 14 Mar. 1854; and to Father, 13 Nov. 1853, 12 Feb. 1854, Bayard Papers; *Official Register of the Officers and Cadets of the U.S. Military Academy* (West Point, N.Y.: USMA [pub. annually, 1833–66]), 1841, 23; 1852, 21–22; SR, 4:56–57; U.S. Congress, Senate Misc. Doc. no. 3, *Report of the Commission . . . to examine into the . . . course of instruction of the United States Military Academy . . .*, 36th Cong., 2nd sess., 1860, 219–22; hereafter cited as *Davis Report*, 1860.

19. *Davis Report*, 1860, 219–20; Cajori, 121–24; John Pemberton to Parents, 8 Mar. 1834, Pemberton Family Papers.

20. Appendix II; Order no. 12, 20 Jan. 1833, USMA Post Orders, 6; Report of Committee of the Academic Board, 1 Feb. 1842, ALR, Box E; SR, 3:24–31; Superintendent to Chief of Engineers, 26 Aug. 1851, SLB, 2; Bayard to Mother, 12 Dec. 1852, Bayard Papers; SR, 4.57, 122–23; Superintendent to Chief of Engineers, 24 Feb. 1853, SLB, 2; SR, 2:108–16; *Official Register USMA*, 1838–54; *USMA Regulations*, 1832, Table A; 1839, Table A; 1853, Table A; *Centennial* 1:317.

21. SR, 2:242–43, 228–29; *Centennial* 1:320–23; *Davis Report*, 1860, 210–11.

22. H. B. Du Pont to Sister, 3 Feb. 1833, H. B. Du Pont Papers; Order no. 106, 23 Sept. 1835, USMA Post Orders, 6; SR, 2:99, 315, 335; Jacob W. Bailey to Mother, 4 Feb. 1832, MS. 1546, Bailey Papers; SR, 3:69–74; Chief of Engineers to Superintendent, 14 Nov. 1843, ALR, Box 1, 237; Order no. 25, 29 Oct. 1838, Hq. Engr. Dept., OCE, Record of Orders and Letters, RG 94, NA; *USMA Regulations*, 1839, 15; Report of Board of Visitors, June 1842, USMA Archives, SR, 2:242–43; *USMA Regulations*, 1832, Table A, 17, 139; 1839, Table A; 1853, Table A; Isaac Stevens to Father, 11 Mar. 1836, quoted in Stevens, 1:44; *Davis Report*, 1860, 166–67; Bayard to Sister, 4 Sept. 1852, Bayard Papers.

23. *Centennial* 1:317; *USMA Regulations*, 1832, Table A; 1839, Table A; 1853, Table A; SR, 3:70–72; Report of the Board of Visitors, June 1842, USMA Archives, SR, 2:242–43; Morrison, "Getting Through West Point," 319.

24. Report of Board of Visitors, June 1842, USMA Archives; Isaac Stevens to Father, 11 Mar. 1836, Stevens, 1:44; *Davis Report*, 1860, 166–67.

25. SR, 2:103; Board of Visitors Report, 1839, USMA Archives; *USMA Regulations*, 1839, 12, Table A; 1853, 8–9, Table A; *Davis Report*, 1860, 166–67; *USMA Regulations*, 1832, 9; 1839, 12; 1853, 8–9. Report of Board of Visitors, 1839, USMA Archives; Morrison, "Getting Through West Point," 321; *Centennial* 1:95; SR, 2:244–45, 388; U.S. Congress, Senate, *Reports of Explorations and Surveys*, 33d Cong., 2nd sess., 1854, vol. 13, pt. 3, 1–84;

ibid., *Report of the Superintendent of the Coast Survey,* 34th Cong., 1st sess., 1855, Exec. Doc. 22, 101; Goetzmann, *Army Explorations,* 15.

26. *USMA Regulations,* 1832, 16; 1839, 19; 1853, 16; Morrison, "Getting Through West Point," 321; *Davis Report,* 1860, 239–40.

27. *Davis Report,* 1860, 239–40; Robert Kane, *Elements of Chemistry, Theoretical and Practical* (London: Longman, Brown, 1849), xi–xx (USMA text); Professor of Chemistry to Superintendent, 31 Aug. 1839, 20 Mar. 1840, ALR, Box 11; Morrison, "Getting Through West Point," 321.

28. Superintendent to Chief of Engineers, 13 Feb. 1840, SLB; *USMA Regulations,* 1832, 20; 1839, 23; 1853, 21; SR, 1835–41, 228–29; *USMA Regulations,* 1832, 11; 1839, 12; 1853, 9; J. D. Dana, *Manual of Mineralogy* (Philadelphia: Theodore Bliss, 1864), v–vi, (USMA text); Professor of Chemistry to Superintendent, 16 Oct. 1841, ALR, G, Box C, 161; Emory Upton to Sister, 21 Dec. 1860, quoted in Michie, 29; H. A. Du Pont to Mother, 17 Oct. 1858, H. A. Du Pont Papers; Morrison, "Getting Through West Point," 321, Bliss, Reminiscences, M55, 2:1, Bliss Papers; Goetzmann, *Army Explorations,* 16.

29. *Davis Report,* 1860, 186; Order no. 4, Mar. 1834, USMA Post Orders, 6; *USMA Regulations,* 1832, Table A; 1839, Table A; 1853, Table A; *Davis Report,* 1860, 188; *Centennial* 1:265–68.

30. James McPherson to Catherine Stem, 11 June 1852, Stem Papers, 106; Report of Board of Visitors, June 1842, USMA Archives; *Davis Report,* 1860, 187; Crary, 37–38; Morrison, "Getting Through West Point," 320; *Centennial* 1:268; Pemberton to Father, 20 May 1836, Pemberton Family Papers; Thomas Rowland to Mother, 11 Feb. 1861, "Letters of a Virginia Cadet," 208; William Harris to Father, 27 Mar. 1859, Harris Papers.

31. Griess, 174–75, 177, 180, 197, 223, 359–60, 377; *Davis Report,* 1860, 218–19; "Tabular Statement of Studies," 4 Aug. 1854, ALR, Box E; SR, 2:183, 192–99; SR, 3:84; Monte A. Calvert, *The Mechanical Engineer in America* (Baltimore: Johns Hopkins Press, 1967), 23–28; SR, 4:49, 267.

32. Griess, 253–61; G. W. Cullum to Alfred Huidekoper, 24 Jan. 1833, Cullum MSS.

33. Griess, 173, 224, 217–25; Morrison, "Getting Through West Point," 322; Tully McCrea to Belle McCrea, 21 Sept. 1861 and 5 Oct. 1861, quoted in Crary, 35–36; Report of Board of Visitors, June 1836, USMA Archives; *USMA Regulations,* 1832, 11–12; 1839, 13–15; 1853, 13.

34. David Donald, *Lincoln Reconsidered,* 2d ed. (New York: Alfred A. Knopf, 1966), 87–89; Marcus Cunliffe, *Soldiers and Civilians: The Martial Spirit in America, 1775–1865* (Boston: Little, Brown and Co., 1968), 389–92; Walter Millis, *American Military Thought* (New York: Bobbs-Merrill, 1966), 133–36; J. D. Hittle, *Jomini and His Summary of the Art of War* (Harrisburg, Pa.: Telegraph Press, 1947), 2; T. Harry Williams, "The Military Leadership of North and South," David Donald, ed., *Why the North Won the Civil War* (New York: Collier Macmillan, 1971), 16–54; T. Harry Williams, *The History of American Wars from Colonial Times to World War I* (New York: Alfred A. Knopf, 1981), 195–97, 248–51. For a more balanced view see Grady McWhiney, *Braxton Bragg and Confederate Defeat,* 2 vols. (New York: Columbia Univ. Press, 1969), 1:17–22; Thomas L. Connelly and Archer Jones, *The Politics of Command: Factions and Ideas in Confederate Strategy* (Baton Rouge: Louisiana State Univ. Press, 1973), xii, 3–31; "From Jomini to Dennis Hart Mahan: The Evolution of Trench Warfare and the American Civil War," John T. Hubbell, ed., *Battles Lost and Won: Essays from Civil War History* (Westport, Conn.: Greenwood Press, 1975), 35–40; Weigley, *The American Way of War,* 87–90; Grady McWhiney, "Jefferson Davis and the Art of War," *Civil War History* 21 (June 1975): 102–11. For a rebuttal and a partial summary of the debate see T. Harry Williams, "The Return of Jomini—Some Thoughts on Recent Civil War History," *Military Affairs* 39 (Dec. 1975): 204ff.

35. *Davis Report,* 1860, 82–83, 93, 108; Frank E. Vandiver, *Mighty Stonewall* (New York: McGraw Hill, 1957), 44; Maury, 29–31, 63; Freeman, 1:456–58; Warren W. Hassler, Jr., *George B. McClellan, Shield of the Union* (Baton Rouge: Louisiana State Univ. Press, 1957), 15; Grant, 1:41–42; William T. Sherman, *Memoirs,* 2 vols. (New York: D. Appleton Co., 1875), 1:82; T. Harry Williams, *P. G. T. Beauregard, Napoleon in Gray* (Baton Rouge: Louisiana State Univ. Press, 1955), 33; Morrison, *Heth's Memoirs,* 24–25, 53–54, 75–76, 112–13, 135, 140; Weigley, *American Way of War,* 90; Connelly and Jones, 29–30; Elliott, 734; Wilson, 1:59; Crary, 14.

36. Sherman once claimed that his moves had not been influenced by the study of Jomini: "Address to the Graduating Class of the U.S. Military Academy," (New York: D. Van Nostrand, 1869), 11; T. Harry Williams, "Military Leadership," 40–54; Williams, *History of American Wars,* 248–52; Williams, "The Return of Jomini," 204ff.

37. Utley, 33.

38. Mahon, *History of the Second Seminole War,* 118, 164–65, 229, 297; Williams, *History of American Wars,* 190; Griess, 306–7.

39. Griess, 213, 225; Cadet Drawing, "Top View of Permanent Fortification," USMA MSS; James B. McPherson to Catherine Stem, 13 Feb. 1853, Stem Papers, 106.

40. Chief of Engineers to Superintendent, 1 Nov. 1849, OCELS, 16:401–2, RG 94, NA; U.S. Congress, Senate Exec. Document no. 1, "Report of the Chief Engineer," 32nd Cong., 1st sess., 360; Special Order no. 112, 14 Aug. 1849, USMA Post Orders, 3; SR, 4:32; Superintendent to Chief of Engineers, 7 July 1851, SLB, 2; Order no. 76, 17 July 1851, USMA Post Orders, 3; *Official Register USMA,* 1852, 20.

41. *Official Register USMA,* 1852, 20; *USMA Regulations,* 1853, 2–3, 11; SR, 5:32, 36–40; *Davis Report,* 1860, 175–76; "Tabular Report of Studies," 4 Aug. 1854, ALR, Box E.

42. Bailey to Mother, 4 Feb. 1832, Bailey Papers, MS. 1546; USMA MSS; H. B. Du Pont to Sister, 11 Sept. 1832, H. B. Du Pont Papers; *Centennial* 1:374–77, 382, 263; Superintendent to Chief of Engineers, 25 June 1839, 1; 20 Sept. 1839, 10 Feb. 1840, SLB, 1; 23 Dec. 1850, SLB, 2; Instructor of Artillery and Cavalry to Adjutant, 3 Feb. 1846; ALR, Box 7; SR, 5:343–44.

43. SR, 5:343–44; *Official Register USMA,* 1854, 7–8; Fitz-John Porter, "Obituary of James M. Hawes," *Twenty-First Annual Reunion of the Association of Graduates, 12 June 1890* (Saginaw, Mich.: Evening Press and Binding House, 1890), 25–27; Lt. Hawes to Major Shover, 23 Aug. 1849, ALR (unnumbered); Order no. 117, 18 Aug. 1849, USMA Post Orders, 3.

44. "Tabular Statement of Studies," 4 Aug. 1854, ALR, Box E; *USMA Regulations,* 1853, Table A; *Centennial* 1:897; U.S. Congress, Senate Executive Document no. 1, "Report of the Chief of Engineers," 32nd Cong. 2nd sess., 167; SR, 5:343–44; Order no. 28, 10 Mar. 1833 and Order no. 40, 7 Apr. 1833, USMA Post Orders, 6; Report of Board of Visitors, June 1835, USMA Archives; Report of Board of Visitors [Officers], 1843, USMA Archives; Instructor of Artillery and Cavalry to Adjutant, 3 Feb. 1846, ALR, Box 7, Strong, 184, 205; Edward C. Boynton, *History of West Point and its Military Importance During the American Revolution: and the Origin and Progress of the United States Military Academy* (New York: D. Van Nostrand, 1863), 270.

45. *USMA Regulations,* 1832, 8–16; 1839, 10–19, Table A; SR, 2:229–30, 247.

46. Strong, 279; Maury, 23–24; Morrison, "Getting Through West Point," 231; Bayard to Mother, 14 Mar. 1854 and to Sister, 6 June 1855, Bayard Papers; H. A. Du Pont to Father, 28 Apr. 1861, and to Mother, 25 Feb. 1860, H. A. Du Pont Papers; Order no. 54, 13 May 1851, USMA Post Orders, 3.

47. According to antebellum American military usage, the squadron was a tactical formation smaller than a battalion. U.S. Army, *Cavalry Tactics . . . School of the Trooper, of*

the Platoon, of the Squadron, and the Evolutions of a Regiment (Washington, D.C.: J. & S. Gideon, 1841, reprinted by GPO in 1864), i–xvi; Strong, 279–82.

48. Cadets were appointed on official orders; they wore the appropriate chevrons on their riding jackets only. These appointments were not related to the ranks held by cadets in the regular corps organization. Orders no. 117, 18 Oct. 1849, USMA Post Orders, 3; Lt. James M. Hawes to Superintendent, 5 June 1850, ALR, 5, Box G; Special Order no. 92, 3 Aug. 1850, USMA Post Orders, 3; Hawes to Major Shover, Instructor of Artillery and Cavalry, 10 Aug. 1850, ALR, G, Box H; Special Order no. 134, 29 Aug. 1855, USMA Post Orders, 2; Chief of Engineers to Superintendent, 28 May 1852, OCELS, xviii, RG 94, NA: Special Order no. 106, 28 Aug. 1853, USMA Post Orders, 4; Special Order no. 115, 28 Aug. 1857, USMA Post Orders, 4.

49. "Remarks on the present state of the Artillery," *Military and Naval Magazine of the United States* (June 1834), 267; Hawes to Instructor of Artillery and Cavalry, 8 June 1850, ALR, Box G; SR, 5:179–83; Tidball Memoirs, 111–15, Tidball Papers; J. W. Bailey to Mother, 4 Feb. 1832, Bailey Papers, MS. 1546; Report of Board of Visitors [Officers], 1843, USMA Archives; Superintendent to Chief of Engineers, 9 Aug. 1850, SLB, 2:104; Superintendent to Chief of Engineers, 7 Oct. 1864, SLB, 4:195; Chief of Engineers to Superintendent, 17 Aug. 1844, ALR, Box 2, 224; SR, 5:178–83; Superintendent to Quartermaster General, 17 Mar. 1853, SLB, 3.

CHAPTER SEVEN

1. Theodore W. Crane, ed., *The Colleges and the Public, 1787–1862* (New York: Columbia Teachers' College, 1963), 83; Richard Hofstadter and C. D. Hardy, *The Development and Scope of Higher Education in the United States* (New York: Columbia Univ. Press, 1952), 15–16, 32; John S. Brubacher and Willis Rudy, *Higher Education in Transition: An American History, 1636–1936* (New York: Harper and Bros., 1958), 20, 86, 101–2, et passim; George P. Schmidt, *The Liberal Arts College: A Chapter in American Cultural History* (New Brunswick, N.J.: Rutgers Univ. Press, 1957), 55–57, 239; Frederick Rudolph, *The American College and University: A History* (New York: Alfred A. Knopf, 1962), 130–35.

2. Crane, 82–99.

3. SR, 3:197–99, 206–7.

4. Philip A. Bruce, *History of the University of Virginia, 1819–1919,* 4 vols. (New York: MacMillan, 1921), 2:73, 77, 78, 131, 248–52, 315; Walter B. Kolesnick, *Mental Discipline in Higher Education* (Madison: Univ. of Wisconsin Press, 1958), 6–11; Hofstadter and Hardy, 14–17; Samuel Eliot Morison, *Three Centuries at Harvard, 1636–1936* (Cambridge: Harvard Univ. Press, 1936), 260–61, 277, 296; Palmer C. Ricketts, *History of the Rensselaer Polytechnic Institute, 1824–1894* (New York: John Wiley & Sons, 1895), 29–46; Merle Curti and Vernon Carstensen, *The University of Wisconsin, 1848–1925,* 2 vols., (Madison: Univ. of Wisconsin Press, 1949), 1:173–76; E. M. Coulter, *College Life in the Old South* (Athens: Univ. of Georgia Press, 1951), 61, 63, 72, 101; Thomas J. Wertenbaker, *Princeton, 1746–1896* (Princeton: Princeton Univ. Press, 1946), 234–35, 243, 244; Horace Coon, *Columbia, Colossus on the Hudson* (New York: E. P. Dutton, 1947), 67, 84, 85; Charles F. Thwing, *A History of Higher Education in America* (New York: D. Appleton & Co., 1906), 300; George W. Pierson, *Yale College, An Educational History, 1871–1921* (New Haven: Yale Univ. Press, 1952), 3–5; Virginius Dabney, *Mr. Jefferson's University, A History* (Charlottesville: Univ. Press of Virginia, 1981), 9, 12, 13–20.

5. The figures cited for the University of Virginia and the other colleges are the gross rates of attrition. Bruce, 2:71–72; 3:3–8; Dabney, 18.

6. Clyde B. Stover and Charles W. Beachem, *The Alumni Record of Gettysburg College, 1832–1932* (Gettysburg, Pa.: Gettysburg College, 1932), 3–35; James H. Easterby, *A History of the College of Charleston* (New York: Scribner Press, 1935), appendix II, 290–328; Ricketts, 130–32; William S. Tyler, *History of Amherst College During Its First Half-Century, 1821–1871* (Springfield, Mass.: Clark W. Bryan Co., 1873), 626–27; Nora C. Chaffin, *Trinity College, 1839–1892: The Beginnings of Duke University* (Durham, N.C.: Duke Univ. Press, 1950), 520.

7. William A. Ellis, *Register of Graduates and Past Cadets of Norwich University, 1819–1907* (Bradford, Vt.: Opinion Press, 1907), 19–30; *Register of Former Cadets, Virginia Military Institute* (Lexington: Virginia Military Institute Alumni Association, 1957), 7–19; Olive J. Bond, *The Story of the Citadel* (Richmond, Va.: Garrett and Massie, 1936), 25, 27; *Register of Alumni, U.S. Naval Academy* (Annapolis: U.S. Naval Academy Alumni Association, 1966), 4–6; Boynton, 320–22.

8. Rudolph, 104–5; Schmidt, 79–80; Wertenbaker, 244; Bruce, 2:248–52, 268–311; 3:96–97; Coulter, 63–80; Curti and Karstensen, 173–75; Dabney, 9, 10, 20.

9. Edward P. Cheyney, *History of the University of Pennsylvania, 1740–1940* (Philadelphia: Univ. of Pennsylvania Press, 1940), 196, 226; Bruce, 2:268–311; Coulter, 74–80; Curti and Karstensen, 175; Rudolph, 104–5; Schmidt, 79–83; Dabney, 2, 10, 21.

10. Schmidt, 78–79, 96; Coon, 95; Morison, 277; Coulter, 61; Curti and Karstensen, 186.

11. Tyler, 197, 274–79; W. H. S. Damarest, *A History of Rutgers College, 1766–1924* (New Brunswick, N.J.: Rutgers College Press, 1924), 317; Brubacher, 42–44; Rudolph, 77–85; Schmidt, 27–28; Dabney, 12–13, 20.

12. Rudolph, 92, 103–5; Schmidt, 12, 78–79; Wertenbaker, 185–86, 243, 247; Curti and Karstensen, 1:173–74, 188; Coulter, 48, 63, 72.

13. Bruce, 171, 320, 339, 353–61; Hofstadter and Hardy, 21; Rudolph, 141–42, 151–52, 370; Schmidt, 80, 85, 97; Damarest, 299–300; Thwing, 375–76, 62, 328; Coulter, 78, 118–19; Morison, 202, 272; Dabney, 10, 121, 20, 21.

14. Bruce, 1:60; Schmidt, 95; Curti and Karstensen, 71, 173, 176–77; Brubacher, 26–31; Hofstadter and Hardy, 126–29; Dabney, 7, 9.

15. Rudolph, 158–64; Bruce, 2:96–97; Schmidt, 70–71, 94–96; Curti and Karstensen, 1:178; Brubacher, 80–81, 208–9.

16. *Register of Graduates,* 1963 (no. 966), 224; (no. 1259), 232; Morison, 260; Ricketts, 29; Hofstadter and Hardy, 17; Bruce, 2:128; Schmidt, 92; Wertenbaker, 234; Curti and Karstensen, 2:177.

17. Ricketts, 29; Hofstadter and Hardy, 20; Demarest, 292; Curti and Karstensen, 1:80–81.

18. Morison, 260, 262; Schmidt, 100–101; Bruce, 2:132–33; Wertenbaker, 237–38; Curti and Karstensen, 1:197; Coulter, 53.

19. Schmidt, 101; Curti and Karstensen, 1:200; Coulter, 20, 134–35.

20. Morrison, "Getting Through West Point," 323; Order no. 42, 19 June 1847, USMA Post Orders, 3; Special Order no. 69, 17 June 1853, ibid., 4.

21. Bruce, 2:194; 3:104; Demarest, 326; Thwing, 409–10; Coulter, 41; Brubacher, 951; Curti and Karstensen, 1:348–49.

22. Coulter, 131–32; Schmidt, 71, 97; Rudolph, 143; Bruce, 2:186; Demarest, 299–300; Thwing, 375–76; Morison, 202; Wertenbaker, 228–29.

23. Wertenbaker, 228–29; Bruce, 3:105; 2:201–6; Schmidt, 71–72; Coulter, 41.

24. Coon, 69, 84, 250; Morison, 235, 261–62, 279–90; Thwing, 300–301; Rudolph, 113–15; Schmidt, 45–46; Coulter, 165; Hofstadter and Hardy, 11–15.

25. Ricketts, 78–80; Daniel H. Calhoun, *The American Civil Engineer, Origins and Conflicts* (Cambridge: Harvard Univ. Press, 1960), viii, 44–46, 208; Charles R. Mann, *A Study of Engineering Education* (Boston: E. P. Dutton, 1917), 4–7, 15–16.

26. Rudolph, 203–5, 207–8; Dale Hruby, "The Civilian Careers of West Point Graduates: Classes of 1802 Through 1833,"(Master's essay, Columbia University, 1965), 1622, appendix B; Hostadter and Hardy, 21; Griess, 203–5, 207–8; Forman, 74–89; *Centennial* 1:835–37; *Register,* 1963, 217–55.

27. U.S. Congress, Senate, Doc. 247, 23d Cong., 1st sess., 1834, 1; U.S. Congress, House, Report 303, 24th Cong., 2nd sess., 1837, 15–30; U.S. War Department, *Annual Report of the Secretary of War,* 1861, 27–28; White, *The Jacksonians,* 208–12; Mahan to Totten, 11 Feb. 1843, Mahan Papers; Forman, 62–69.

28. Rudolph, 212–20.

29. Richard Hofstadter, *Anti-Intellectualism in American Life* (New York: Vintage, Alfred A. Knopf, 1963), 164.

30. Rudolph, 212, 220.

31. Christopher Jenks and David Reisman, *The Academic Revolution* (Garden City, N.Y.: Doubleday and Co., 1968), 220.

CHAPTER EIGHT

1. "Report of the Board of Visitors," *The North American Review* 34 (Jan. 1832): 26.

2. "Reports of Boards of Visitors," June 1833, June 1838, June 1842, USMA Archives; "Report of Board of Officers," June 1843, June 1844, USMA Archives; U.S. Congress, Senate, Exec. Doc. no. 1, *Report of the Chief Engineer,* 31st Cong., 2nd sess., 1850, 271–72; U.S. Congress, Senate, Exec. Doc. no. 2, *Report of the Chief Engineer,* 32nd Cong., 1st sess., 1851, 367; U.S. Congress, Senate, Exec. Doc. no. 1, *Report of the Chief Engineer,* 32nd Cong., 2nd sess., 1852, 171–83.

3. SR, 4:37–60, (Feb. 1845), 158 (June 1846); U.S. Congress, Senate, Exec. Dec. no. 1, *Report of the Chief Engineer,* 29th Cong., 2nd sess., 1846, 134.

4. U.S. Congress, Senate, Exec. Doc. no. 98, *Report of the Secretary of War,* 32nd Cong., 1st sess., 1852, 1.

5. Chief of Engineers to Superintendent, 5 June 1854, OCELS, 20:8, RG 94, NA.

6. *Congressional Globe,* 51, pt. 2, 36th Cong., 1st sess., 15 Mar. 1860, 1142–45; Dunbar Rowland, ed., *Jefferson Davis, Constitutionalist, His Letters, Papers, and Speeches,* 10 vols. (Jackson: Mississippi Department of Archives, 1923), 2:307–8.

7. Boynton, 320–21; U.S. Congress, Senate, Exec. Doc. no. 1, *Report of the Chief Engineer,* 32nd Cong., 2nd sess., 1854, 117.

8. Bayard to Mother, 30 Aug. 1854, Bayard Papers; Superintendent to Chief of Engineers, 8 Sept. 1854, SLB, 3; SR, 5, (Sept. 1854): 455; Special Order no. 131, 18 Sept. 1854, USMA Post Orders, 4.

9. SR, July 1854, 432–37; Chief of Engineers to Secretary of War, 8 Aug. 1854, OCE. Abstract of Letter Book, 2:21, RG 94, NA.

10. Special Order no. 132, 18 Sept. 1854, USMA Post Orders, 4; SR, 5, July 1854, 437–38.

11. SR, 6, June 1856, 122; U.S. Congress, *An Act Making Appropriations for the Support of the Military Academy for the year ending the thirtieth of June one thousand eight hundred and fifty-eight,* Sec. 2, approved 16 Feb. 1857; Professor of French to Adjutant, 5 May 1856, ALR, Box 4A; Bratt diary, 16 Apr. 1857; MSS; *Centennial* 3:311, 325.

12. SR, 6, June 1856, 122; "Tabular Statement of Studies," 4 Aug. 1854, ALR, Box E; *Davis Report,* 1860, 115–18.

13. "Tabular Statement of Studies," 4 Aug. 1854, ALR, Box E.

14. *Davis Report,* 1860, 288–91.

15. Ibid., 244, 438; SR, 5, July 1854, 432–38; SR, 5, Dec. 1856, 198–99.

16. "Tabular Statement of Studies," 9 Aug. 1854, ALR, Box E; SR, 5, July 1854, 438; SR, 6, Dec. 1856, 198–99; Secretary of War to Acting Chief of Engineers, 26 Aug. 1859, OSWLSMA, 61:383, RG 107, NA; Secretary of War to Chief of Engineers, 10 Sept. 1859, ibid., 403; Special Order no. 164, 13 Sept. 1859, USMA Post Orders, 5; SR, 7, Sept. 1859, 31.

17. Professor of Engineering to Superintendent, 15 July 1858, OCEMA, 1841–58, RG 104, NA.

18. Professor of Engineering to Superintendent, 2 Oct. 1854, ALR, Box A9M.

19. SR, 5, July 1854, 437–38; Report of Instructor of Practical Military Engineering, 21 Apr. 1859, ALR, Box 12; "Tabular Report of Studies," 4 May 1854, ALR, Box E; *Davis Report,* 1860, 31, 175–76; *USMA Regulations,* 1857, 16, 20, 36; SR, 6, Dec. 1856, 191–93.

20. U.S. Congress, *An Act Making Appropriations for the Support of the Army, June 12, 1858, for the year ending the thirtieth of June, eighteen hundred and fifty-nine,* chap. 156, approved 12 June 1858; *Centennial* 1·374, 379–80; Special Order no. 117, 6 Aug. 1856, USMA Post Orders, 6.

21. "Tabular Statement of Studies," 4 Aug. 1854, ALR, Box E; USMA, "Endorsements and Memorandums," 1 (10 June 1857): 69, USMA Archives; *Centennial* 1:426.

22. Griess, 223; *Official Registers USMA,* 1860, 17; 1859, 9, 16; *Centennial* 2:114; SR, 7, Sept. 1859, 35–37; Chief of Engineers to Superintendent 19 Oct. 1859, ALR; SR, 7, Sept. 1859, 25–31.

23. Figures reflect the total number of drills for the entire five years. "Tabular Statement of Studies," 4 Aug. 1854, ALR, Box E; Instructor of Small Arms to Adjutant, 22 July 1859, ALR, Box 5A; USMA, "Endorsements and Memorandums," 1 (11 Apr. 1859): 124, USMA Archives; *Davis Report,* 1860, 218.

24. Instructor of Small Arms to Adjutant, 22 July 1859, ALR, Box 5A; USMA, "Endorsements and Memorandums," 1 (11 Aug. 1859): 124; Special Order no. 106, 25 June 1859, USMA Post Orders, 5; *Davis Report,* 1860, 31, 218, 229.

25. *Davis Report,* 1860, 218, 229–31.

26. *Davis Report,* 1860, 31; *USMA Regulations,* 1857, 20–21, 55.

27. *Davis Report,* 1860, 31, 218, 203, 229; H. A. Du Pont to Father, 8 Oct. 1859, H. A. Du Pont Papers; SR, 7, Sept. 1859, 31; *Official Registers USMA,* 1860, 18; *USMA Regulations,* 1857, 55.

28. *Davis Report,* 1860, 31, 229, 238; *USMA Regulations,* 1857, 55.

29. Nathaniel C. Hughes, Jr., *General William J. Hardee, Old Reliable* (Baton Rouge: Louisiana State Univ. Press, 1965), 41–49, 67; *Davis Report,* 1860, 87, 200–203, 218; H. A. Du Pont to Mother, 4 Oct. 1856, 28 Mar. 1857, H. A. Du Pont Papers.

30. U.S. Congress, Senate, Exec. Doc. no. 12, *Report of the Chief Engineer,* 34th Cong., 2nd sess. 1856, 301–2; *Davis Report,* 1860, 130, 189; Chief of Engineers to Secretary of War, 20 Sept. 1858, OCE, Abstract of Letter Book, 2:79–80, RG 94, NA.

31.

Math	3	Law	1	Mil Engr, Sci War	3
Natl Phil	3	Ethics & Log	1	Ord & Gunnery	1½
Min & Geol	1	Rhetoric	½	Inf Tactics	1
Chem	1½	Lit, Hist, Geog.	½	Arty Tactics	1
Civl Engr	1	Drawing	1	Cav Tactics	1
Prac Engr	½	French	1	Total	7½
Total	10	Spanish	1		
		Conduct	1½		
		Total	7½		

Sources: *USMA Regulations,* 1857, 36; Schaff, 273.

32. *USMA Regulations,* 1853, 21.

33. U.S. Congress, Senate, Exec. Doc. no. 1, *Report of the Chief Engineer,* 34th Cong., 1st sess., 1855, 250; Special Order no. 206, 10 Nov. 1855, USMA Post Orders, 4; Superintendent to Chief of Engineers, 16 Oct. 1855, SLB, 3:249; Chief of Engineers to Superintendent, 8 Dec. 1855, ALR, Box 3, no. 373; *USMA Regulations,* 1857, 37.

34. Secretary of War to Chief of Engineers, 12 Apr. 1860, ALR, Box F; Order no. 9, 14 Apr. 1860, USMA Post Orders, 5; Special Order no. 64, 7 May 1860, ibid.; SR, 7, May 1860, 65–69.

35. U.S. Congress, Senate, Exec. Doc. no. 1, Report of the Chief Engineer, 36th Cong., 2nd sess., 1860, pt. 2, 275; SR, 7, Jan. 1861, 140; Mar. 1861, 156–57.

36. Superintendent to Chief Engineer, 5 Oct. 1855, SLB, 3; Chief Engineer to Superintendent, 30 Oct. 1855, 17 Nov. 1855, OCELS, 20:414, RG 94, NA; Acting Chief Engineer to Superintendent, 30 June 1860, OCELS, 23:163, RG 94, NA.

37. Special Order no. 211, 21 Dec. 1855, USMA Post Orders, 4.

38. Special Order no. 173, 8 Dec. 1858, USMA Post Orders, 5; Special Order no. 8, 17 Jan. 1859, ibid.; Special Order no. 95, 20 June 1859, ibid.; Special Order no. 144, 12 Aug. 1859, ibid.; Adjutant to William Conner, 25 Mar. 1859, ALB, 3:60; H. A. Du Pont to Mother, 25 Dec. 1859, H. A. Du Pont Papers; Thomas Rowland to Mother, 29 Apr. 1860, "Letters of a Virginia Cadet," 344; Michie, "Reminiscences of Cadet and Army Service," 194; George A. Custer to Adjutant, 18 Aug. 1860, ALR, Box C.

39. Superintendent to Chief of Engineers, 3 Aug. 1856, SLB, 3:332; Chief of Engineers to Superintendent, 18 Aug. 1856, ALR, Box 3, no. 155; Special Order no. 59, 25 Apr. 1857, USMA Post Orders, 5; Chief of Engineers to Secretary of War, 11 May 1857, OCE, Abstract of Letters Sent, 2:13, RG 94, NA; Edward Anderson to Mother, 29 June 1860, "Letters of a Virginia Cadet," 603.

40. Special Order no. 86, 16 June 1856, USMA Post Orders, 4; Order no. 20, 14 June 1857, ibid., 5; Special Order no. 69, 17 June 1853, ibid., 4; Bratt diary, 10 June 1857; *New York Times,* 15 Jan. 1859, 4; Order no. 18, 14 June 1860, USMA Post Orders, 5.

41. Bayard to Sister, 20 Nov. 1855, Bayard Papers; Special Order no. 32, 1 Mar. 1856, USMA Post Orders, 4; Forman, 148; Album, Class of 1857, USMA Collection of Class Albums.

42. William H. Harris to Father, 4 Apr. 1859, 10 Apr. 1859, 4 Mar. 1860, Harris Papers; SR, 6, Aug. 1858, 348–50, 353–64; Oct. 1858, 385–86; Special Order no. 143, 11 Oct. 1858, USMA Post Orders, 5; Boynton, 250.

43. Secretary of War to Chief of Engineers, 31 Mar. 1859, OSWLSMA, 41:184, RG 107, NA; Chief of Engineers to Superintendent, Apr. 1859, ALR, Box 5, no. 5; Circular, 4 Apr. 1859, USMA Post Orders, 5; Special Order no. 54, 5 Apr. 1859, ibid.; Bratt diary, 5 Apr. 1859.

44. H. A. Du Pont to Mother, 10 June 1859, 14 Oct. 1860, H. A. Du Pont Papers; Letters, Bratt diary, 5 Apr. 1859; William H. Harris to Father, 10 Apr. 1859, Harris Papers; Boynton, 250; "John B. Floyd," *The Encyclopedia of Southern History,* ed. David C. Roller and Robert W. Twyman (Baton Rouge: Louisiana State Univ. Press, 1979), s.v. Floyd, John B.; Morrison, *Heth's Memoirs,* xxxiii–xxxvii, 138, 151–59, 160–62.

45. Denton, 260, citing Thayer to Gratiot, (Chief of Engineers), 27 Jan. 1832, Thayer Papers, and Gratiot to Drayton, 2 Feb. 1832, OSWLSMA, 3:20–22; U.S. Congress, *Journal of the House of Representatives,* 22nd Cong., 1st sess., 1831–32, 307.

46. Acting Chief of Engineers to Capt. H. G. Wright, 15 Sept. 1858, Thayer Papers, 20.

47. Thayer to Cullum, 25 Feb. 1860, Thayer Papers, 20; Secretary of War to Superintendent, 7 Apr. 1860, ELS, 23:109, RG 94, NA; Thayer to Mordecai, 30 Apr. 1860, Thayer Papers, 20; Superintendent to Secretary of War, 1 May 1860, OSW, Register of Letters Received, 96, A-312, RG 107, NA; *Davis Report,* 1860, 132, 148, 272, 338–41, 320–27.

48. *Davis Report,* 1860, 1; Rowland, 4:519; *Congressional Globe,* 51, pt. 2, no. 114, 36th Cong., 1st sess. 19 Apr. 1860, 1810; U.S. Congress, Senate, *Senate Journal,* 36th Cong., 1st sess., June 1860, 785.

49. *Davis Report,* 1860, 2.

50. Ibid., 1, 12–19; *Congressional Globe,* 36th Cong., 2nd sess., Jan. 1861, no. 29, 463.

51. *Davis Report,* 1860, 12–19.

CHAPTER NINE

1. Wofford to Adjutant, USMA, 19 Dec. 1860, ALR.

2. Tully McCrea to Belle McCrea, 29 Dec. 1860, in Crary, 73; Schaff, 83; Joseph P. Farley, *West Point in the Early Sixties* (Troy, N.Y.: Palfrey's Book Co., 1902), 24; William H. Harris to Clara, 30 Dec. 1860, Harris Papers; Robert G. Carter, *Four Brothers in Blue, Or Sunshine and Shadows of the War of the Rebellion* (Austin: Univ. of Texas Press, 1978), 2.

3. *Register of Graduates,* 1963, 251–55. "Southern" and "South" as used herein refer to the eleven Confederate States.

4. H. A. Du Pont to Mother, 10 Apr. 1861, H. A. Du Pont Papers; Edward W. Anderson to Mother, 18 Apr. 1861, "Letters of a West Pointer, 1860–1861," 61; A. G. Marchbanks to Chief of Engineers, 22 Apr. 1861, ALR.

5. Thomas Rowland to Mother, 27 Dec. 1860 and to Aunt, 16 Apr. 1861, "Letters of a Virginia Cadet at West Point, 1859–1861," *South Atlantic Quarterly* 15 (July 1915): 154–56, 214.

6. Beauregard to Chief of Engineers, 23 Jan. 1861, SLB, 4; Special Order 6, 23 Jan. 1861, USMA Post Orders, 5; Chief of Engineers to Delafield (Message), 24 Jan. 1861, and Chief of Engineers to Delafield, 28 Jan. 1861, ELS, 23.288, RG 94, NA; Bratt diary, 19 Jan. 1861; Gouvernour Kemble to Winfield Scott, Jan. 1861, A. J. Swift Papers, USMA Archives; Williams, *P. G. T. Beauregard,* 44–47; Hamilton Basso, *Beauregard, the Great Creole* (New York: Charles Scribner's Sons, 1933), 60–62.

7. Tully McCrea to Belle McCrea, 27 Apr. 1861, in Crary, 88–89; Schaff, 247.

8. Stevens, 1:37–55; Tidball, "Getting Through West Point," 65–69, Tidball Papers; Oliver Otis Howard, *Autobiography,* 2 vols., (N.Y.: Taylor Co., 1908), 1:48–55; John A. Carpenter, *Sword and Olive Branch: Oliver Otis Howard* (Pittsburgh: Univ. of Pittsburgh Press, 1964), 8–9; Stuart to George Hairston, 6 Mar. 1851, MS. 2, St. 922–b–2, Va. Historical Society, Richmond; Walter Sherwood to Jacob T. Garthwaite, 29 June 1833, USMA MSS.

9. Tidball Papers, 65–69, USMA MSS; Schaff, 82, 139–65; Wilson, 1:19–21, 27; Carter, 5–7; Crary, 64, 69, 77–78, 82.

10. Morgan to Adjutant, 7 Apr. 1857, ALR.

11. Schaff, 85–86; Edward W. Anderson to Mother, 3 July 1860, "Letters of a West Pointer," 604; Crary, 78; Miohic, 26, Thomas Rowland to Mother, 9 Aug. 1859, "Letters of a Virginia Cadet," 213.

12. USMA Dialectic Society Journal, 1840–44, USMA MSS; Stevens, 1:38; SR, 2 Dec. 1841, 332, USMA Archives; ibid., 3, Feb. 1842, 10; Superintendent to Chief of Engineers, 10 Dec. 1841, ELS, 10:8–10, RG 94, NA; Superintendent to Inspector, 12 Apr. 1858, ALB, 3; Chief of Engineers to Superintendent, 3 June 1865, OCELS, 10:8–10, RG 94, NA.

13. Reports, Boards of Visitors, 1838, 1848, USMA Archives; U.S. Congress, Senate Documents, 1:1, *Report of the Chief Engineer,* 31st Cong., 1st sess., 1849, 244.

14. Rowland, 2:351, 3:560. Davis graduated from West Point in 1828: *Register of Graduates,* 1963, 251.

15. Truman Seymour, "Politics and West Point," reprint from *Army and Navy Journal*

and *New York Times,* 8 Sept. 1864, USMA Cullum Files; Stuart to George Hairston, 6 Mar. 1851; Crary, 63–64; Schaff, 137–38; Wilson, 1:23–27.

16. *Congressional Globe,* 37th Cong., 3d sess., Jan. 1863 324–27; Williams, "Attack on West Point," 491–504.

17. Franklin, 138–44; Huntington, 211, et passim; Marcus Cunliffe believes the idea of a "Militant South" needs revision; see *Soldiers and Civilians,* 25, 211–21, 320, et passim.

18. *Annual Report of the Secretary of War,* 1861, 27–36, 46–48; Williams, "Attack on West Point," 491–93.

19. Williams, "Attack on West Point," 492–501; White, *The Jacksonians,* 208–12; U.S. Congress, Senate Doc. 247, 23d Cong., 1st sess., 1834, 1; U.S. Congress, House, Report no. 303, 24th Cong., 2nd sess., 1837, 15–20; "Miscellany," *Army and Navy Chronicle* 9 (Sept. 1839): 182–83; Weigley, *History of the Army,* 154–57.

20. "History of West Point," *North American Review* 98 (Apr. 1864): 540–50; Griess, 298, 330, et passim; Forman, 128–29; Boynton, 251–52, 324; *Congressional Globe,* 37th Cong., 3d sess., Jan. 1863, 324, 34; *New York Times,* 23 Jan. 1863, 4; 16 May 1864, 4; 26 May 1864, 2, 4; 16 Sept. 1864, 5; *Army and Navy Journal,* 24 Sept. 1864, 69, 70; 19 Dec. 1863, 265.

21. Chief of Engineers to Secretary of War, 23 Jan. 1866, OCE Abstract of Letter Book, 3:112, RG 94, NA; *Congressional Globe,* House, pt. 3, 39th Cong., 1st sess., Mar. 1866, 119.

22. *Register of Graduates,* 1948, 386–87. The classes in this group included 85.4 percent of the total number of graduates who joined the Confederacy and 77.1 percent of those who served on the Union side.

23. Heitman, 2:180–84, lists a total of 99 regular officers, not graduates of the Military Academy, who resigned to join the Confederacy. There were 343 such officers on duty at the time. *Army Register,* 1861, 1–31; Weigley, *History of the Army,* 199; Ganoe, 250.

24. SR, 7, 24 Apr. 1861, 158–59, and 3 May 1861, 160–69, 210–12; Superintendent to Chief of Engineers, 24 Apr. 1861, SLB, 4; Chief of Engineers to Superintendent, 29 Apr. 1861, ELS 23, 384, RG 94, NA; USMA Order no. 13, 2 May 1861, USMA Post Orders, 6.

25. Members of the Class of June 1861 to Secretary of War, 24 Apr. 1861, ALR; Superintendent to Chief of Engineers, 16 Apr. 1861, SLB, 4; Members of the First Class to Secretary of War, 15 Apr. 1861, ALR.

26. Superintendent to B. R. Petriken, 25 Mar. 1862, SLB, 4; Superintendent to Chief of Engineers, 18 Mar. 1861, ALR; Chief of Engineers to Superintendent (telegram), 29 Aug. 1861, ELS 23, 510, RG 94, NA.

27. "Program of a course of studies for four years," 30 May 1861, SR, 7, May 1861, 183–87; Chief of Engineers to Superintendent, 26 Aug. 1861, ALR; Chief of Engineers to Superintendent (telegram), 29 Aug. 1861, OCELS, 23, 510, RG 94, NA.

28. *Congressional Globe,* 12 June 1862, 37th Cong., 2nd sess., 1862, pt. 3, 2646–59, 3371; Chief of Engineers to Superintendent (telegram), 16 June 1862, OCELS, 23, 142, RG 94, NA.

29. Chief of Engineers to Superintendent, 9 July 1863, OCELS, 24, 344, RG 94, NA; ibid., 18 July 1863, 349; Superintendent to Chief of Engineers, n.d., July 1863, SLB, 4:119; Capt. S. T. Cushing to Superintendent, 20 Oct. 1863, ALR; SR, 7, Apr. 1864, 35–354.

30. U.S. Congress, *An Act Providing for the Better Organization of the Military Establishment,* chap. 42, sec. 8, approved 3 Aug. 1861; *Congressional Globe,* 37th Cong., 1st sess., July 1861, 437–38; Archivist USMA to Florence Lyons, 29 Nov. 1956, USMA Archives, *USMA Regulations,* 1866, 7; *Congressional Globe,* 37th Cong., 2nd sess., (1862), appendix, 385.

31. Special Order no. 56, 14 July 1863, USMA Post Orders, 6; Bowman to Totten, 23 July 1863, SLB, 4; Cullum to Col. H. F. Clarke, 22 Nov. 1864, Private and Confidential, SLB, 4.

32. Bowman to Totten, 5 Sept. 1861, and 30 May 1861, SLB, 4; Bowman to B. R. Petri-

kin, 25 Mar. 1862, and to A. L. Twining, 17 Mar. 1862, SLB, 4; Bowman to Totten, 6 Dec. 1861, SLB. 4; Bowman to Totten, Endorsements and Memos, 1:201, USMA Archives.

33. *New York Times,* 21 Jan. 1863, 4; *North American Review* 98 (Apr. 1864): 546; *Army and Navy Journal,* 20 Sept. 1864, 402; Superintendent to Senator Ira Harris, n.d., Mar. 1864, SLB, 4: 152; *Congressional Globe,* 38th Cong., 1st sess., pt. 2, 66, Mar. 1864, 1053–84, 1086, 1088, 1091; ibid., pt. 2, 77, Mar. 1864, 1266; *New York Times,* 9 June 1864, 4; Report of Committee of Academic Board, SR, 7, June 1865, 450–51; Thayer to Cullum, 23 Jan. 1865, Thayer Papers, 2; Superintendent to Secretary, Board of Visitors, 21 June 1865, SLB, 4; *United States Service Magazine* 4 (Sept. 1865): 194; U.S. Congress, *Joint Resolution Relative to Appointments to the Military Academy of the United States,* no. 49, June 1866, sec. 3; U.S. Congress, *An Act Making Appropriations for the Year Ending June Thirtieth, Eighteen Hundred and Sixty-Eight and for Other Purposes,* chap. 152, sec. 3, approved 2 Mar. 1867; *Centennial* 2:120.

34. Delafield to Tower, 13 Aug. 1864, OCELS, 25:25, RG 94, NA; Tower to Delafield, 16 Aug. 1864, SLB, 4; Special Order 124, 2 Sept. 1864, USMA Post Orders, 6; Kirk, 443.

35. U.S. Congress, *An Act for the Better Organization of the Military Establishment,* chap. 42, sec. 8, 3 Aug. 1861, 38th Cong., 1st sess.; Superintendent to Chief of Engineers, 21 Dec. 1861, SLB, 4; SR, 7, June 1863, 303; U.S. Congress, *An Act Making Appropriations for. . . the Military Academy,* chap. 75, sec. 2, 38th Cong., 2nd sess., 2 Mar. 1865; *Congressional Globe,* 38th Cong., 2nd sess., pt. 1, no. 19, Jan. 1865, 301, and appendix, 128.

36. Superintendent to Chief of Engineers, 30 July 1861, 30 May 1861, 18 Mar. 1861, SLB, 4:30, 17, 5; 5 Dec. 1861, USMA Endorsements and Memos, 1:201; 6 Dec. 1861, 10 Sept. 1861, 31 Dec. 1861, 21 Jan. 1864, 7 Aug. 1862, 10 Aug. 1865, SLB, 4; Superintendent to Governor of Conn., 29 Apr. 1861, SLB, 4:11; Special Orders no. 185, 26 Oct. 1861, no. 80, 19 Oct. 1861, USMA Post Orders, 6; *Register of Graduates,* 1860–65; Chief of Engineers to Superintendent, 4 Sept. 1861, 12 Aug. 1865, OCELS 24:5–6, and 25, RG 94, NA; 15 Jan. 1864, ALR; Crary, 121–22; Superintendent to A. L. Twining, 17 Mar. 1862, SLB, 4; U.S. Congress. House, Doc. 21, *Report of the Chief Engineer,* 37th Cong., 3d sess., June 1862, 102; Adjutant USMA to Adjutant Fifth Artillery, 8 July 1862, ALB, 3; Adjutant to Capt. W. P. Chambliss, 13 Feb. 1864, ALB, 3.

37. Superintendent to Chief of Engineers, 4 Nov. 1864, SLB, 4; Chief of Engineers to Superintendent, 10 Nov. 1864, OCELS, 25:63, RG 94, NA; Special Orders no. 293, 5 Dec. 1864; no. 102, 6 July 1865; no. 22, 9 Feb. 1866, USMA Post Orders, 6; no. 103, 11 Aug. 1866, ibid., 7; Boynton, 219; *Centennial* 2:77, 120; *USMA Regulations,* 1866, 51–52; Frederick P. Todd, *Cadet Gray, A Pictorial History of Life at West Point As Seen Through Its Uniforms,* (New York: Sterling Publishing Co., 1955), 111; *The Howitzer,* yearbook of the Corps of Cadets, various publishers, issues 1897 through 1914.

38. *New York Times,* 4 Jan. 1865, 4; 17 June 1865, 1; Special Orders no. 100, 30 June 1861; no. 75, 14 June 1862; no. 50, 10 June 1863; no. 68, 10 June 1864, USMA Post Orders, 6.

39. Mahan to Totten, 13 July 1861, Mahan Papers, Engineer Department, MA 2524–1861, RG 94, NA; Mahan to Salmon P. Chase, 22 Oct. 1861, Chase Papers; Edwin M. Stanton to Mahan, 25 July 1863, and Mahan, undated memo, Mahan Papers; Herman Hattaway and Archer Jones, *How the North Won, A Military History of the Civil War* (Urbana: Univ. of Illinois Press, 1983), 97, 99, 107; Williams, *History of American Wars,* 253; Weigley, *History of the Army,* 227, 449; Matloff, 205, 264.

40. *New York Times,* 25 Dec. 1861, A3; Totten to Bowman, 6 May 1863, OCELS, 24:299, RG 94, NA; Totten to Bowman, 29 July 1863, OCELS, 24:355, RG 94, NA; Delafield to Cullum, 29 Sept. 1864, OCELS, 25:49, RG 94, NA; David L. Ogden to Bowman, 30 Aug. 1861, ALR; "Papers Relating to Beardsley Electro-Magnetic Apparatus," 3 Dec. 1864-17 Nov. 1865, ALR; Thomas C. Scott (Asst. Sec. War) to Chief of Ordnance, 24 Oct. 1861, ALR.

41. First annual report as secretary of war, quoted by Millis, 175.

42. Confederate: 41 killed, 32 wounded. Union: 54 killed, 109 wounded.

43. *Register of Graduates,* 1963, 218–55.

44. Dennis Hart Mahan, "West Point Training—The True Point of View," *New York Times,* 3 Mar. 1866, 4.

CHAPTER TEN

1. Ganoe, 306.

2. U.S. Congress, Senate, Exec. Doc. no. 88, *Report of the Secretary of War,* 16th Cong., 1st sess., 1820, 4–26; Denton, 182–87; Huntington, 216.

3. Chief of Engineers to Mahan, 9 Mar. 1852, OCELS, 7:364, RG 94, NA; *Congressional Globe,* pt. 2, 31st Cong., 1st sess., July 1852, 1858, 2045.

4. U.S. Congress, House, Doc. no. 1, *Report of the Secretary of War,* 34th Cong., 1st sess., 1855, 10; Rowland, 2:561; U.S. Congress, House, Exec. Doc. no. 12, *Report of the Board of Visitors,* 34th Cong., 3d sess., 1856, 300–301; Chief of Engineers to Delafield, (Private), 19 July 1856, ALR; A. J. Swift Memoirs, 17 Aug. 1855, 276, Swift Papers; Swift to Thayer, 28 Oct. 1855, ibid.; Bayard to Sister, 30 May 1856, Bayard Papers; Thayer to Cullum, 23 June 1856, Thayer Papers, 2.

5. Local rank applied only at West Point, *Congressional Globe,* 35th Cong., 1st sess., 1858, appendix, 572–73; U.S. Congress, *An Act Making Appropriations . . . for . . . eighteen hundred and fifty-nine,* chap. 156, approved 12 June 1858.

6. *Davis Report,* 1860, 181, 199, 203, 208, 226–27, 236–37.

7. Ibid., 139, 143, 149, 195, 197, 308–9, 313, 317.

8. Ibid., 12–13.

9. James L. Morrison, Jr., "Educating the Civil War Generals: West Point, 1833–1861," *Military Affairs* 38 (Oct. 1974): 108.

10. Ibid. Ames later became one of the "boy generals" of the Civil War; in the 1870s he served as a "carpetbag" governor of Mississippi.

11. Sherman, *Memoirs,* 2:405; U.S. Congress, House, Reports of Committees, Report no. 74, *Army-Staff Reorganization,* 42nd Cong., 3d sess., 1873, 10:277–88.

12. Chief of Engineers to Superintendent, 7 July 1865, OCELS, 25:170, RG 94, NA; Superintendent to Chief of Engineers, 10 Aug. 1865, 1 Sept. 1865, SLB, 4.

13. U.S. Congress, House, Exec. Doc. no. 1, *Report of the Secretary of War, Report of the Chief of Engineers,* 39th Cong., 1st sess., 1865, 2:983–93.

14. Ibid., 987.

15. Chief of Engineers to Secretary of War, 22 Jan. 1866, OCE, Abstract of Letter Book, 3:112, RG 94, NA; *Congressional Globe,* House, pt. 3, 39th Cong., 1st sess., Mar. 1866, 1191.

16. U.S. Congress, House, Exec. Doc. no. 1, *Report of the Secretary of War,* 39th Cong., 1st sess., 1865, 993.

17. U.S. Congress, House, Exec. Doc. no. 1, *Report of the Secretary of War,* 39th Cong., 1st sess., 1865, 984, 988–93; *New York Times,* 1 Aug. 1865, 1; Chief of Engineers to Secretary of War, 20 June 1865, OCE, Abstract of Letter Book, 3:73–77, RG 94, NA; *United States Service Magazine* 4 (Sept. 1865): 193–95.

18. Ibid., 20.

19. W. T. Sherman, George G. Meade, and George H. Thomas to Major General J. A. Rawlins, 1 Feb. 1866, MS 1056, USMA MSS.

20. "The Board of Visitors at West Point," *United States Service Magazine* 4 (Sept.

1865): 193–94; *New York Times,* 19 June 1866, 8; Superintendent to Senator Henry Wilson, 12 Jan. 1866, SLB, 4; Mahan to Senator Edwin D. Morgan, 10 Apr 1866, Morgan MSS, New York State Library (USMA photocopy); Mahan to Sherman, 21 Mar. 1866, 5 Feb. 1866, Sherman Papers, General Correspondence, 18:2481–82, 2424.

21. *Congressional Globe,* 39th Cong., 1st sess., May 1866, pt. 3, 2795–96; ibid., pt. 4, 3255, 3575; ibid., pt. 5, 338; Order, Headquarters Engineer Department, 8 Aug. 1866, ALR; General Order no. 54, AGO, 30 July 1866, OCE, Record of Letters and Orders, 632, RG 94, NA.

22. *Congressional Globe,* 39th Cong., 1st sess., 1866, pt. 4, 3575, 3589, 3590, 3255; U.S. Congress, *An Act Making Appropriations For the Support of the Army for the Year Ending the Thirtieth of June Eighteen Hundred and Sixty-Seven,* chap. 176, sec. 6.

23. General Order no. 54, AGO, 30 July 1866, OCE, Record of Orders and Letters, 632, RG 94, NA; Special Orders no. 110 and 111, 28 Aug. 1866, USMA Post Orders, 7; Superintendent to Inspector, Military Academy, 28 Aug. 1866, SLB, 4.

24. *Register of Graduates,* 1963, 232. Cadets in the last section of the class were called "Immortals" (see chapter 6).

25. *USMA Regulations,* 1866, 4–5.

26. SR, 8:60–63, 133, 134; *USMA Regulations,* 1866, 8–15.

27. *USMA Regulations,* 1866, 32. SR, 8:60–63, 133, 134, passim.

28. Weigley, *History of the Army,* 272; Matloff, 289; Forman, 135–36; Ambrose, 192–93; William P. Randel, *Centennial: American Life in 1876* (New York: Chilton Book Co., 1969), 273.

29. Rudolph, 241–46, 290–95; Brubacher and Rudy, 155–57; Thwing, 436–37.

30. *USMA Regulations,* 1853, 7–12, 13, 14; 1873, 12–21; *Official Registers USMA,* 1853, 22–24; 1866, 24, 25; 1873, 27, 28.

31. Rudolph, 230–32, 246; Brubacher and Rudy, 87, 262; Thwing, 436–37. For conflicting views on the efficacy of West Point education at the turn of the twentieth century see Charles W. Eliot, "From the President of Harvard University," *Army and Navy Journal* 39 (14 June 1902): 1023, and William R. Harper, "American Universities and Colleges," *Centennial* 1:713–16.

32. *Centennial* 1:292, 314, 325; Forman, 135–36, USMA Cullum Files, no. 494 (George L. Andrews), and 2339 (Charles W. Larned).

33. Mahan to Superintendent, 20 Sept. 1869, and 1 Nov. 1869, ALR; Superintendent to Mahan, 9 Mar. 1866, SLB, 4; Mahan to Sherman, 8 Sept. 1865, Sherman Papers, General Correspondence, 17:2315–16; Mahan to Chief of Engineers, 28 Jan. 1867, OCE, Mahan Papers, M-21, RG 77, NA; William E. Merrill to Mahan, 8 Mar. 1867, MS. 1455, USMA MSS.

34. Mahan to Superintendent, 12 Sept. 1867, ALR.

35. Report, Peter S. Michie to Adjutant, USMA, 25 July 1873, ALR.

36. Williams, *History of American Wars,* 196–97. Anyone who attaches such importance to the impact of a single course has never taught West Point cadets.

37. William H. Ashbaugh, "The Therapeutic Curriculum, Personality Outcomes of the Academic Disciplines," *Psychology In the Schools* 2 (Apr. 1965): 126–29. A more extensive bibliography of studies on the subject is contained in a manuscript by the same author, former Professor of Psychology, York College of Pennsylvania.

Bibliography
★

PRIMARY SOURCES

Manuscripts

Allen, Jesse K. Letters. U.S. Military Academy, West Point, New York.
Anderson, Robert. Letters. U.S. Military Academy, West Point, New York.
Ayres, Romeyn B. Papers. U.S. Military Academy, West Point, New York.
Bailey, Jacob W. Papers. U.S. Military Academy West Point, New York.
Bailey, William W. Scrapbook. U.S. Military Academy West Point, New York.
Bayard, George D. Papers. U.S. Military Academy, West Point, New York.
Beauregard, Pierre G. T. Papers. U.S. Military Academy, West Point, New York.
Bliss, W. S. Letters (microfilm). U.S. Military Academy, West Point, New York.
Bliss, Zenas R. Papers. U.S. Army Military History Institute. Carlisle Barracks, Pennsylvania.
Bonaparte, Jerome N. Letters. U.S. Military Academy, West Point, New York.
Bratt, John. Diaries, 1833–1889. U.S. Military Academy, West Point, New York.
Brooke, W. T. H. Letters. U.S. Army Military History Institute. Carlisle Barracks, Pennsylvania.
Carr, Eugene A. Papers. U.S. Army Military History Institute. Carlisle Barracks, Pennsylvania.
Church, Albert E. Letters. U.S. Military Academy, West Point, New York.
Cullum, George W. Papers. U.S. Military Academy, West Point, New York.
———. Papers relative to Association of Graduates. U.S. Military Academy, West Point, New York.
Custer, George A. Papers. U.S. Military Academy, West Point, New York.
Davis, Jefferson. Papers. U.S. Military Academy, West Point, New York.
Delafield, Richard. Papers. U.S. Military Academy, West Point, New York.
Dialectic Society. Journal. U.S. Military Academy, West Point, New York.
D'Oremieulx, Theophile. Papers. U.S. Military Academy, West Point, New York.
Du Pont, Henry A. Papers. Hagley Museum and Library, Wilmington, Delaware.
Du Pont, Henry B. Papers. Hagley Museum and Library, Wilmington, Delaware.
Ela, Richard K. Papers (microfilm). U.S. Military Academy, West Point, New York.
Ellis-Allen. Papers (microfilm). U.S. Military Academy, West Point, New York.

Ewing, Philemon. Papers. Ohio Historical Society, Columbus, Ohio.

Fish, Williston. "Memories of West Point." U.S. Military Academy, West Point, New York.

French, John W. "Report to Superintendent," 2 September 1859. U.S. Military Academy, West Point, New York.

French, Samuel G. Letters. U.S. Military Academy, West Point, New York.

Gilmore, Quincy A. Letters, 21 March 1846. U.S. Military Academy, West Point, New York.

Grant, Ulysses S. Papers. U.S. Military Academy, West Point, New York.

Harris, David B. Papers. William R. Perkins Library, Duke University, Durham, North Carolina (USMA photocopy).

Harris, William A. Letters. U.S. Military Academy, West Point, New York.

Heth, Henry. Memoirs and papers. University of Virginia, Charlottesville, Virginia.

Howard, Oliver O. Letter, 8 September 1850. U.S. Military Academy, West Point, New York.

Irons, Joseph J. Letters. U.S. Military Academy, West Point, New York.

Kautz, August V. Papers. U.S. Army Military History Institute, Carlisle Barracks, Pennsylvania.

Knight, John G. D. Medal for Academic Merit. U.S. Military Academy, West Point, New York.

Lee, Robert E. Papers. U.S. Military Academy, West Point, New York.

———. Papers. Virginia Historical Society, Richmond, Virginia.

Mahan, Dennis H. Papers. U.S. Military Academy, West Point, New York.

Martin, Joseph J. Journal, 1838–1841 (microfilm). U.S. Military Academy, West Point, New York.

Michie, Peter S. Papers. U.S. Military Academy, West Point, New York.

Mordecai, Alfred. "Journal of Experiments." U.S. Military Academy, West Point, New York.

Pemberton, John C. Papers (microfilm). U.S. Military Academy, West Point, New York.

Poinsett, Joel R. Papers. The Historical Society of Pennsylvania, Philadelphia, Pennsylvania.

Scott, Mrs. Winfield and Cadet Daniel M. Beltzhoover. "Graduation Song, Class of 1847." U.S. Military Academy, West Point, New York.

Sherman, William T. Papers. U.S. Military Academy, West Point, New York.

———. Letters. General Correspondence Series. MSS Division, Library of Congress, Washington, D.C.

Sheridan, Philip H. Papers. U.S. Military Academy, West Point, New York.

Sherwood, Walter. Letters. U.S. Military Academy, West Point, New York.

Smith, Francis H. Papers. Preston Library, Virginia Military Institute, Lexington, Virginia.

Stanley, David S. Memoirs. West-Stanley-Wright Papers. U.S. Army Military History Institute, Carlisle Barracks, Pennsylvania.

Stem Family. Papers. Rutherford B. Hayes Presidential Center, Fremont, Ohio.

Stevens, Isaac I. Letters. U.S. Military Academy, West Point, New York.

Stuart, James E. B. Letter, 1 September 1852. U.S. Military Academy, West Point, New York.

———. Letters. Virginia Historical Society, Richmond, Virginia.

Swift, Joseph G. Papers. U.S. Military Academy, West Point, New York.

Thayer, Sylvanus. Letter, 15 September 1858. U.S. Military Academy, West Point, New York.

———. "The West Point Thayer Papers, 1808–1872," Cindy Adams, ed. U.S. Military Academy, West Point, New York.

Tidball, John C. Papers. U.S. Military Academy, West Point, New York.

Tillman, Samuel E. Typescript, "Anecdotes of Cadet Life." U.S. Military Academy, West Point, New York.

Toner, John M. Letterbook, diary, notes on field fortifications (microfilm). U.S. Military Academy, West Point, New York.

Turner, John W. Journal, 1856. (Photocopy). In possession of author.

Wool, John E. Letter. U.S. Military Academy, West Point, New York.

Unpublished Government Documents

Adjutant General, U.S. Army. Correspondence Relating to the Military Academy, 1819–1866. Record Group 94, National Archives.

———. Letters Sent Relating to the Military Academy, 1812–1867. 29 vols. Record Group 94, National Archives.

———. Papers Relating to the Court of Inquiry to Examine into the Moral Condition of the Academy and the Conduct of Lt. Shiras, Assistant Professor, 1840. Record Group 94, National Archives.

———. Records Relating to the Military Academy, 1812–1867, Abstract of Letter Book. 3 vols. Record Group 94, National Archives.

———. Records Relating to the Military Academy, 1812–1867, Records of Orders and Letters, (1814–1867). 26 vols. Record Group 94, National Archives

Chief of Engineers, U.S. Army. Letters and Reports of Joseph G. Totten. 10 vols. Record Group 77, National Archives.

———. Letters Received, 1826–1866. Record Group 77, National Archives.

———. Letters Sent, 1812–1867. Records Relating to the United States Military Academy, Military Academy Letters. Record Group 77, National Archives.

———. Military Academy Orders, 1856–1866. Archives, U.S. Military Academy, West Point, New York.

Secretary of War, War Department. Confidential and Unofficial Letters Sent, 1814–1847. 2 vols. Record Group 107, National Archives.

———. Letters Received. Main Series, 1800–1870. Record Group 107, National Archives.

———. Letters Received, Unregistered Series, 1789–1860. Record Group 107, National Archives.

———. Letters Sent, Military Affairs, 1800–1899. Record Group 107, National Archives.

_____. Letters Sent to the President, 1800–1863. Record Group 107, National Archives.

_____. Register of Letters Received, Main Series, 1800–1870. Record Group 107, National Archives.

U.S. Military Academy. Adjutant's Letters, 1838–1902. 11 vols. Archives, U.S. Military Academy, West Point, New York.

_____. "Casualties, U.S. Corps of Cadets." Archives, U.S. Military Academy, West Point, New York.

_____. Consolidated Morning Reports, 1838–1945. 78 vols. Archives, U.S. Military Academy, West Point, New York.

_____. Descriptive Lists of New Cadets, 1838–1909. 4 vols. Archives, U.S. Military Academy, West Point, New York.

_____. Endorsements and Memoranda, 1853–1870. 5 vols. Archives, U.S. Military Academy, West Point, New York.

_____. Laws and regulations relative to the appointment, examination, and admission of candidates to the U.S. Military Academy, 1854–1871. Archives, U.S. Military Academy, West Point, New York.

_____. Letters Received, 1840–1890. Archives, U.S. Military Academy, West Point, New York.

_____. Letters relating to the United States Military Academy in reply to reports of various committees, 1836–1844. Archives, U.S. Military Academy, West Point, New York.

_____. Library Circulation Records, 1824–1902. MSS Collection, U.S. Military Academy, West Point, New York.

_____. Monthly Returns, 1818–1903. 13 vols. Archives, U.S. Military Academy, West Point, New York.

_____. Muster Rolls, United States Corps of Cadets, 1817–1839. 4 vols. Archives, U.S. Military Academy, West Point, New York.

_____. Orders, Commandant of Cadets, 1839–1899. 29 vols. Archives, U.S. Military Academy, West Point, New York.

_____. Orders, 1817–1839. 7 vols. Archives, U.S. Military Academy, West Point, New York.

_____. Orders, General, Special, Engineer, and Military Academy, 1838–1855. 15 vols. Archives, U.S. Military Academy, West Point, New York.

_____. Orders, General Orders, Special Orders, Memoranda and Circulars, 1838–1877. 16 vols. Archives, U.S. Military Academy, West Point, New York.

_____. Post Orders, 1838–1877, 1882–1904. 16 vols. Archives, U.S. Military Academy, West Point, New York.

_____. Register of Delinquencies, 1819–1913. 59 vols. Archives, U.S. Military Academy, West Point, New York.

_____. Register of Letters and Orders Received, 1838–1858. 2 vols. Archives, U.S. Military Academy, West Point, New York.

_____. Register of Letters from various sources, 1853–1866. 1 vol. Archives, U.S. Military Academy, West Point, New York.

_____. Register of Punishments, 1838–1900. 9 vols. Archives, U.S. Military Academy, West Point, New York.

————. Reports of Boards of Visitors, 1826–1850. Archives, U.S. Military Academy, West Point, New York.

————. Semi-Annual Roll of Cadets, 1840–1907. Archives, U.S. Military Academy, West Point, New York.

————. Staff Records, 1818–1875. 9 vols. Archives, U.S. Military Academy, West Point, New York.

————. Superintendent's Letter Books, 1838–1840, 1845–1902. 12 vols. Archives, U.S. Military Academy, West Point, New York.

Published Government Documents

American State Papers, Class V. Military Affairs. 7 vols. Washington, D.C.: Gales and Seaton, 1832–1861.

Annual Report of the Board of Visitors of the United States Military Academy, West Point, New York, June 20, 1839. Washington, D.C.: A. B. Claxton, 1839.

U.S. Army, Adjutant General's Office. *Official Army Registers.* 1833–1866. Washington, D.C.: various printers, published annually.

U.S. *Congressional Globe.* Washington, D.C.: Blair and Rives, 1834–1866.

U.S. Congress, House. *Report of the Board of Visitors.* Exec. Docs. 3 and 21. 37th Cong., 3d sess., 1863.

————. *Report of the Inspector of the Military Academy.* Exec. Doc. no. 1, 39th Cong., 2d sess., 1866.

————. *Report of the Colonel of Engineers.* Exec. Doc. no. 1, 34th Cong., 1st sess., 1855.

————. *Report of Mr. Fish relative to the Military Academy.* House Report no. 476, 28th Cong., 1st sess., 1844.

————. *Report of the Secretary of War.* Exec. Doc., vol. 5. 38th Cong., 1st sess., 1863.

————. *Report of the Secretary of War.* Exec. Doc., vol. 2. 39th Cong., 1st sess., 1865.

————. Report of the Secretary of War *Ad Interim* and General, U.S. Army. Exec. Doc. no. 1, pt. 1, vol. 2. 40th Cong., 2d sess., 1868.

U.S. Congress, Senate. *Report from the Engineer Department.* Exec. Doc. no. 22, 35th Cong., 2d sess., 1858.

————. *Report of the Chief Engineer.* Exec. Doc. no. 1, no. 6, 28th Cong., 1st sess., 1844.

————. *Report of the Chief Engineer.* Vol. 1, Exec. Doc. no. 1, no. 6, 29th Cong., 1st sess., 1845.

————. *Report of the Chief Engineer.* Exec. Doc. no. 1, no. 18, 30th Cong., 1st sess., 1847.

————. *Report of the Chief Engineer.* Exec. Doc. no. 1, 30th Cong., 2d sess., 1848.

————. *Report of the Chief Engineer.* Vol. 1, Exec. Doc. no. 1, no. 12, 31st Cong., 1st sess., 1849.

————. *Report of the Chief Engineer.* Vol. 2, Exec. Doc. no. 1, no. 7, 31st Cong., 2d sess., 1850.

_____. *Report of the Chief Engineer.* Vol. 2, Exec. Doc. 1, pt. 2, 33d Cong., 1st sess., 1853.

_____. *Report of the Chief Engineer.* Exec. Doc., vol. 2, Doc. 1, pt. 2, 33d Cong., 2d sess., 1854.

_____. *Report of the Chief Engineer.* Exec. Doc., vol. 3, no. 12, 34th Cong., 3d sess., 1856.

_____. *Report of the Chief Engineer.* Exec. Doc., vol. 3, no. 10, 35th Cong., 1st sess., 1857.

_____. *Report of the Colonel of Engineers.* Exec. Doc., vol. 1, no. 1, pt. 1, 32d Cong., 1st sess., 1851.

_____. *Report of the Colonel of Engineers.* Exec. Doc., vol. 1, no. 1, pt. 2, 33d Cong., 2d sess., 1852.

_____. *Report of the Commission on the U.S. Military Academy* (Hon. Jefferson Davis, President). Misc. Doc. no. 3, 36th Cong., 2d sess., 1860.

_____. *Report of the Engineer Bureau.* Exec. Doc., vol. 2, no. 17, 36th Cong., 2d sess., 1860.

_____. *Report of the Engineer Department.* Exec. Doc., vol. 2, no. 18, 36th Cong., 1st sess., 1859.

_____. *Report of the Engineer Bureau.* Exec. Doc., vol. 2, 37th Cong., 2d sess., 1861.

U.S. Military Academy. *A Catalogue of the Graduates of the U.S. Military Academy from its Establishment in 1801 to 1847 Giving the Present Rank of Them in Service, Together with the Regulations for the Admission of Cadets, and a Synopsis of the Course of Study Pursued at that Institution.* New York: W. H. Graham, 1848.

_____. *Catalogue of Books in the Library of the Military Academy, August 1822.* Newburgh, N.Y.: Ward H. Gazlay, 1822.

_____. *Catalogue of the Library of the U.S. Military Academy Exhibiting its Condition at the Close of the Year 1852.* New York: John F. Trow, 1853.

_____. *Catalogue of the Library of the U.S. Military Academy, May 1830.* New York: J. Desnoues, 1830.

_____. *Laws of Congress Relative to West Point and the United States Military Academy from 1786 to 1877.* N.p., n.d.

_____. *Official Register of the Officers and Cadets of the U.S. Military Academy.* West Point, N.Y.: USMA, pub. annually, 1833–1866.

_____. *Register of Graduates and Former Cadets of the United States Military Academy.* 1948. Reprint. West Point, N.Y.: West Point Alumni Foundation, 1956.

_____. *Regulations of the U.S. Military Academy at West Point.* New York: J. and J. Harper, 1832.

_____. *Regulations Established for the Organization and Government of the Military Academy at West Point, New York.* New York: Wiley and Putnam, 1839.

_____. *Regulations for the U.S. Military Academy at West Point, New York.* New York: John F. Trow, 1853.

_____. *Regulations for the United States Military Academy at West Point, New York.* New York: John F. Trow, 1857.

————. *Regulations for the United States Military Academy at West Point, New York*. New York: Baldwin and Jones, 1866.

United States. *The Public Statutes at Large of the United States of America, 1789–1873*. 17 vols. Boston: Little, Brown, published on various dates, vol. 17 published in 1873.

U.S. Secretary of War. *Report of the Board of Visitors, West Point*. June 22, 1840.

————. *Report of Board of Visitors of Military Academy*. 21 June 1861; 26 June 1865.

————. *Report of the Chief Engineer*. 30 October 1865.

U.S. War Department. *Cavalry Tactics*. Washington, D.C.: J. & G. S. Gideon, 1841.

————. *General Regulations for the Army of the United States: Also, the Rules and Articles of War*. Washington, D.C.: Globe, 1835.

————. *General Regulations for the Army of the United States: 1841*. Washington, D.C.: J. & G. S. Gideon, 1841.

————. *Regulations for the Army of the United States, 1857*. New York: Harper Bros., 1857.

The War of the Rebellion: A Compilation of the Official Records of the Union and Confederate Armies. Series 1, 53 vols.; series 2, 8 vols.; series 3, 4 vols.; series 4, 3 vols. Washington, D.C.: Government Printing Office, 1880–1902.

Contemporary Newspapers, Periodicals, and Pamphlets

"Academy at West Point." *American Quarterly Review* 16 (December 1834): 358–75.

Addresses Delivered Before the Graduating Classes of the U.S. Military Academy. 1825–1897.

Alexander, J. E. "United States Military Academy, West Point." *United Service Magazine* 3 (September 1854): 7–23.

Alvord, Benjamin. *Address Before the Dialectic Society of the Corps of Cadets*. New York: Wiley & Putnam, 1839.

American Quarterly Review. 11 (1832), 16 (1834), 22 (1837).

Appelles, A. *Graduating Song of 1852*. New York: Firth, 1852.

Army and Navy Chronicle. 11 vols. 1835–1841.

Army and Navy Chronicle and Scientific Repository. 3 vols. 1842–1844.

Army and Navy Journal. 9 vols. 1863–1872.

Beltzhoover, Daniel, and Mrs. Winfield Scott. *Graduating Song, Dedicated to the West Point Graduates of 1847*. New York: Firth, 1847.

Cadets' Graduating Song, 1848. New York: Firth, 1848.

Hammond, Marcus C. *An Oration on the Duties and the Requirements of an American Officer*. New York: Baker Co., 1852.

234

BIBLIOGRAPHY

Harper's New Monthly Magazine. 33 vols. 1850–1866.

Hunt, Ezra M "West Point and Cadet Life." *Putnam's Monthly* 4 (August 1864): 192–204.

Johnson, Richard M. "Military Academy." *Military and Naval Magazine of the United States* 4 (October 1834): 136–51.

"Life of the West Point Cadet," *Eclaireur* 1 (December 1853): 40.

McClellan, George B. *Oration by General McClellan.* New York: C. S. Westcott Co., 1864.

Military and Naval Magazine of the United States. 6 vols. 1833–1835.

"Military Academy, West Point." *Military and Naval Magazine of the United States* 2 (November 1833): 135–36.

Lossing, Benson J. "West Point." *Scribner's Monthly,* 4 (July 1872): 257–84.

New York Times. 1851–1866.

Niles Weekly Register. (Also *Niles National Register.*) 1833–1849.

North American Review. 1832–1864.

Northrup, Birdsey G. "The United States Military Academy at West Point." *Massachusetts Board of Education, Annual Report.* 1864, 90–124.

Porter, Horace. *West Point Life.* West Point: Dialectic Society, 1859.

"Quiff" [pseud.]. "A Plebe's Account of Himself: My Reception." *Military and Naval Magazine of the United States* 2 (October 1833): 83–87.

Report of the Committee of the Academic Board of the United States Military Academy in Relation to the Restoration of Cadets who have been Discharged from the Institution. New York: Van Nostrand, 1862.

Schofield, John M. "An Address to the Corps of Cadets, U.S.M.A., 11 August 1879." West Point: 1879.

Smith, Francis H. "United States Military Academy." *Southern Literary Messenger* 9 (November 1843): 665–70.

Seymour, Truman. *Military Education: A Vindication of West Point and the Regular Army.* Williamstown, Mass.: 1864.

Southern Literary Messenger. 1-36 (1834–1864).

Symmes, John G. "A Fragment from the Journal of a Cadet of the USMA." *Eclaireur* 1 (September 1853): 9–10, 77–78.

"The United States Military Academy at West Point." *American Journal of Education* 6 (June 1828): 328–38.

United States Service Magazine. 1-4 (1864–1866).

"West Point." *American Journal of Scientific and Useful Knowledge* 1 (October 1835): 41–45.

"West Point." *Military and Naval Magazine of the United States* 3 (March 1834): 68–72.

"West Point." *Family Magazine or Monthly Abstract of General Knowledge* 3 (1836): 423–27.

"West Point and the United States Military Academy." *New England Magazine* 3 (October 1832): 265–78.

"West Point and the War, Dedicated by a Western Officer to his Eastern Fellow-Soldiers." (St. Louis, Mo.: n.p., 1863).

Published Letters, Memoirs, and Diaries

Alexander, Edward P. *Military Memoirs of a Confederate.* 1907. Reprint. Bloomington: Univ. of Indiana Press, 1962.

Alexander, James E. *Passages in the Life of a Soldier.* London: Hurst, 1857.

Anderson, Edward W. "Letters of a West Pointer, 1860–1861." *American Historical Review* 33 (April 1928): 599–617.

Bailey, William W. *My Boyhood at West Point.* Providence, R.I.: Soldiers and Sailors Historical Society, 1891.

Barnard, John G. "Letters to Editors of National Intelligencer." New York: D. Van Nostrand, 1862.

Bassett, John S., ed. *Correspondence of Andrew Jackson.* 7 vols. Washington, D.C.: Carnegie Institute, 1928.

Butler, Benjamin F. *Butler's Book.* Boston: A. M. Thayer, 1892.

Carter, Robert G. *Four Brothers in Blue.* Austin: Univ. of Texas Press, 1979.

Church, Albert E. *Personal Reminiscences of the United States Military Academy.* West Point: U.S. Military Press, 1879.

Cox, Jacob D. *Military Reminiscences of the Civil War.* 2 vols. New York: Charles Scribner's Sons, 1900.

Crary, Catherine S. ed. *Dear Belle: Letters from a Cadet and Officer to his Sweetheart, 1858–1865.* Middletown, Conn.: Wesleyan Univ. Press, 1965.

D'Oremieulx, Mrs. Theophile M. "Recollections of West Point in 1853." *Bulletin, Association of Graduates, U.S. Military Academy* 3 (May 1903): 39–46.

Grant, Ulysses S. *Personal Memoirs.* 2 vols. New York: Charles Webster & Co., 1885.

Hamlin, Percy G., ed. *The Making of a Soldier, The Letters of General R. S. Ewell.* Richmond: Whittet and Sheperson, 1935.

Howard, Oliver O. *Autobiography.* 2 vols. New York: Taylor & Co., 1908.

"Justitia" [pseud.]. "Letter to the Honorable Mr. Hawes in Reply to His Strictures on the Graduates of the Military Academy." New York: Wiley and Long, 1836.

Latrobe, John H. *Reminiscences of West Point from September 1818 to March 1882.* East Saginaw, Mich.: Evening News Printers, 1887.

Leslie, Miss. "Recollections of West Point." *Graham's Magazine,* April 1882, 207–09, 290–95.

Maury, Dabney H. *Recollections of a Virginian in the Mexican, Indian, and Civil Wars.* 3d ed. New York: Charles Scribner's Sons, 1894.

McClellan, George B. *McClellan's Own Story.* New York: Charles L. Webster & Co., 1887.

Morrison, James L., Jr., ed., *The Memoirs of Henry Heth.* Westport, Conn.: Greenwood Press, 1974.

Mosby, John S. *The Memoirs of Colonel John S. Mosby.* 1917. Reprint. Millwood, N.Y.: Kraus Reprint, 1975.

Postprandial Dream of an Old-Time West Pointer. N.p., n.d.

Quaife, Milo, ed. *The Diary of James K. Polk During His Presidency.* 4 vols. Chicago: A. C. McClurg Co., 1910.

Rowland, Dunbar, ed. *Jefferson Davis, Constitutionalist, His Letters, Papers, and Speeches.* 10 vols. Jackson: Mississippi Department of Archives and History, 1923.

Rowland, Thomas. "Letters of a Virginia Cadet at West Point, 1859–1861." *South Atlantic Quarterly* 14 (July and October 1915): 201–19, 330–47; 15 (January, April, and July 1916): 1–17, 143–55, 201–15.

Schofield, John M. *Forty-Six Years in the Army.* New York: Century Co., 1897.

Scott, Winfield. *Memoirs.* New York: Sheldon & Co., 1864.

Sheridan, Philip H. *Personal Memoirs.* 2 vols. New York: Charles L. Webster & Co., 1888.

Sherman, William T. *Memoirs.* 2 vols. New York: D. Appleton Co., 1875.

Simon, John Y., ed. *The Papers of Ulysses S. Grant.* Carbondale: Southern Illinois Univ. Press, 1967. To date only volume 1, 1837–1861, has been published.

Smith, Francis H. *West Point Fifty Years Ago.* New York: D. Van Nostrand, 1879.

Swift, Joseph G. *The Memoirs of General Joseph Gardner Swift.* Worcester, Mass.: F. S. Blanchard Co., 1890.

Thorndike, Rachel S., ed. *The Sherman Letters.* New York: Charles Scribner's Sons, 1894.

Viele, Mrs. Egbert L. *Following the Drum: A Glimpse of Frontier Life.* New York: Rudd & Carleton, 1858.

Wilson, James H. *Under the Old Flag.* 2 vols. New York: Appleton Co., 1912.

SECONDARY ACCOUNTS

Books

Alexander, Thomas A. *Sectional Stress and Party Strength, A Computer Analysis of Roll-Call Voting Patterns in the United States House of Representatives, 1836–1860.* Nashville, Tenn.: Vanderbilt Univ. Press, 1967.

Ambrose, Stephen E. *Duty, Honor, Country: A History of West Point.* Baltimore: Johns Hopkins Univ. Press, 1966.

Annual Report of the Superintendent of the United States Military Academy, 1896. Washington, D.C.: Government Printing Office, 1896.

Arnold, Thomas J. *Early Life and Letters of General Thomas J. Jackson.* Richmond: Dietz Press, 1957.

Baker, George A. *West Point, A Comedy in Three Acts.* New York: Frederick A. Stokes Co., 1875.

Bandel, Eugene. *Frontier Life in the Army.* Glendale, Calif.: A. H. Clark, 1932.

Barnard, Henry. *Military Schools and Courses of Instruction in the Science and Art of War, in France, Prussia, Austria, Russia, Sweden, Switzerland, Sardinia, England, and the United States.* Rev. ed., New York: Steiger, 1872.

Bartlett, David W. *The Life of General Frank Pierce of New Hampshire.* Buffalo: George H. Derby Co., 1852.

237

Basso, Hamilton. *Beauregard, the Great Creole.* New York: Charles Scribner's Sons, 1933.

Bauer, K. Jack. *The Mexican War, 1846–1848.* New York: Macmillan, 1974.

Baumer, William H., Jr. *Not All Warriors: Portraits of 19th Century West Pointers Who Gained Fame in other than Military Fields.* New York: Smith & Durrell, 1941.

Bayard, Samuel J. *The Life of George Dashell Bayard.* New York: G. Putnam's Sons, 1874.

Berard, Augusta B. *Reminiscences of West Point in the Olden Times.* East Saginaw, Mich.: Evening News Printing and Binding House, 1886.

Berman, Myron. *Richmond's Jewry, 1769–1976.* Charlottesville: Univ. Press of Virginia, 1979.

Bernardo, C. S., and E. H. Bacon. *American Military Policy: Its Development Since 1775.* Harrisburg, Pa: Military Service Publishing Co., 1955.

Bingham, Robert. *Sectional Misunderstandings.* Asheville, N.C.: Hackney and Moale Co., 1904.

Birkhimer, William E. *Historical Sketch of the Organization, Administration, Materiel and Tactics of the Artillery, United States Army.* Washington, D.C.: J. J. Chapman, 1884.

Boatner, Mark M. *The Civil War Dictionary.* New York: David McKay Co., 1959.

Bond, Oliver J. *The Story of The Citadel.* Richmond, Va.: Garrett and Massie, 1936.

Boynton, Edward C. *History of West Point and its Military Importance During the American Revolution: and the Origin and Progress of the United States Military Academy.* New York: D. Van Nostrand, 1863.

Bruce, Philip A. *History of the University of Virginia, 1819–1919.* 4 vols. New York: Macmillan, 1920.

Brubacher, John S. and Willis Rudy. *Higher Education in Transition: An American History, 1636–1956.* New York: Harper Bros., 1958.

Cajori, Florian. *The Teaching and History of Mathematics in the United States.* Washington, D.C.: Government Printing Office, 1890.

Calhoun, Daniel H. *The American Civil Engineer: Origins and Conflict.* Cambridge: Harvard Press, 1960.

Callan, John F. *The Military Laws of the United States.* Philadelphia: George W. Childs, 1863.

Calvert, Monte. *The Mechanical Engineer in America, 1830–1910.* Baltimore: Johns Hopkins Univ. Press, 1967.

Carpenter, John A. *Sword and Olive Branch: Oliver Otis Howard.* Pittsburgh: Univ. of Pittsburgh Press, 1964.

Catton, Bruce. *U. S. Grant and the American Military Tradition.* Boston: Little, Brown, 1954.

———. *Reflections on the Civil War.* Ed. by John Leekely. Garden City, N.Y.: Doubleday, 1981.

Centennial of the United States Military Academy at West Point, New York. 2 vols. Washington, D.C.: Government Printing Office, 1904.

238

Chaffin, Nora C. *Trinity College, 1839–1892: The Beginnings of Duke University.* Durham, N.C.: Duke Univ. Press, 1950.

Chambers, Lenoir. *Stonewall Jackson.* 2 vols. New York: William Morrow, 1959.

Cheyney, Edward P. *History of the University of Pennsylvania: 1740–1940.* Philadelphia: Univ. of Pennsylvania Press, 1940.

Clausewitz, Karl von. *Principles of War.* Trans. Hans W. Gatzke. Harrisburg, Pa.: Military Service Publishing Co., 1945.

———. *On War.* Ed. and trans. by Michael Howard and Peter Paret. Princeton, N.J.: Princeton Univ. Press, 1976.

Clendenen, Clarence C. *Blood on the Border: The United States Army and the Mexican Irregulars.* New York: Macmillan, 1969.

Coffman, Edward M. *The Old Army: A Portrait of the American Army in Peacetime, 1784–1898.* New York: Oxford University Press, 1986.

Connelly, Thomas L., and Archer Jones. *The Politics of Command: Factions and Ideas in Confederate Strategy.* Baton Rouge: Louisiana State Univ. Press, 1973.

Cooke, Philip St. George. *Scenes and Adventures in the Army. Or Romance of Military Life.* Philadelphia: Lindsay and Blakiston, 1857.

Coon, Horace. *Columbia, Colossus on the Hudson.* New York: E. P. Dutton, 1947.

Coulter, Ellis M. *College Life in the Old South.* Athens: Univ. of Georgia Press, 1951.

Couper, William C. *One Hundred Years at V.M.I.* 4 vols. Richmond: Garrett and Massie, 1939.

Crane, Theodore R., ed. *The Colleges and the Public, 1787–1862.* (Classics in Education, no. 15). New York: Teachers' College, Columbia, 1963.

Cremin, Lawrence. *American Education.* 2 vols. New York: Harper and Row, 1980.

Cullum, George W. *Biographical Register of the Officers and Graduates of the United States Military Academy at West Point, New York.* 2d ed. 3 vols. New York: James Miller, 1879.

Cunliffe, Marcus. *Soldiers and Civilians: The Martial Spirit in America, 1775–1865.* Boston: Little, Brown & Co., 1968.

Curti, Merle and Vernon Carstenson. *The University of Wisconsin, 1848–1925, A History.* 2 vols. Madison: Univ. of Wisconsin Press, 1942.

Dabney, Virginius. *Mr. Jefferson's University, A History.* Charlottesville: Univ. Press of Virginia, 1981.

Davis, Burke. *Gray Fox: Robert E. Lee and the Civil War.* New York: Rinehart & Co., 1956.

———. *Jeb Stuart: The Last Cavalier.* New York: Rinehart & Co., 1957.

Davis, William C. *Jefferson Davis: The Man and His Hour.* New York: Harper Collins, 1991.

Demarest, William H. S. *A History of Rutgers College, 1766–1924.* New Brunswick, N.J.: Rutgers College, 1924.

Desmazes, Rene. *Saint-Cyr, son histoire-ses gloires-ses leçons.* Paris: La Saint-Cyrienne, 1948.

Donald, David H. *Lincoln Reconsidered: Essays on the Civil War Era.* 2d ed. New York: Knopf, 1966.

————. *Why the North Won the Civil War.* New York: Macmillan, 1971.

Dowdey, Clifford. *Lee.* Boston: Little, Brown & Co., 1965.

Dunn, Jacob P. *Massacres of the Mountains. A History of the Indian Wars of the Far West, 1815–1875.* New York: Archer House, 1958.

DuPuy, R. Ernest. *The Compact History of the United States Army.* Rev. ed. New York: Hawthorn Books, 1961.

————. *Men of West Point. The First 150 Years of the United States Military Academy.* New York: Sloane, 1951.

————. *The Story of West Point: 1802–1943: The West Point Tradition in American Life.* Washington, D.C.: The Infantry Journal, 1943.

Dutcher, George M. *An Historical and Critical Survey of the Curriculum of Wesleyan University and Related Subjects.* Middletown, Conn.: Wesleyan Univ. Press, 1948.

Dyer, Frederick H. *A Compendium of the War of the Rebellion.* 3 vols. 1908; reprint, New York: Thomas Yoseloff, 1959.

Earle, Edward M., ed. *Makers of Modern Strategy: Military Thought from Machiavelli to Hitler.* New York: Atheneum, 1966.

Easterby, James H. *A History of the College of Charleston.* New York: Scribner Press, 1935.

Eaton, Clement. *Jefferson Davis.* New York: The Free Press, 1977.

L'École Polytechnique, livre du centenaire, 1794–1894. 3 vols. Paris: Gauthier-Villars et fils, 1895.

Eliot, Ellsworth. *West Point in the Confederacy.* New York: G. A. Baker & Co., 1941.

Elliott, Charles W. *Winfield Scott, The Soldier and the Man.* New York: Macmillan, 1937.

Ellis, Joseph, and Robert Moore. *School for Soldiers: West Point and the Profession of Arms.* New York: Oxford University Press, 1974.

Ellis, W. A. *History of Norwich University, 1819–1898.* Concord, N.H.: Rumford Press, 1898.

————. *Register of the Graduates and Past Cadets of Norwich University.* Bradford, Vt.: Opinion Press, 1907.

Farley, Joseph P. *West Point in the Early Sixties with Incidents of the War.* Troy, N.Y.: Palfrey's Book Co., 1902.

Farrow, Edward S. *West Point and the Military Academy.* 3d ed. New York: Military-Naval Publishing Co., 1895.

Fleming, Thomas J. *West Point: The Men and Times of the United States Military Academy.* New York: William Morrow, 1969.

Forman, Sidney B. *Cadet Life Before the Mexican War.* West Point: U.S.M.A. Printing Office, 1945.

————. *West Point, A History of the United States Military Academy.* New York: Columbia Univ. Press, 1950.

Franklin, John H. *The Militant South, 1800–1861.* Cambridge: Harvard Univ. Press, Belknap Press, 1956.

Freeman, Douglas S. *R. E. Lee: A Biography.* 4 vols. New York: Charles Scribner's Sons, 1936.

Galpin, W. F. *Syracuse University.* 2 vols. Syracuse, N.Y.: Syracuse Univ. Press, 1952.

Galvin, John, ed. *Western American In 1846–1847: The Original Travel Diary of Lieutenant J. W Abert.* San Francisco: John Howell, 1966.

Ganoe, William A. *The History of the United States Army.* Ashton, Md.: Eric Lundberg, 1964.

Goetzmann, William H. *Army Explorations in the American West, 1803–1863.* Lincoln: Univ. of Nebraska Press, 1979.

————. *Exploration and Empire: The Explorer and the Scientist in the Winning of the American West.* New York: W. W. Norton & Co., 1978.

Guggisberg, Frederick G. *The Shop: The Story of the Royal Military Academy.* London: Cassell and Co., 1900.

Hagan, Kenneth J., and William R. Roberts, eds. *Against All Enemies: Interpretations of American Military History from Colonial Times to the Present.* Westport, Conn.: Greenwood Press, 1986.

Halleck, Henry W. *Elements of Military Art and Science.* New York: D. Appleton, 1862.

Hamersley, Thomas H. *Complete Regular Army Register of the United States for One Hundred Years, (1779–1879).* Washington, D.C.: T. H. Hamersley, 1880.

Hardee, William J. *Rifle and Light Infantry Tactics for the Exercise and Manoeuvres of Troops When Acting as Light Infantry or Riflemen.* Philadelphia: Lippincott, Grambo & Co., 1855.

Hart, Herbert M. *Pioneer Forts of the West.* Seattle: Superior Publishing Co., 1968.

Hassler, Warren G., Jr. *Commanders of the Army of the Potomac.* Baton Rouge: Louisiana State Univ. Press, 1962.

————. *General George B. McClellan: Shield of the Union.* Baton Rouge: Louisiana State Univ. Press, 1957.

Hattaway, Herman and Jones, Archer. *How the North Won, A Military History of the Civil War.* Urbana: Univ. of Illinois Press, 1981.

Heitman, Francis B. *Historical Register and Dictionary of the United States Army.* 2 vols. Washington, D.C.: Government Printing Office, 1903. Reprint, Urbana: Univ. of Illinois Press, 1965.

Henderson, G. F. R. *Stonewall Jackson and the American Civil War.* New York: Longmans, Green & Co., 1949.

Historical Statistics of the United States, Colonial Times to 1957. Washington, D.C.: Department of Commerce, Government Printing Office, 1961.

Hittle, J. D. *The Military Staff, Its History and Development.* 2d ed. Harrisburg, Pa.: The Military Service Publishing Co., 1952.

Hofstadter, Richard. *Anti-Intellectualism in American Life.* New York: Vintage Books, 1963.

Hofstadter, Richard and C.D. Hardy. *The Development and Scope of Higher Education in the United States.* New York: Columbia Univ. Press, 1952.

Hofstadter, Richard and Wilson Smith, eds. *American Higher Education, A Documentary History.* 2 vols. Chicago: Univ. of Chicago Press, 1961.

Holzman, Robert. *Stormy Ben Butler.* New York: Macmillan, 1954.

Howard, Michael, ed. *The Theory and Practice of War.* Bloomington: Univ. of Indiana Press, 1965.

Howitzer. Yearbook of the Corps of Cadets, various publishers, 1897–1914.

Hubbell, John T., ed. *Battles Lost and Won: Essays From Civil War History.* Westport, Conn.: Greenwood Press, 1975.

Hubbell, John T., and James W. Geary, eds. *Biographical Dictionary of the Union: Northern Leaders of the Civil War.* Westport, Conn.: Greenwood Press, 1995.

Hughes, Nathaniel C., Jr. *General William J. Hardee, Old Reliable.* Baton Rouge: Louisiana State Univ. Press, 1965.

Huntington, Samuel P. *The Soldier and the State: The Theory and Politics of Civil-Military Relations.* Cambridge: Harvard Univ. Press, Belknap Press, 1959.

Janowitz, Morris. *The Professional Soldier: A Social and Political Portrait.* Glencoe, N.Y.: Free Press, 1960.

Jazet, Paul. *Histoire de l'école spéciale militaire de Saint-Cyr.* Paris: Delagrave, 1893.

Jenks, Christopher and David Reisman. *The Academic Revolution.* New York: Doubleday & Co., 1968.

Jomini, Antoine H. *Summary of the Art of War.* Trans. by J. D. Hittle. Harrisburg, Pa.: Military Service Publishing Co., 1947.

Karsten, Peter. *The Military in America from the Colonial Era to the Present.* New York: Free Press, 1980.

Kilpatrick, H. Judson. T*he Blue and the Grey; or, War is Hell.* Ed. by Christopher Morley. Garden City, N.Y.: Doubleday, 1930.

Klein, Maury. *Edmund Porter Alexander.* Athens: Univ. of Georgia Press, 1971.

Kolesnik, Walter B. *Mental Discipline in Modern Education.* Madison: Univ. of Wisconsin Press, 1958.

Kriedberg, Marvin A. and Merton G. Henry. *History of Military Mobilization in the United States Army, 1775–1945.* (Department of the Army Pamphlet no. 20–212). Washington, D.C.: Government Printing Office, 1955.

Lenney, John J. *Caste System in the American Army, A Study of the Corps of Engineers and Their West Point System.* New York: Greenberg Publishers, 1949.

Lewis, Lloyd. *Captain Sam Grant.* Boston: Little, Brown & Co., 1950.

———. *Sherman: Fighting Prophet.* New York: Harcourt, Brace & Co., 1932.

Liddell Hart, B. H. *Sherman: Soldier-Realist-American.* New York: Frederick A. Praeger, 1958.

Livermore, Thomas L. *Numbers and Losses in the Civil War in America, 1861–1865.* Bloomington: Indiana Univ. Press, 1957.

Logan, John A. *The Volunteer Soldier of America.* Chicago: R. S. Peale, 1887.

Luvaas, Jay. *The Militant Legacy of the Civil War.* Chicago: Univ. of Chicago Press, 1959.

Mackler-Ferryman, Augustus H. *Annals of Sandhurst: A Chronicle of the Royal Military College from its Foundation to the Present Day.* London: William Heineman, 1900.

BIBLIOGRAPHY

Mahan, Dennis H. *A Complete Treatise on Field Fortifications, with the General Outlines of the Principles Regulating the Arrangement, the Attack, and the Defence of Permanent Works.* New York: Wiley, 1836.

———. *Advanced Guard, Outpost and Detachment Service of Troops, with the Essential Principles of Strategy and Grand Tactics for the Use of Officers of the Militia and Volunteers.* 1847. New ed. New York: Wiley, 1864.

———. *An Elementary Treatise on Advanced-Guard, Out-Post, and Detachment Service of Troops, and the Manner of Posting and Handling them in the Presence of an Enemy.* New York: J. Wiley, 1853.

Mahon, John K. *History of the Militia and the National Guard.* New York: Macmillan, 1983.

———. *History of the Second Seminole War, 1835–1842.* Gainesville: Univ. of Florida Press, 1967.

Malone, Dumas. *Jefferson and His Time.* 6 vols. Boston: Little, Brown & Co., 1948–1981.

Mann, Charles R. *A Study of Engineering Education.* New York: Carnegie Foundation for the Advancement of Teaching, 1917.

Mansfield, Edward D. *The United States Military Academy at West Point.* Hartford, Conn.: H. Barnard, 1863.

Marshall, Edward C. *Are the West Point Graduates Loyal?* New York: Van Nostrand, 1862.

Marszalek, John F. *Sherman: A Soldier's Passion for Order.* New York: The Free Press, 1993.

Matloff, Maurice, ed. *American Military History.* Rev. ed. Washington, D.C.: Office of the Chief of Military History, 1973.

McClellan, Henry B. *The Life and Campaigns of Major-General J.E.B. Stuart.* Boston: Houghton, Mifflin, 1885.

McFeely, William S. *Grant, A Biography.* New York: W. W. Norton & Co., 1981.

———. *Yankee Stepfather: General O. O. Howard and the Freedmen.* New York: W. W. Norton & Co., 1968.

McMaster, Richard K. *West Point's Contribution to Education, 1802–1952.* El Paso, Tex.: McMath Printing Co., 1951.

McMurry, Richard M. *John Bell Hood and the War for Southern Independence.* Lexington, Ky.: Univ. Press of Kentucky, 1982.

McWhiney, Grady. *Braxton Bragg and Confederate Defeat.* 2 vols. New York: Columbia Univ. Press, 1969.

Michie, Peter S. *The Life and Letters of Emory Upton.* New York: D. Appleton Co., 1885.

Millis, Walter. *Arms and Men: A Study of American Military History.* New York: G. P. Putnam's Sons, 1956.

Morison, Samuel E. *Three Centuries of Harvard, 1636–1936.* Cambridge: Harvard Univ. Press, 1936.

Nichols, James L. *General Fitzhugh Lee: A Biography.* Lynchburg, Va.: H. E. Howard, 1989.

Nichols, Roy F. *Franklin Pierce: Young Hickory of the Granite Hills.* Philadelphia: Univ. of Pennsylvania Press, 1931.

Pappas, George S. *To the Point: The United States Military Academy, 1802–1902.* Westport, Conn.: Praeger Press, 1995.

Park, Roswell. *A Sketch of the History and Topography of West Point and the U.S. Military Academy.* Philadelphia: Henry Perkins, 1840.

Patton, John S. *Jefferson, Cabell, and the University of Virginia.* New York: Neale Publishing Co., 1906.

Pennell, E. R. and J. Pennell. *The Life of James McNeill Whistler.* 5th ed. Philadelphia: J. B. Lippincott, 1911.

Phisterer, Frederick. *Statistical Record of the Armies of the United States.* New York: Charles Scribner's Sons, 1883.

Pinet, G. *Histoire de L'École Polytechnique.* Paris: Georges Chamerot, 1887.

Pierson, George W. *Yale College, An Educational History, 1871–1921.* New Haven: Yale Univ. Press, 1952.

Poore, Benjamin Perley. *The Life and Public Services of Ambrose E. Burnside.* Providence, R.I.: J. A. & R. A. Reid, 1882.

Prucha, Francis P., ed. *Army Life on the Western Frontier: Selections from the Official Reports Made Between 1826 and 1845 by Colonel George Croghan.* Norman: Univ. of Oklahoma Press, 1958.

————. *Broadax and Bayonet: The Role of the United States Army in the Development of the Northwest, 1815–1860.* Madison: Historical Society of Wisconsin, 1953.

————. *The Sword of the Republic: The United States Army on the Frontier, 1783–1846.* New York: Macmillian, 1969.

Randall, James G. *The Civil War and Reconstruction.* Boston: D. C. Heath, 1953.

Randel, William P. *Centennial, American Life in 1876.* New York: Chilton Book Co., 1969.

Rapp, Kenneth W. *West Point.* New York: North River Press, 1978.

Register of Graduates and Former Cadets, United States Military Academy, 1802–1948. West Point: West Point Alumni Foundation, 1948.

Register of Graduates and Former Cadets of the United States Military Academy, 1802–1963. West Point: West Point Alumni Foundation, 1963.

Richardson, James D., ed. *A Compilation of the Messages and Papers of the Presidents.* 10 vols. Washington, D.C.: Bureau of National Literature and Art, 1896–1899.

Ricketts, Palmer C. *History of Rensselaer Polytechnic Institute, 1824–1894.* New York: John Wiley and Sons, 1895.

Rippy, J. Fred. *Joel R. Poinsett, Versatile American.* Durham, N.C.: Duke Univ. Press, 1935.

Robertson, James I. *General A. P. Hill: The Story of a Confederate Warrior.* New York: Random House, 1987.

————. *Stonewall Jackson: The Man, the Soldier, the Legend.* New York: Macmillan, 1997.

Rodenbough, Theodore F. and William L. Haskins, eds. *The Army of the United States.* New York: Maynard, Merrill, and Co., 1896.

Rudolph, Frederick. *The American College and University, A History.* New York: Alfred A. Knopf, 1962.

244

Rudy, Willis. *The Evolving Liberal Arts Curriculum: A Historical Review of Basic Themes.* New York: Teachers' College Press, 1965.

Schaff, Morris. *The Spirit of Old West Point, 1858–1862.* Boston: Houghton, Mifflin, 1908.

Schmidt, George P. *The Liberal Arts College: A Chapter in American Cultural History.* New Brunswick, N.J.: Rutgers Univ. Press, 1957.

Scott, Winfield. *Infantry Tactics, or, Rules for the Exercise and Manoeuvres of the United States Infantry.* 3 vols. New York: Harper, 1846–1847.

Seager, Robert. *And Tyler Too: A Biography of John and Julia Tyler.* New York: McGraw-Hill, 1963.

Shannon, Fred A. *The Organization and Administration of the Union Army, 1861–1865.* 2 vols. 1928. Reprint. Gloucester, Mass.: Peter Smith, 1965.

Singletary, Otis A. *The Mexican War.* Chicago: Univ. of Chicago Press, 1960.

Smith, George W. and Judah, Charles. *Chronicles of the Gringos, The U. S. Army in the Mexican War, 1846–1848, Accounts of Eye-Witnesses and Combatants.* Alburquerque: Univ. of New Mexico Press, 1968.

Smith, Justin H. *The War with Mexico.* 2 vols. New York: Macmillan, 1919.

Smyth, John. *Sandhurst: The History of the Royal Military Academy, Woolwich, the Royal Military College, Sandhurst, and the Royal Military Academy, Sandhurst, 1741–1961.* London: Weidenfield and Nicolson, 1961.

Spaulding, Oliver L. *The United States Army in War and Peace.* New York: G. P. Putnam's, 1937.

Stevens, Hazard. *The Life of Isaac Ingells Stevens.* 2 vols. Boston: Houghton, Mifflin, 1901.

Stover, Clyde B. and Beacham, Charles W. *The Alumni Record of Gettysburg College, 1832–1932.* Gettysburg, Pa.: Gettysburg College, 1932.

Strode, Hudson. *Jefferson Davis.* 3 vols. New York: Harcourt, Brace and World, 1955–1964.

Strong, George C. *Cadet Life at West Point.* Boston: T. O. H. P. Burnham, 1862.

Tewksbury, Donald G. *The Founding of American Colleges and Universities Before the Civil War.* Hamden, Conn.: Archon Books, 1965.

Thomas, Emory M. *The Confederate Nation, 1861–1865.* New York: Harper and Row, 1979.

———. *Bold Dragoon: The Life of J. E. B. Stuart.* New York: Harper and Row, 1986.

Thomas, Hugh. *The Story of Sandhurst.* London: Hutchinson, 1961

Thomas, Wilbur. *General George H. Thomas, The Indomitable Warrior.* New York: Exposition Press, 1964.

Thomason, John W. *Jeb Stuart.* New York: Charles Scribner's Sons, 1948.

Thwing, Charles F. *A History of Higher Education in America.* New York: D. Appleton and Co., 1906.

Todd, Frederick P. *Cadet Grey, A Pictorial History of Life at West Point as Seen Through Its Uniforms.* New York: Sterling Publishing Co., 1955.

Todorich, Charles. *The Spirited Years: A History of the Antebellum Naval Academy.* Annapolis, Md.: Naval Institute Press, 1984.

Tucker, Glenn. *Hancock the Superb.* Dayton, Ohio: Morningside Bookshop, 1980.

Tyler, William S. *History of Amherst College During Its First Half Century, 1821–1871.* Springfield, Mass.: Clark W. Bryan & Co., 1873.

Upton, Emery. *The Military Policy of the United States.* Washington, D.C.: Government Printing Office, 1907.

Utley, Robert M. *Frontiersmen in Blue: The United States Army and the Indian, 1848–1865.* New York: Macmillan, 1967.

Vagts, Albert. *A History of Militarism, Civilian and Military.* Rev. ed. New York: Free Press, 1967.

Van Amringe, John H. *A History of Columbia University, 1754–1904.* New York: Macmillan, 1904.

Vandiver, Frank E. *Mighty Stonewall.* New York: McGraw-Hill, 1957.

———. *Rebel Brass, The Confederate Command System.* Westport, Conn.: Greenwood Press, 1969.

———. *Their Tattered Flags, the Epic of the Confederacy.* New York: Harper's, 1970.

Veysey, Laurence R. *The Emergence of the American University.* Chicago: Univ. of Chicago Press, 1965.

Warner, Ezra J. *Generals In Blue.* Baton Rouge: Louisiana State Univ. Press, 1964.

———. *Generals In Gray.* Baton Rouge: Louisiana State Univ. Press, 1959.

Waugh, John C. *The Class of 1846: From West Point to Appomattox: Stonewall Jackson, George McClellan and Their Brothers.* New York: Warner Books, 1994.

Weigley, Russell F. *History of the United States Army.* New York: Macmillan, 1967.

———. *Quartermaster General of the Union Army, A Biography of M. C. Meigs.* New York: Columbia Univ. Press, 1959.

———, ed. *The American Military: Readings in the History of the Military in American Society.* Reading, Mass.: Addison-Wessley Publishing Co., 1969.

———. *The American Way of War, A History of United States Military Strategy and Policy.* New York: Macmillan, 1973.

———. *Towards An American Army, Military Thought from Washington to Marshall.* New York: Columbia Univ. Press, 1962.

Weir, Irene. *Robert W. Weir.* New York: Doubleday & Co., 1947.

Wertenbaker, Thomas J. *Princeton, 1746–1896.* Princeton, N.J.: Princeton Univ. Press, 1946.

West, Richard S., Jr. *Lincoln's Scapegoat General, A Life of Benjamin F. Butler, 1818–1893.* Cambridge, Mass.: Houghton, Mifflin, 1965.

White, Leonard D. *The Jacksonians: A Study in Administrative History, 1829–1861.* New York: Free Press, Macmillan, 1965.

———. *The Jeffersonians: A Study in Administrative History, 1801–1829.* New York: Macmillan, 1951.

Whitman, S. E. *The Troopers, An Informal History of the Plains Cavalry, 1865–1890.* New York: Hastings House, 1962.

Wilcox, Cadmus M. *History of the Mexican War.* Washington, D.C.: Church News Publishing Co., 1892.

BIBLIOGRAPHY

Williams, T. Harry. *McClellan, Sherman, Grant.* 2d ed. New Brunswick, N.J.: Rutgers Univ. Press, 1962.

———. *P. G. T. Beauregard, Napoleon in Gray.* Baton Rouge: Louisiana State Univ. Press, 1955.

———. *The History of American Wars from Colonial Times to World War I.* New York: Alfred A. Knopf, 1981.

Articles

Ashbaugh, William H. "The Therapeutic Curriculum." *Psychology in the Schools* 2 (April 1965): 126–29.

Boynton, Edward C. "History of West Point: Its Military Importance During the American Revolution and the Origin and Purposes of the U.S. Military Academy." *North American Review* 97 (April 1864): 530–50.

Crackel, Theodore J. "The Founding of West Point: Jefferson and the Politics of Security." *Armed Forces and Society* 7 (Summer 1981): 529–41.

Dudley, Edgar S. "Was Secession Taught at West Point? What the Records Show." *Century Magazine,* August 1909, 629–36.

Falk, Stanley L. "Divided Loyalties in 1861: The Decision of Major Alfred Mordeccai." *American Jewish Historical Society* 472 (March 1959): 154–55.

Holden, Edward S. "Biographical Memoir of William H. C. Bartlett, 1804–1893." *National Academy of Sciences Biographical Memoirs* 7 (June 1911): 174–93.

King, Charles. "Cadet Life at West Point." *Harper's New Monthly Magazine* 75 (July 1887): 196–219.

———. "West Point in the Old Days." *Illustrated Sunday Magazine:* (10 July 1910), 12–13; (17 July 1910), 10–11; (24 July 1910), 12–13, (31 July 1910), 12–13; (7 August 1910), 10–13.

Maury, Dabney H. "West Point and Secession." *Southern Historical Society Papers* 6 (July-December 1878): 249.

Michie, Peter S. "Reminiscences of Cadet and Army Service." *Personal Recollections of the War of the Rebellion.* 2d ser. New York: G. P. Putnam's Sons, 1897, 183–97.

———. "West Point: Its Purpose, its Training, and its Results." *Union College Practical Lectures, Butterfield Course.* New York: F. T. Neely, 1895. 1.13–42.

Morrison, James L., Jr. "Educating the Civil War Generals: West Point, 1833–1861." *Military Affairs* 38 (October 1974): 106–11

———. "Getting Through West Point: The Cadet Memoirs of John C. Tidball, Class of 1848." *Civil War History* 26 (December 1980): 304–25.

———. "The Struggle Between Sectionalism and Nationalism at Ante-Bellum West Point." *Civil War History* 19 (June 1973): 138–48.

Padgett, James A. "The Life of Alfred Mordeccai as Related by Himself." *The North Carolina Historical Review* 22 (January 1945): 58–108.

Preston, R. A. "A Letter from a British Military Observer of the American Civil War." *Military Affairs* 16 (Summer 1952): 49–60.

Prucha, Francis P. "Distribution of Regular Army Troops Before the Civil War." *Military Affairs* 16 (Winter 1952): 169–73.

———. "The United States Army as Viewed by British Travelers, 1825–1860." *Military Affairs* 17 (Fall 1953): 113–24.

Skelton, William B. "Officers and Politicians: The Origins of Army Politics in the United States Before the Civil War." *Armed Forces and Society* 6 (Fall 1979): 22–48.

Tierney, John J., Jr. "Samuel F. Huntington and the American Military Tradition." *The Political Science Review* 8 (Fall 1978): 205–34.

Viollet, Claude. "West Point a cent cinquante ans." *St. Cyr* 15 (April 1952): 84–89.

Watson, Richard. "Congressional Attitudes Toward Military Preparedness, 1829–1835." *Mississippi Valley Historical Review* 34 (March 1948): 611–36.

Welch, M. L. "Early West Point French Teachers and Influences." *The American Society Legion of Honor Magazine* 26 (Spring 1955): 27–43.

Wheeler, Joseph. "West Point Fifty Years Ago." *The Golden Age,* February 1906, 66–70.

Williams, T. Harry. "The Attack Upon West Point During the Civil War." *Mississippi Valley Historical Review* 25 (March 1939): 491–504.

Wright, John M. "West Point Before the War." *Southern Bivouac* 4 (June 1885): 13–21.

Theses and Dissertations

Denton, Edgar, III. "The Formative Years of the United States Military Academy, 1775–1833." Ph.D. diss., Syracuse University, 1964.

Griess, Thomas E. "Dennis Hart Mahan: West Point Professor and Advocate of Military Professionalism, 1830–1871." Ph.D. diss., Duke University, 1968.

Hruby, Dale E. "The Civilian Careers of West Point Graduates, Classes of 1802 through 1833." Master's essay, Columbia University, 1965.

Index

251

Halleck, Henry W., 57, 73, 133, 138; influence of Mahan's teaching on, 97
Hammond, Marcus M., 26
Hardee, William, 19, 59, 119–20
Hardy, Arthur, 52
Harney, William S., 12
Harris, William, 89
"Hash," 80–82, 212 n.25
Haupt, Hermann, 9, 10
Hawes, James M., 59, 98, 99–100
Hayden, Ferdinand V., 6
Hazing, 66–68, 84, 122
Heth, Henry, x, 10, 19, 66, 67, 71, 77, 78, 81; and frontier duties, 21
"High Privates," 72, 210 n.47. *See also* Corps of cadets, command structure of
Holden, Edward S., 51
Honor system, 82–85
Howard, Oliver O., x, 59, 85, 89, 129
Humphreys, Andrew A., 125
Huse, Caleb, 176

"Immortals," 91–92, 146–47
Insignia, 138, 210 nn. 44, 45, 218 n.48
Ives, Joseph C., 6

Jackson, Andrew: intervention in academy affairs, 26–27; praise of academy, 26–27
Jackson, Thomas J. ("Stonewall"), 71, 73, 76
Jefferson, Thomas: and establishment of academy, 2
Jesup, Thomas, 14, 58–59
Jomini, Antoine: influence on cadets, 96–97, 153, 217 n.36
Jones, Roger, 14

Kautz, August V., 21
Kendrick, Henry, 48 (photo), 53, 60; academic achievements, 54; relationship with cadets, 54

Lane, James H., 131
L'École Polytechnique, 3, 23, 25, 102; description of program, 192–93
Lee, Fitzhugh, 59, 78, 100; leaves academy for Civil War, 127–28
Lee, Robert E., 8; and establishment of five-year course, 115; influence of Mahan's teaching on, 96; as superintendent of academy, 39, 77

Library, academy, 76–77, 89–91, 95 (drawing of), 110–11
Loyalty oaths, 135

McClean, John, 30
McClellan, George B., 5–6, 19, 42, 59, 133; influence of Mahan's teaching on, 96
Macomb, Alexander, 31
Macomb, John C., 6
McCrea, Tully, 129
McLean, Thomas F., 67
McPherson, James B., 73
Mahan, Dennis Hart, 16, 25, 44, 45 (photo), 70, 109, 133, 140; academic achievements, 47–49; courses of, 94–98; and five-year course, 117–18; influence on academic policies, 59–60; and molding of Civil War military thought, 153; relationship with cadets, 49; relationship with Chase and Stanton, 138; as representative of old regime, 148–49; supports engineers' hegemony, 146
Mansfield, Jared, 32
Marchbank, John, 126–27
Marcy, Randolph, 5
Marcy, William L., 30
Marshall, Humphrey, 141
Maury, Dabney, 21, 59
Meade, George G., 5
Meade, Richard K., 128, 128 (photo)
Meigs, Montgomery, 8
Mexican War, 7, 11, 14
Michie, Peter S., 58; as representative of postwar academy faculty, 148–50
"Militant South," 131–32
Military academy. *See* United States Military Academy
Military tactics, instruction in, 94–97, 119–20; limitations of instruction, 100–101. *See also* Curriculum
Mordecai, Alfred, 120, 124
Morgan, Charles, 130
Morgan, Edwin D., 146
Morison, Samuel Eliot, 110

Newton, John, 9
New York draft riots, 136
Norris, Ariel, 26
Nugen, John, 81 (photo)

Stanton, Edwin M., 137, 144; and removal of engineers' hegemony, 144, 146
Stevens, Isaac I., 5, 129
Stone, Charles P., 9
Strong, George C., 65, 67–68, 69, 78
Stuart, James E. B., x, 21, 73, 76, 100, 129, 131; and fight incident, 80
Summer encampment, 118, 119; daily schedule of, 69; description of, 64–71; recreational and social activities of, 69–71
Sumner, Charles, 132, 133
Sumner, Edwin V., 12
Superintendency of academy: and engineers' hegemony, 141–46; limitations on, 37, 39; responsibilities of, 39; role at academy, 37, 39–42
Swift, Joseph, 3, 23, 36, 57; innovations at academy, 3

Taylor, Zachary, 17
Thayer, Sylvanus, x–xi, 3, 37, 124, 141; contributions as superintendent, 23–26; influences on academy, 26; innovations at academy, 4; "Thayer mystique," 4
"Thayer System," 23–26, 87–89, 113, 150, 151. See also Thayer, Sylvanus
"Thing." See Plebes
Thomas, J. Addison, 74
Thompson, Mrs. Alexander R. ("Mammy"), 78
Tidball, John C.: comments on academy, 21, 41, 52, 64, 65, 68, 71, 73, 74, 79, 85–86, 89, 93, 100, 129, 142–43
"Topogs" (topographical engineers), 8–9
Totten, Joseph G., 14, 33 (photo), 63; and appointment of Beauregard as superintendent, 127; as chief of engineers, 32–36; contributions to academy, 34–36, 152; criticized by Thayer, 25–26; and establishment of military engineering course, 97–98; and five-year course, 115–20; scientific contribution of, 34
Traditions, at academy, 110, 122, 138. See also Hazing; Insignia; Order of merit; Plebes
Trumbull, Lyman, 132
Turner, John W., 21
Turner, W. W., 6
Twiggs, David E., 12, 21

United States Military Academy: academic atmosphere of, 113, 147–48; achievements of graduates, 5–10; as bastion of aristocracy, 61–63, 153–54; command structure of, 31–32, 109, 141–47; compared to American colleges, 104–13; compared to European military colleges, 102–4; and concept of a "militant South," 131–32; contributions to military science during Civil War, 138–39; criticisms of, 114, 133, 152–54; establishment of, 2; "Golden Age" of, 150; "monopoly" of officers in regular army, 15–16, 112, 133; postwar changes in, 141–54; postwar decline of, 148–49; and problems created by Civil War, 134–38; purpose of, 1, 105, 111; "Radical Republicans'" attempt to abolish, 133; reforms in during Civil War, 137–38; regular army officers at, 58–59; and rise of military professionalism, 18–20; sectional tensions at, 80–81, 129–31; and testing of military materials and tactics, 19–20, 138–39; and U.S. presidents, 26–28; and U.S. secretaries of war, 28–31. See also Academic departments; Academic policies; Appointment system; Cadet life; Corps of cadets; Curriculum; Discipline; Faculty; Failure rate; Sectionalism; Superintendency; Traditions
Upton, Emory, 73, 81, 85
Utley, Robert, 97

Valentine, Jesse, 66
Van Buren, Martin, 27
Vigilante justice: origin of, 83
Voltigeurs (light infantry), 11
von Humboldt, Alexander, 7

Wade, Benjamin F., 131
"Walk-a-heaps," 11, 12
Walker, William H. T., 142
Warner, Thomas, 57
Warren, Gouverneur K., 6, 73, 78
Weir, Robert, 48 (photo), 54, 60, 70; artistic achievements, 55–56; relationship with cadets, 55–56; confrontation with James Whistler, 55
West Point. See United States Military Academy

254